THE MODEL AIRCRAFT HANDBOOK

William Winter

THE MODEL AIRCRAFT
HANDBOOK
Fourth Edition

ILLUSTRATED BY:

H. A. THOMAS, PAUL PLECAN, and BRUCE WENNERSTROM

THOMAS Y. CROWELL COMPANY: New York

The author wishes to thank *Aero Modeller* for permission to reprint figures 8–4, the glow engine, and 8–5, the diesel engine.

CONTENTS

1. TYPES OF MODEL PLANES   1
2. PREPARATION OF WORKING PLANS   8
3. AERODYNAMICS AND PROPORTIONS   14
4. CONSTRUCTION   40
5. LANDING GEARS AND PONTOONS   62
6. PROPELLERS   74
7. COVERING   81
8. MINIATURE GAS ENGINES   90
9. TANKS   104
10. RUBBER MODELS   110
11. CONTROL-LINE MODELS   118
12. JET MODELS   135
13. FREE-FLIGHT MODELS   144
14. RADIO CONTROL   153
15. FLYING AND ADJUSTING   170
16. SCALE MODELS   180
17. PAYLOAD MODELS   186
    GLOSSARY   193
    INDEX   203

ILLUSTRATIONS

1-1. TYPES OF MODELS 3
1-2. FREAK MODELS 5

2-1. PREPARATION OF WORKING PLANS 10
2-2. RIBS AND BULKHEADS 12

3-1. VARIOUS AXES 15
3-2. FORCES ACTING ON A PLANE 16
3-3. TYPES OF AIRFOILS 18
3-4. POPULAR AIRFOIL SECTIONS 20
3-5. PLOTTING AIRFOILS 22
3-6. WING PLANFORMS 23
3-7. ASPECT RATIOS 24
3-8. CENTER OF PRESSURE MOVEMENT 26
3-9. STABILIZER SECTIONS 27
3-10. AIRFLOW AT STALL 28
3-11. ANGULAR DIFFERENCE 29
3-12. STABILIZER PLANFORMS 31
3-13. RUDDER SHAPES 32
3-14. DIHEDRAL FORMS 33
3-15. FUSELAGE PROFILE 36
3-16. FORCE DIAGRAMS 38

4-1. TOOLS 41
4-2. BALSA WOOD SIZES 42
4-3. FUSELAGE TYPES 43

4-4. Free-Flight Wings 44
4-5. Box Fuselage Construction 45
4-6. Fuselage Cross Sections 46
4-7. Typical Noses 48
4-8. Fuselage Planking 50
4-9. Crutch Construction 52
4-10. Wing Structure Details 57
4-11. Dihedral Joints 59

5-1. Landing Gear Design and Construction 63
5-2. Gas Model Landing Gear 64
5-3. Control-Line Landing Gears 65
5-4. Sea Wing, or Sponson 66
5-5. Float Arrangements 67
5-6. Booton Floats 70
5-7. Sea Sled Construction 71
5-8. Flying Boat Proportions 72

6-1. How Propellers Work 75
6-2. How to Carve a Propeller 76
6-3. Typical Folding Propeller 78

7-1. Tools and Materials for Covering 81
7-2. Methods of Covering 83
7-3. Fuselage Covering 84
7-4. Wing Covering 86
7-5. Grain of Paper Covering 87
7-6. Lettering of Wing Covering 88

8-1. Two-Cycle Engine 91
8-2. Ignition Engine 92
8-3. Spark and Glow Plugs 93
8-4. Glow Engine 94
8-5. Diesel Engine 95
8-6. One- and Three-Volt Wiring 96
8-7. Venturi Restriction 102
8-8. Engine Mounts 103

9-1. Free-Flight Tanks 105
9-2. Wedge, or Stunt, Tank 106
9-3. Balloon Tank 108

10-1. Rubber Model Proportions 112
10-2. Joe Bilgri's Duster 116

11-1. PARTS OF TYPICAL CONTROL-LINE MODEL   119
11-2. CONTROL SYSTEMS   120
11-3. CONTROL-LINE TYPES   121
11-4. TEAM RACER   122
11-5. SPEED-MODEL PROPORTIONS   123
11-6. BELLCRANK AND LINKAGE   124
11-7. HINGES AND HORNS   125
11-8. MONO-LINE ELEVATOR CONTROL UNIT   126
11-9. MONO-LINE CONTROL HANDLE   127
11-10. DETAILS OF MONO-LINE CONTROL UNIT   128
11-11. STUNT MODEL PROPORTIONS   131
11-12. TWO-SPEED IGNITION   132
11-13. TWO-SPEED LINES   133
11-14. SPEED TANK   134

12-1. TYPES OF JET ENGINES   136
12-2. JETEX TYPE MODELS   137
12-3. ENGLISH JETEX SKYROCKET   139
12-4. JETEX DELTA   141
12-5. DUCTED FAN ENGINE   142

13-1. TYPES OF FREE-FLIGHT GAS MODELS   145
13-2. TORQUE EFFECTS   146
13-3. PYLON MODEL   148
13-4. DIHEDRAL MEASUREMENT   149
13-5. DETHERMALIZERS   151

14-1. TYPICAL RADIO INSTALLATION   160
14-2. TYPICAL RADIO AND CONTROL INSTALLATIONS   161
14-3. RADIO-CONTROL PROPORTIONS   165
14-4. TWO-SPEED HOOKUP   167

15-1. FREE-FLIGHT ADJUSTMENTS   173
15-2. TURN ADJUSTMENTS   176
15-3. TABLE OF TURNS   178

16-1. SOLID SCALE   181
16-2. FREE-FLIGHT SCALE   182
16-3. CONTROL-LINE SCALE   183
16-4. FREE-FLIGHT JETEX SAILPLANE   184
16-5. CONTROL-LINE SCALE JET   185

17-1. PAA LOAD MODEL   187
17-2. CARGO CLIPPER   189

THE MODEL AIRCRAFT HANDBOOK

TYPES OF MODEL PLANES

REAR ADMIRAL Thomas S. Combs, U.S. Navy, Chief of the Bureau of Aeronautics, speaking before the 1952 annual convention of the National Exchange Clubs in Atlantic City, N.J., pointed out the important relationship between our national air power and model aviation. That the Admiral confined his speech to model airplanes and model builders is not surprising when you consider that for five consecutive years—it is now nine—the Navy had provided the facilities (which means the use of the naval air station, barracks, work hangars, personnel, and so on) for the full week required to run off the National Model Airplane Championships. The National Exchange for years sponsored the Nationals.

Nor is the Navy alone in its observation that model building is worthwhile. The Air Force annually arranges a series of world-wide elimination contests for its personnel at many scattered bases, then flies the winners to its own nationals in America. Winners from there compete in the regular Nationals. For years the Plymouth Corporation sponsored numerous contests with a final Internationals in Detroit. Each year American teams compete internationally in such famous international events as the Wakefield, for rubber-powered models; FAI gas for free-flight models; Nordic, for high-performance sailplane gliders.

The first model plane was built centuries ago! For hundreds of years models were used in an effort to discover a means of flight. This process culminated in success when the Wright brothers first flew an airplane at Kitty Hawk in 1903. Miniature aircraft had been flown many years before the Wrights were successful with a full-scale machine. And, after the Wrights, hobbyists began to build models not so much to find answers for intended big planes—though that is done even today—but to imitate in true flying-model form the big planes that began to fly across the skies.

It was only a few years after the flights of the Wrights, Glenn Curtiss, Louis Bleriot, Alberto Santos-Dumont, and others, that people found interest in making miniatures of real flying machines. Even before the first World War at least one manufacturer catered to the needs of the infant hobby. But Charles Lindbergh's flight to Paris in 1927 was the spark that touched off the fireworks. For since that day the ranks of the aeromodelers have swelled year by year—even through the depression—until there are now between one and a half and two million enthusiasts supplied by more than 100 manufacturers who have grossed as much as 30 million dollars in a year.

At the hobbyist's beck and call is an elaborate system of distribution. In any fair-sized town in the country a hobby dealer stocks a full line of equipment and supplies. This includes balsa wood, cement, dope, paper, wire, and all the materials needed for putting together original designs. His shelves are crammed with all manner of kits for stunt jobs, free-flight models, scale models, and so on, all of them beautifully prefabricated from materials that catch the eye. He has engines in all classes, from the tiny Infant to the big sixties. Glow Plugs. Tanks. Props. Wheels.

A good dealer is able to guide his young customer's choice to items that suit   age and ability level. As time goes by the customer completes various lines of models and graduates to things more interesting and difficult. A spectacular recent trend has been the plastic model. Beautifully detailed kits of famous military planes and the "crates" of yesteryear are sold by the millions. Practically every air-minded American boy has tried at least one of these easily glued together replicas. Plastics have invaded the ready-to-fly field, too. Various manufacturers have produced real-looking gas-engined flying models that circle the flier on the ends of thin wires or cords. Comet, Cox, Stanzel, Wen Mac are notable examples. In the scale field many firms are active, such as Revell, Aurora, Lindberg, Hawk, Monogram, Comet, and so on.

Still other manufacturers specialize in the more complex models,

2

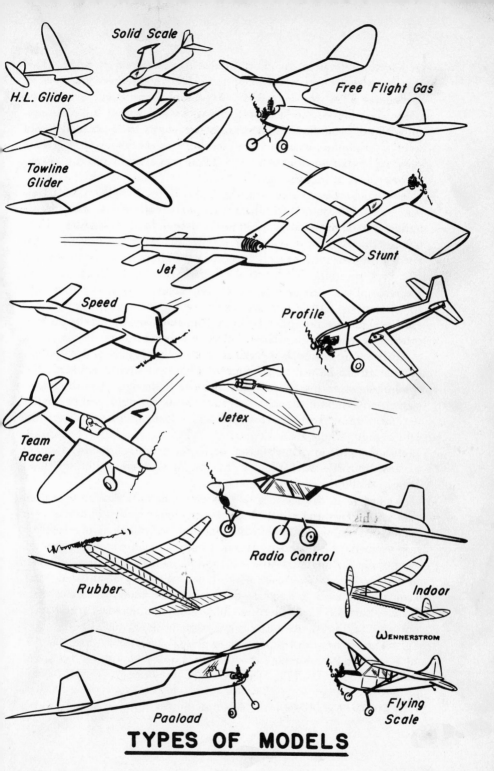

H.L. Glider

Solid Scale

Free Flight Gas

Towline Glider

Stunt

Jet

Speed

Profile

Team Racer

Jetex

Radio Control

Rubber

Indoor

Wennerstrom

Paaload

Flying Scale

TYPES OF MODELS

Fig. 1–1.

3

such as Sterling, with a wide range of working boats and planes; DMECO, with its radio-controlled planes; Berkeley, with numerous flying scale jobs of all sizes and shapes; Top Flite, with its propellers and beginners fliers; Guillow, with its control-line stunt and trainer planes; and other firms too numerous to mention. All these manufacturers, making anything from a line of small engines to wheels or other accessories, advertise in the three magazines that are devoted to this field. Powerful little one-cylinder engines, developing as much as one horsepower (sometimes more!) range in price from less than 5 dollars to more than 50. Some of these engines have cylinders smaller than thimbles, yet they scream at better than 10,000 rpm. Featuring glow ignition, these engines have no spark plug, coil, or batteries as of old. They use a glow plug which is heated by temporarily attaching a booster battery.

Even jet planes are possible. American Telasco imports from England, for national distribution via hobby shops, the famous Jetex powerplants. These are little cylindrical affairs which hold a small charge of special solid fuel. This fuel is ignited with a fuse and burns with a hiss. Thrust is developed exactly as it is with a big jet motor. Jetex powerplants can be put on solid balsa gliders, in small-scale versions of real jet fighters, and other special designs. Patterned after the Nazi "buzz bomb" is the Dynajet, a longish tubelike jet which burns gasoline. Developing great thrust, it has driven control-line speedsters at better than 160 mph.

What the individual purchaser does not see in a hobby shop—which is very little—he can order by mail through the magazines that feature model-airplane building and flying.

The purpose of this book is to provide an orderly plan of action, a guide, not for the expert, but for the average fan who continually seeks to add to his knowledge. His aim is to build better-looking and better-flying models. The beginner, too, will profit by gaining an appreciation of technique in design, construction, and flying methods. The modeler who has made a start but lacks the experience to be gained from years of constant building and flying, will gain by the experience of others, reflected in this book in the form of information on what to do and what not to do in designing, building, and flying. A complete picture is given of current practices, theories, and technique. Things the author knows the average builder will ask about are set forth in planned order, making this book a handy reference work. Expressed in a nutshell, the author's idea has been to pass on everything known to the expert but not known by the general run of hobbyists.

Most unusual of all models are ornithopters-crankshaft and rods actuate wings which feature flexible trailing edges

Helicopters vary greatly in design — successful both indoor and out-proponents claim great possibilities

Autogiro models with non-powered vanes have had most success indoors-very difficult to adjust

Many early models were pushers — some rudderless-all had positive incidence in front elevator - slight negative incidence in wing

Early champs in speed and duration were twin pushers — used long powerful motors — props rotated in opposite directions — sometimes equipped with landing gear

Tailless or flying wing types obtain stability by sweepback and decreased incidence in wing tips — designs vary greatly

Rubber-powered racing models have flown over 60 m.p.h. — generally use low pitch hardwood propeller with wing area cut to a minimum

Tandem models also vary greatly in design- wings are sometimes equal in area - fuselage contains two rubber motors with torque neutralized

Amphibian models can operate off water or, with wheels extended, from the ground- most frequently are twin-motored

Fig. 1–2.

5
Thomas

The beginner and the inexperienced hobbyist are urged to start at the beginning and not to put the cart before the horse, as too many do today, by building a gas-powered model without amassing the all-important experience to be gained in making the simpler types first.

A simple glider can be assembled in minutes from sheet balsa for wings and tail and a hard balsa strip for the body. It can be launched by hand, thrown into the air like a ball. Well-made hand-launched gliders have flown out of sight! Increased a little in size and sometimes fitted with a paper-covered wood framework, a hand-launched glider can be flown like a regular sailplane by means of a towline. By looping a cord around a wire hook fastened into the bottom of the fuselage, the builder tows his miniature sailplane aloft by running with it like a kite. As the ship gains altitude, the cord drops off, and the glider is on its own.

Getting back to our small all-balsa glider with its stick fuselage, we can equip it with a propeller and a rubber-strand motor by fitting one end of the stick with a wire hook for holding the rubber and the other end with a special fixture, called a propeller hangar or thrust bearing, and fly the little ship like a real airplane. We can make it climb and turn. By fitting a pair of small wheels close to the nose of the stick (using a wire axle bent to fit around the stick) we enable our ship to take off the ground and to land on its wheels at the end of the flight.

But perhaps our builder prefers something that more closely resembles a real airplane, something with a high degree of flying ability. Then he can purchase a more advanced construction set, or, if he has even a passing knowledge of what makes a plane fly, he can design his own ship. Only when he comes to gas-powered models does it become essential to have a complete working knowledge of flight. A small rubber-powered model may have a 2-foot wing, although it is almost as easy to build one with a 4-foot wing. The fuselage may embody a cabin and a windshield. The sturdy framework is covered with paper doped to a drumlike surface. Ability. No! And still the cost remains considerably less than a dollar.

Control-line flying is the big thing. Here it is that prefabrication has been carried to the ultimate, where structures fall together by clever interlocking design. The builder has a choice of speed, sport, stunt, or scale types. They may be as little as 10 inches or as big as 4 feet. They may fly on the end of 35-foot, .008 flexible steel wires or on 70-foot, .016 wires. Every movement is in response to a control handle held in the flier's hand. He tilts the handle back to make the plane climb or zoom, dips it to make the plane dive. With some experience

6

he can make the model do such advanced maneuvers as square loops, vertical 8's, overhead 8's, inverted flight, and so on.

Solid-scale exhibition models should satisfy even the fanatic. Although attractive solid designs can be turned out from a couple of soft balsa blocks, there really is no limit to the amount of detail the fan can put into his ship. The writer has seen miniatures built from pieces of wire soldered into an exact duplicate of a real airplane, with even the gas and oil tanks in their proper places. It is not unusual to see exhibition models with such details as rivets, working controls in the cockpit, a lighting system, and shock absorbers. Enterprising modelers have fitted dummy pilots, togged in goggles and the rest, complete to a seatpack parachute.

Flying scale ships are the happy medium. They look realistic, yet fly surprisingly well. A well-built scale airplane based on a logical selection for flying ability can be sent out of sight by a veteran flyer. Most rubber-powered scale jobs range from 24 to 36 inches in wing span, although the practical limits seem to be 15 to 50 inches.

Gas-powered free flight is at last coming into its own due to the very small Half-A class engines, such as the Thermal Hopper, Wasp, and Cub. Engines of approximately .049 displacement work out well in scale ships having a wing area of 150 to 250 square inches respectively.

During the last few years great strides have been made in the development of radio-controlled model airplanes. A few experts competing each year at the national contests have done the pioneering work. They have encountered the problems, discovered some entirely new ones, and have evolved the basic principles required in the ship itself for successful control, the best receivers and transmitters, and the most practical ways of installing radio equipment in the ship.

Many radio plane construction kits are on the market. Plans for planes also are available from the magazines. The Federal Communications Commission has granted two frequencies, 27.255 and 465 megacycles, for examination-free operation of model planes and boats.

There is little risk of boredom in this hobby. Should the hobbyist grow tired of looking at the conventional type of airplane, he can always try a pusher instead of a tractor or puller, or he can place the tail in front of the wing instead of behind it for a canard or tail-first airplane. Or he can go off the deep end entirely with a combination push-puller with a prop at both front and rear, a flying wing (pterodactyl), a helicopter, an autogiro, or an ornithopter "wing-flapping" airplane.

2

PREPARATION OF WORKING PLANS

To BEGIN WITH, plans that are not full size usually are drawn to a definite scale—say ¼ inch to the foot, or perhaps ½, ³⁄₁₆, or ⅛ inch to the foot. Sometimes a bar scale is conveniently divided to indicate scaled-up equivalents of small-plan measurements. Usually, model scales are even—⅛ or ¼ inch to the foot—and can be multiplied an even number of times for full-scale dimensions. Quarter-scale dimensions are multiplied by four, eighth-scale dimensions by eight, half-scale dimensions by two. But if an odd scale is used—for example, ⁵⁄₃₂ inch to the foot— there is tough sledding ahead. Every dimension must be calculated. A draftsman's rule with its various scales is a help. So is a table of decimal equivalents, giving decimal equivalents of fractions and mixed numbers and vice versa. Such a table speeds up arithmetical calculations of full-scale parts. Decimal equivalents are a boon if a full-scale plan is to be reduced, say, to 60 per cent of full size.

Enlarging plans is a cinch if you know how to go about it. Do you have trouble drawing the long sweeping bottom curve of a fuselage? Then pin a square strip of balsa in the proper curve on the drawing, and trace its outline with pencil. Or is it the intricate curve of a wing-tip that bothers you? Just draw a screen of horizontal and vertical lines over the curve in question on the small plan, spacing the lines ⅛, ¼, or ½ inch apart, depending on the scale. Make a similar screen or grid over the full-scale working drawing, but space the lines a full

8

inch apart. Then count off squares on the small plan to find points of intersection of the curve and the screen lines; repeat the count on the large plan; and mark all intersection points. With a freehand motion, lightly sketch in the curve, going over it heavily when it takes on a satisfactory appearance. A draftsman's French curve or a ship's curve are ideal for drawing model plans.

Suppose we draw up a hypothetical full-sized working drawing. The fuselage is usually the first thing to be constructed, so we'll start there. The simplest procedure is to draw a reference line lengthwise through the small plan's fuselage side view; then, at regular intervals, draw cross lines at right angles—at crosspiece stations if given, otherwise spaced ½ inch or 1 inch apart, depending on the size of the original drawing. Another reference line is drawn on the blank paper to start the full-sized working plan. Then, if the large plan is to be four times the small one, for example, the vertical cross lines are spaced 2 inches, or 4 inches, apart on the reference line, depending on the line spacing used on the small plan. The idea is to measure each cross line out from the reference line to both top and bottom fuselage edges, then to multiply these measurements the required number of times to achieve full scale, transferring each measurement in turn to the proper cross line on the large working plan. After all these fuselage outline points have been found, pin a strip of balsa in the indicated shape and draw in the final outline.

It's a lengthy job, but not too difficult. Depending on the drafting tools or similar equipment available to the individual builder, the job can be simplified greatly. A large drawing board, a T-square, a triangle, and a French curve are indispensable to anyone who does much model designing. These drawing tools not only speed up a tedious job, they insure accuracy. A proportion divider is a great help in scaling up plans, especially those having an odd scale. A pantograph, an automatic device that draws plans to any desired proportion when a pointer is moved over the outlines of a small plan to be enlarged, can be purchased reasonably at an art supply store.

However, any accurately squared flat object, sheet metal for instance, will substitute in a pinch for both T-square and triangle. Even a scrap of plain white paper will substitute for dividers. Just place the margin of the paper over the part on the plan to be enlarged; mark the dimensions with two pencil dots; then transfer the paper to the full-scale plan; and measure off the two pencil marks as many times as is required. Another clever trick is to make a cardboard copy —really a scaled-down ruler—of the bar scale found on the small plan.

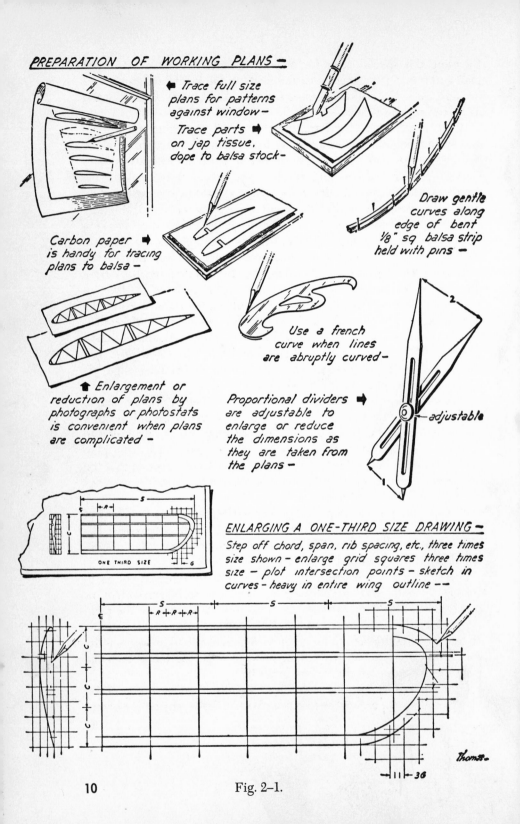

PREPARATION OF WORKING PLANS —

← Trace full size plans for patterns against window —

Trace parts → on jap tissue, dope to balsa stock —

Carbon paper → is handy for tracing plans to balsa —

Draw gentle curves along edge of bent 1/8" sq balsa strip held with pins —

↑ Enlargement or reduction of plans by photographs or photostats is convenient when plans are complicated —

Use a french curve when lines are abruptly curved —

Proportional dividers → are adjustable to enlarge or reduce the dimensions as they are taken from the plans —

adjustable

ONE THIRD SIZE

ENLARGING A ONE-THIRD SIZE DRAWING —

Step off chord, span, rib spacing, etc., three times size shown — enlarge grid squares three times size — plot intersection points — sketch in curves — heavy in entire wing outline — —

—11—36

Thomas

10   Fig. 2–1.

By using this special ruler for measuring various parts of the small plan and transferring these measurements to the identical figure on an ordinary rule, the builder obtains full-scale dimensions almost as fast as he can measure them.

Wings of constant chord are scaled up easily by using the leading and trailing edges as reference lines. Rib spacing is measured off along one wing edge, and rib lines are drawn in at the indicated positions. Curved tips, stabilizers, and rudders are enlarged by making the screen of squares already described. Tapered wings are scaled up by drawing a rectangle around the small wing to be enlarged, the long side being the span, the short side the maximum chord. Still working with the small plan, the builder draws lines through the leading and trailing edges, extending them until they intersect one side of the reference rectangle. Then it is a simple matter to measure back from the front or leading edge of the rectangle to the point of intersection of the small wing's leading edge, multiplying and transferring the new measurement to a full-sized rectangle drawn on the working-plan sheet. The distance between the leading and trailing edge intersection points with the side of the small rectangle is, in turn, multiplied and transferred to the large plan. Then the leading and trailing edge reference lines are filled in, followed by rib lines.

Sometimes only half a wing is given with a full-sized plan. A simple trick in drawing up the missing half is to trace the given half on thin tissue, then to invert the tissue and paste it down on the plan, end to end with the half wing already shown. Or the given half-wing plan may be rubbed with thin oil making the paper transparent so that the lines can be seen in reverse through the other side. In this way wings can be built one-half at a time.

Making patterns, or templates, of fuselage bulkheads or formers and of ribs in a tapered wing is a tough job. Fortunately, practice has evolved accurate methods. These methods make awkward description, but they are diagrammed clearly.

Full-sized plans are awkward affairs, especially when it comes to cutting out parts of a curved wingtip, rudder, or stabilizer section, or of a bulkhead. It is not always practical to work directly on the plan. It is advisable, for instance, to transfer directly to the wood, patterns of curved parts that are to be cut out. A practical kink is to trace the part in question on thin tissue and then to dope the tissue onto the wood for a cutting guide. Simple, isn't it?

Or, if the builder can place the sheet wood under the section of the plan being used, with a sheet of carbon in between, he can trace

TAPERING RIBS AND BULKHEADS

BY SUPERIMPOSING THE TIP RIB OVER THE CENTER RIB, INTERMEDIATE RIBS CAN BE DRAWN IN. NOTE SEVERAL LINES DRAWN AT RIGHT ANGLES TO THE CAMBER LINES TO AID IN DIVISION OF SPACE BETWEEN ROOT AND TIP RIBS.

FOR SECTIONS WITH A FLAT LOWER CAMBER, THE METHOD SHOWN BELOW IS BEST. DIVIDE "X" & "Y" INTO EQUAL PARTS (AS MANY PARTS AS THERE ARE RIBS).

BY DRAWING A SEMI-SYMETRICAL TIP RIB OVER THE ROOT SECTION AS SHOWN BELOW, RIBS MAY BE DRAWN IN WHICH TAPER FROM AN UNDERCAMBERED AIRFOIL AT CENTER OF WING TO A STREAMLINED SECTION AT THE TIPS.

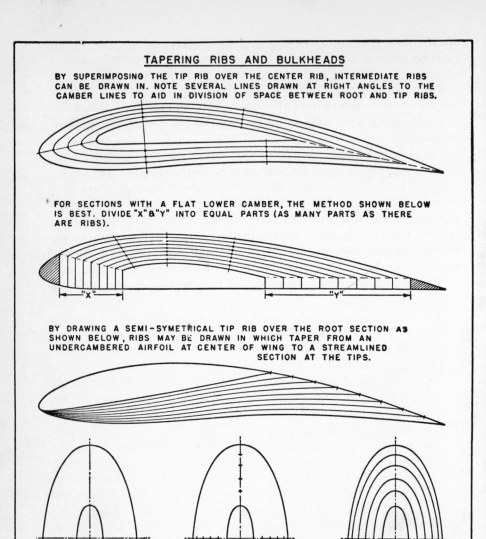

CHOOSE DESIRED CROSS SECTIONS (GET HEIGHT & WIDTH FROM FUSELAGE SIDE & TOP VIEWS)

OBTAIN HEIGHT AND WIDTH OF INTERMEDIATE BULKHEADS.

USING A FRENCH CURVE FAIR IN LINES.

Fig. 2–2.

12

directly onto the wood the outline of the part to be cut out. Care must be taken to have the wood grain running in the direction indicated on the plan. Resourcefulness always pays dividends.

A wing-rib template is advisable if the wing is of constant chord. Such a template insures that all ribs are both accurate and identical. Trace the given wing section on thin cardboard or, better yet, on thin aluminum.

Templates are handy in making solid models. Trace the plan form of the wings and tail and the side view of the fuselage on thin cardboard. Then cut out these patterns or templates and use them for accurate laying out of the wood blocks or blanks. Additional templates for solid-model fuselage cross sections are made to match the sections given on the plans, usually marked A-A, B-B, C-C, and so on. By making these body templates the reverse of those on the plan, so that they can be fitted against and around the rough-cut fuselage, the builder can check carving accuracy quickly and repeatedly.

3

AERODYNAMICS AND PROPORTIONS

It is customary in books of this kind to begin with an airfoil and to show how it creates lifts. However, it is wiser, first, to examine the stability requirements enabling a ship to fly, and then to relate everything else to these requirements. A fresh approach is necessary if control-line planes are to be considered simultaneously with free-flight planes. It is obvious that a machine that is tethered on control wires will have radically different requirements from one that is not captive.

Any airplane whose movements are not artificially restricted as they are on control lines is free to climb or dive, to roll to right or left, to turn to the right or left, or to combine varying amounts of any of these three movements for an infinite number of movements. An aircraft rotates about three different axes. First, for our discussion purpose, is the vertical or directional axis about which the machine turns. This directional or vertical axis pierces the plane from top to bottom through the machine's center of gravity or C.G. A weather vane has a directional or vertical axis. Revolving on this axis, either a weather vane or a plane can be pointed. In the weather vane, most of the side area is distributed behind the axis so that the force of the wind causes the vane to point into the wind. By use of a vertical tail area, the modeler similarly is able to control his plane about its vertical axis. Without the vertical tail, his machine would twist and tumble to the ground.

14

The C.G. can be found by suspending the model by a string from its top center line somewhere forward toward the nose and extending the line indicated by the cord across the fuselage with a pencil. Then, by hanging the model from another point, also along its top center line, and by repeating the process, the designer marks the intersection of the two pencil lines. This is the location of the C.G.

A second axis pierces the plane from nose to tail, also through the C.G. It is called the lateral axis. The ship rolls about this axis. Perhaps you have seen a spit in a restaurant or at a barbecue. Whatever is to be cooked is pierced with the spit and then rotated slowly above an open fire. The spit is a perfect example of a lateral axis. Call this axis anything you want—rolling axis or sideways axis—so long as you fix its existence in your mind.

Successful gas model must have inherent stability about its axes: 1. Directionally (vertical axis), 2. Longitudinally (lateral axis), and 3. Laterally (longitudinal axis)

Fig. 3–1.

The third axis pierces the plane from wingtip to wingtip, again through the C.G. The plane dives or climbs around this spanwise axis; when the nose goes up, the tail goes down and vice versa. Sound like a seesaw, doesn't it? And that is what this axis is. Keeping this seesaw balanced is the toughest job the model designer has!

You cannot see or feel these axes but they are there just the same. The designer's problem is to stop or limit to a controllable degree the undesirable movements of his plane around them. What are the principal things he can do to obtain such stability? To begin with the vertical or directional axis, he utilizes a proper amount of vertical tail area, and possibly offset thrust (to right or left) to assist only when absolutely necessary. Dihedral or uptilted wings hold the plane steady on its rolling or lengthwise axis. A stabilizer or horizontal tail surface, perhaps assisted by an offset thrust line (downthrust) prevents uncontrollable climbs or dives. All these things must be approximately correct in size and amount or the designer creates instability. For an example, an excessively large lifting type of stabilizer will make a fast free-flight gas job nose over when it picks up speed under high power.

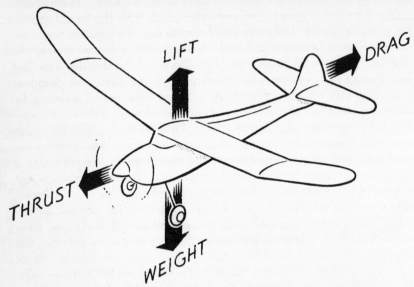

LIFT

DRAG

THRUST

WEIGHT

In level flight, principal forces are equal:
THRUST, forward through thrust line, vs.
DRAG, rearward through line of resistance;
LIFT, upward through center of lift, vs.
WEIGHT, downward through center of gravity

Fig. 3–2.

Let's consider briefly the control-line model because of its special requirements. Like any airplane, the control-liner has three control axes. However, the lines that hold such a machine captive, limiting its flight path to a circle around the flier, prevent its turning right or left. As long as the flier maintains control, the plane will not turn away from him to fly out of the circle, or toward him to come inside the circle. The control wires replace the function of the vertical tail. Proof of this is the speed model which usually has no vertical tail. When control-line jobs have vertical tails, it is to insure that, for beginners, an offset rudder (to the outside of the circle) further minimizes any chance of the ship turning into the circle. On stunt planes, the vertical tail does the same job during overhead 8's and other

16

maneuvers high off the ground where there is danger of a model sliding sideways into the circle if speed and centrifugal force drop below a minimum necessary for sufficient tautness in the control wires. Basically, the control-line plane is able to fly without a vertical tail.

Nor does the designer need concern himself with the lateral or rolling axis that pierces the plane from nose to tail. The control wires are connected to a bellcrank inside the fuselage, or on the wing near the fuselage, and extend toward the flier through a fixed guide attached to the wing near the tip. The wires prevent the ship from dropping a wingtip and rolling either away or toward the flier (assuming he keeps the lines taut through good flying technique). The wires therefore take the place of dihedral wings. Only in the case of the spanwise axis about which an airplane dives or climbs does the control craft have any special requirement and even here that requirement is not exacting. Some horizontal tail surface is necessary but the amount is not critical, provided it does not become unduly small. The movable elevators which the pilot manipulates with his control handle provide any correction for accidental departures of the plane from stable level flight. Here is another interesting difference between the free-flight and the control-line craft. The former must resist, on its own, any tendency to rotate undesirably about any of its three axes. The control job, on the other hand, has elevators which enable the flier to force the plane to rotate about its wingtip or spanwise axis. It is these controlled movements—and the controlled recoveries from them—that create stunt maneuvers. The only stability requirement is that the plane be able to maintain level flight.

With this knowledge of the stability requirements of either free-flying or control-line designs, the ins and outs of airplane design will not prove confusing.

An understanding of elemental aerodynamics is necessary before tackling design. Essentially, flight is attained by means of a wing that is drawn through the air to generate lift (the force that keeps the plane aloft); tail surfaces consisting of a fin and rudder (vertical surface) and a stabilizer and elevator (horizontal surface) that exert a continual leverage to hold the plane on a true flight path, as the feathered tail of an arrow; and a propeller, or airscrew, that screws its way forward through the air, pulling or pushing the plane and developing sufficient thrust (propulsive energy) to overcome the drag (air resistance) created by the plane's forward speed.

Lift is generated, first, because of the airfoil (wing-rib or wing cross-section shape) and, secondly, because of the angle of attack (in-

17

clination or angular setting of the wing), the latter being nothing but the tilting up of the leading edge of the wing. A kite flies because of its angle of attack. Most of the lift at ordinary angles of attack results from the airfoil shape. Inclining the wing to the wind stream does boost lift, but it also increases drag, so much so, as more and more attack is imparted to the wing, that drag increases out of all proportion to lift, thereby destroying efficiency. Thus, for any given airfoil shape, there is a certain best angular setting for the wing, usually between 2 and 6 degrees positive. The flat sheet-balsa wings on a small rubber-powered model, or on a small glider, lacking any wing-rib shape, must get their lift from a small positive angle of attack. Such models automatically seek the necessary angle of flight to develop lift.

Most of the airfoil's lift is created by the passage of air over the highly curved top surface. This stream of air, because it must travel

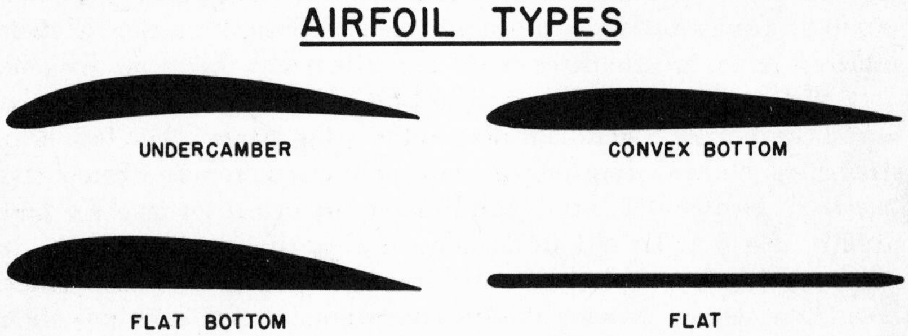

AIRFOIL TYPES

UNDERCAMBER   CONVEX BOTTOM

FLAT BOTTOM   FLAT

Fig. 3–3.

a greater distance than the air stream passing beneath the wing, accelerates or stretches out, thus reducing air pressure immediately above the wing, forming a partial vacuum. This differential of air pressure—that is, less pressure above the wing and more pressure below—is the source of lift. Roughly, $\frac{2}{3}$ of the total lift is due to the upper surface of the wing and only $\frac{1}{3}$ to the lower surface when placed at ordinary angles of attack.

Airfoils vary greatly in appearance. Some are curved, or cambered, on top and flat on bottom; others are cambered on top and under-cambered on the bottom. Still others are cambered convexly on both top and bottom, along the lines of a streamlined object, depending for lift on a slight angle of attack. Generally speaking, the thicker the airfoil the greater the lift and drag; the thinner the airfoil, the less the lift and the greater the speed (owing to less drag). Thus, load-carrying planes of the bomber or transport type have very thick wings.

18

Racers and fighters have thinner wings. So it is with your model. A slow, high-lift model, such as a radio-controlled job with its heavy load of equipment and batteries, has a thick wing, whereas a hand-launched glider has an almost flat wing. High-lift wings have a greater drag. Airfoils must be selected carefully for the purpose the plane is to fulfill. The key to the problem of airfoil selection is a factor called the lift-drag ratio. Lift-drag ratio is nothing more than the relation between the amount of lift and the amount of drag created per square foot of wing area at any given angle of attack. It is a measure of efficiency expressed simply, for example, as 16 to 1, or 22 to 1. The ratio becomes lower, hence less efficient, if the angle of attack is increased beyond certain limits. Comparing a number of airfoils at a like angle of attack, the designer uses known lift-drag ratios as a means of selecting the particular airfoil best suited for his purpose. If, for example, a high-lift airfoil is required, the designer segregates a group of airfoils fulfilling the requirements. Then, by means of their lift-drag ratios he compares them and eliminates them one by one, until he has the most efficient airfoil for the purpose. Naturally the airfoil having the highest lift-drag ratio is his choice. The less drag the better, because drag means more power required and hence less duration. Fortunately, no research is required to determine the best airfoils. The popular airfoils are illustrated in this chapter.

Charts are obtainable to assist in analyzing airfoil sections. These charts plot curves showing the lift coefficients (an offhand indication of relative amounts of lift) at each degree of angle of attack. The charts do the same for drag and for the lift-drag ratio. If a speed model is involved, the builder will select a section that has minimum drag at zero degrees attack (or other chosen angle) provided lift is also developed and a good lift-drag ratio is maintained. For free flight, he would look for a high lift-drag ratio and the angular setting necessary to obtain that efficiency. A really clever designer would consider the size of the lift coefficient at the same time he considered the lift-drag ratio.

While airfoil charts usually indicate the best airfoil for the job, scale effect sometimes plays an upsetting part. Some airfoil sections that look like world-beaters on paper prove to be duds on an airplane. The list of everyday sections that will work successfully is rather well-known. It includes sections that are very old and others that are of recent vintage.

The most famous airfoil section is the Clark Y. It is a good all-round section for modeling, though it has limitations in full scale

POPULAR AIRFOIL SECTIONS

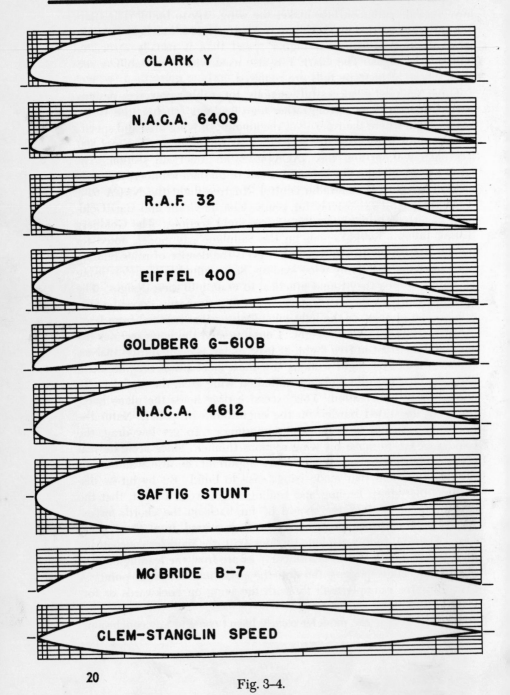

CLARK Y

N.A.C.A. 6409

R.A.F. 32

EIFFEL 400

GOLDBERG G-610B

N.A.C.A. 4612

SAFTIG STUNT

MC BRIDE B-7

CLEM-STANGLIN SPEED

Fig. 3-4.

practice. Of moderate thickness, it compromises lift and drag so that it applies well to all free-flying models although it rarely excels on any. Its flat bottom surface makes the wing easy to build. The Clark Y is good for sport ships, both gas and rubber. It is excellent for radio jobs requiring a somewhat higher speed than is usually associated with such designs. The Clark Y is also used widely as stabilizer sections where lifting-type tails are required.

Three eminently successful sections for rubber-powered designs, particularly for those having rather high loadings (such as the Wakefield design, where the rules limit the amount of wing area and specify a minimum weight) are the RAF 32, a British section; the Eiffel 400, a French section; and the NACA 4612, an American section. The latter can be given a flat bottom instead of an undercamber; it is then an excellent section for radio control. In free flight the NACA 6409 was used almost exclusively for years. Charlie Grant and Carl Goldberg developed special families of free-flight sections. The Goldberg section became world-famous on the Sailplane gas model, noted for its fantastic glide. In late years, however, the demise of rules limiting wing area and specifying wing loading, has resulted in modelers using all the wing area they found practical to cram into their designs. The soaring ability of the machine then became primarily dependent on the amount of area—or the light wing loading that resulted from large areas in relation to gross weight. Consequently, the wing sections became unimportant in free flight, at least as far as comparative analysis is concerned. Free-flight sections now must meet a novel requirement. Consider that in adding almost unlimited wing area, the modeler also adds drag to his creation. This excessive drag holds the plane back, throwing an added burden on the engine and propeller. Naturally, low drag becomes of paramount importance. To get low drag, the builder began to make his wing sections thinner. Since accurate real plane sections were no longer vitally important, he also wanted flat-bottomed sections that made wings easy to build. Bit by bit he discovered that sharp leading and trailing edges were a must, that the deepest point of the wing should be far back on the chord; for example, 40 to 50 per cent of the chord measured from the leading edge. Since no such real plane sections exist, the modeler concocts his own. He merely draws a smooth curve or arc from the leading edge to the trailing edge, passing through the maximum thickness point. A Civy Boy, for example, will fly with the wing on backwards or forwards.

In speed design, the modeler clearly hasn't come to any conclusions.

Apparently several types of sections will work. Some speed builders prefer symmetrical airfoils (ones that have both surfaces convex) because he feels this is the road to minimum drag. Yet other builders, successfully, have employed a Clark Y.

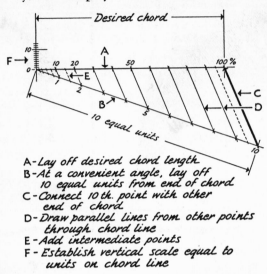

A–*Lay off desired chord length.*
B–*At a convenient angle, lay off 10 equal units from end of chord.*
C–*Connect 10th. point with other end of chord.*
D–*Draw parallel lines from other points through chord line.*
E–*Add intermediate points.*
F–*Establish vertical scale equal to units on chord line.*

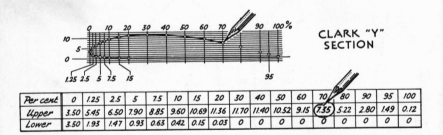

CLARK "Y" SECTION

Per cent	0	1.25	2.5	5	7.5	10	15	20	30	40	50	60	70	80	90	95	100
Upper	3.50	5.45	6.50	7.90	8.85	9.60	10.69	11.36	11.70	11.40	10.52	9.15	7.35	5.22	2.80	1.49	0.12
Lower	3.50	1.93	1.47	0.93	0.63	0.42	0.15	0.03	0	0	0	0	0	0	0	0	0

Fig. 3–5. Plotting Airfoils.

For an extensive list of airfoils and other aerodynamic information available, write the Superintendent of Documents, Washington, D.C.

The amount of lift developed by any wing section is affected by the planform (top view of the wing outline) and by the aspect ratio (relation between wing length—span—and the wing width—chord). Aspect ratio is span divided by chord, thus: a 36-inch span divided by a 6-inch chord (36 ÷ 6 = 6) equals 6, or an aspect ratio of 6:1. The planform may be rectangular, tapered, or elliptical—these are the usual shapes.

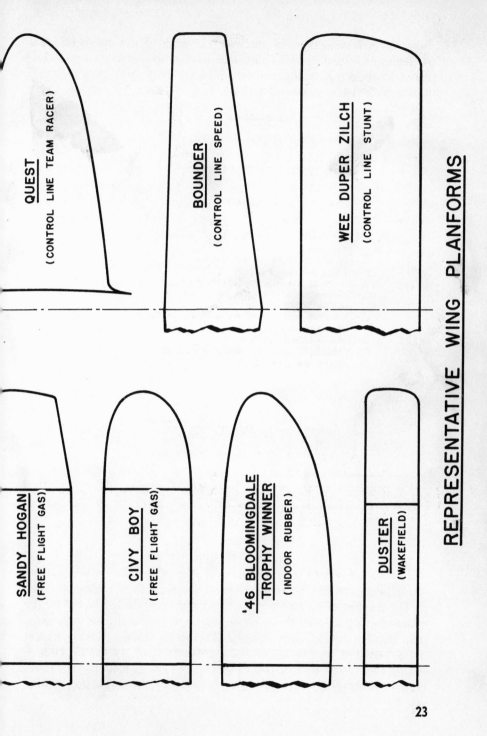

QUEST
(CONTROL LINE TEAM RACER)

BOUNDER
(CONTROL LINE SPEED)

WEE DUPER ZILCH
(CONTROL LINE STUNT)

SANDY HOGAN
(FREE FLIGHT GAS)

CIVY BOY
(FREE FLIGHT GAS)

'46 BLOOMINGDALE
TROPHY WINNER
(INDOOR RUBBER)

DUSTER
(WAKEFIELD)

REPRESENTATIVE WING PLANFORMS

Fig. 3–6.

23

Both tapered and elliptical planforms are said to improve a wing's efficiency, but in view of the consistent success of squarish wings on models, it is doubtful if the added difficulties of plotting a full set of varying wing ribs for tapered or elliptical wings is warranted.

Aspect ratio, however, is much more important than planform. High aspect ratios in real planes mean added efficiency. The narrower the chord, the less the induced drag. In moving forward, a wing disturbs an area of surrounding air. This can be visualized by drawing a wing rib and then, setting apart the points of the compass to the same measurement as the length of the rib, scribing a circle with the trailing edge of the rib as the center. The area of the circle indicates the amount of induced drag. The bigger the rib, the bigger the circle, and hence the greater the induced drag. High-performance sailplanes have extremely high aspect ratios, sometimes in excess of 20:1! For structural reasons, the aspect ratios for transports and bombers usually don't exceed 10:1. Racers and fighters may have ratios of less than 6:1.

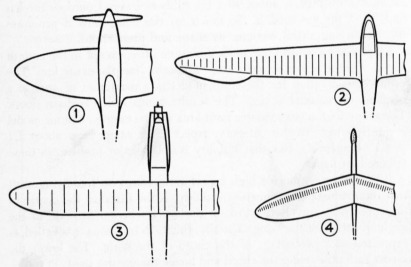

VARIATIONS IN ASPECT RATIO
1. Control-line model   2. Sailplane
3. Rubber model   4. Hand-launched glider

Fig. 3–7.

Total drag of an airplane includes induced drag, mentioned above, and parasite drag, coming from parts exposed to the air stream, such as wheels, struts, tail, and so on. Included in parasite drag is skin friction, caused by the rubbing of the air stream against the plane's surfaces. This explains the elaborate curves on some model fuselages, used to decrease the plane's surface area and hence to cut down drag.

Unfortunately, a foolproof application of real plane practice to models cannot be made accurately in this case. A 6-inch-wide model wing moving at 15 mph does not have a proportionate amount of lift and drag to a real plane wing, which may be many feet wide and traveling at 300 mph or more. This is due to the fact that an infinitely smaller number of air molecules pass over our model wing at its slow speed than pass over the high-speed plane wing ("Reynolds Number"). The larger the model wing's chord, the closer it approaches a true proportion to the real plane. Thus, while high aspect ratios admittedly improve efficiency, model designers compromise between having the largest wing rib (low aspect ratio) for a favorable scale effect, and a high aspect ratio for efficiency. And so, although model records have been made with wings of as high as 18-to-1 and as low as 4:1 aspect ratios, the average is about 10:1 for rubber-powered outdoor models and 6½:1 for gas models. So much for the wing, how it generates lift, its varying airfoil sections, its shape and proportions.

Efficiency on control-line models matters little, except in the case of speed. On the whole, aspect ratios for control-line planes are low. The prime consideration for the stunt model is a maximum of area in a machine of reasonable size. The result: wings look like barn doors. The shape that accommodates most area is a rectangle. A stunt model is mostly wing. In this category, aspect ratios range from about 2:1 to 4:1. Remember, too, that stability is not a major problem in these tethered airplanes.

Still another reason for high aspect ratio wings on free-flying craft that require maximum inherent stability, is the distance the center of pressure (lift) travels forward on the wing with an increase in the angle of attack of the wing. Usually, this C.P. travel, as it is called, is expressed in a percentage of the chord of the wing. The lower the aspect ratio, the wider the chord and hence the greater the C.P. travel. Since the movement of the C.P. forward of the C.G., or center of gravity, creates a larger nose-up or tail-heavy condition, leading to a possible stall, it is important to minimize the C.P. travel. This can be controlled by avoiding low aspect ratios and airfoils whose graphs indicate a relatively large C.P. movement.

The wing alone is too unstable for flight by itself. The technical explanation of this is that the C.P. not only shifts forward toward the leading edge with an increase in angle of attack, but backward toward the trailing edge with decreased attack. This movement of the C.P. is greater with increase in depth of the airfoil, high-lift airfoils usually having a much greater C.P. travel. Glide a wing from your hand and it will twirl edge over edge to the ground. Ordinarily, at zero angle of attack, the C.P. is located at approximately 30 per cent of the wing chord back from the leading edge. Plainly, a stabilizing force is required.

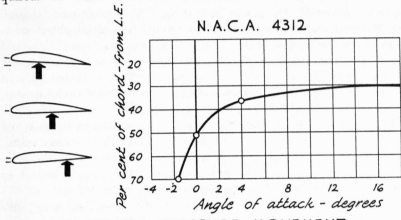

CENTER OF PRESSURE MOVEMENT
(Varies with different sections)

Fig. 3–8.

This is provided by a stabilizer, or horizontal tail, that exerts a powerful pressure or leverage not only to keep the wing at its proper angle but to restore the wing to that angle when the plane dives or stalls. Stabilizer area, shape, cross section, angular setting, and position on the plane, all vary according to the particular design. The area, for example, must be greater when the distance between the wing and tail is shortened, giving a smaller tail moment arm (the distance through which a force is exerted, as in a lever), the area will be less when the distance is increased, giving a greater tail moment arm. The usual range of stabilizer area in free-flight planes is from 30 per cent to 50 per cent of the wing area.

The observing reader may recall that some extremely long free-flight designs have large stabilizer areas. This interesting exception to the rule is found in very high-powered free-flight contest machines which use rather high pylons to support the wings. The high power provides great forward speed, even in the climb. Because of the stress on long glides and soaring ability, these machines also have large wing areas. Since lift is influenced by area and speed (the speed actually is squared in the lift formula!), tremendous excess lift is created while the engine is running. Therefore, the designer depends on a large lifting type of stabilizer which also increases its lift greatly at high speed, and thus prevents the wing from looping or stalling the plane. Why doesn't such a plane dive during the glide, when the forward speed is lowered? The answer is that the C.G. is positioned far back on the wing chord, as much as 75 to 100 per cent of the chord measured from the leading edge. With a nonlifting tail, the C.G. would be further forward although the plane then would stall under power. (When a 50 per cent tail of a lifting cross section cannot prevent loops, the designer removes some of the angle of attack from the wing to reduce its lift at high speed and moves back the C.G.)

Tail moment arm is generally considered the distance between the midpoint of the wing chord and the midpoint of the stabilizer chord. On the average model this tail moment arm is usually ½ the wing span. For example, on a 40-inch wing span a tail moment arm of ½ the span would equal 20 inches. On gas models this tail moment arm is sometimes as small as ⅖ of the span. Tow-launched model sailplanes have moment arms as small as ⅓ and even ¼ of the span. Racing models approach the other extreme, having tail moment arms as great as ⅔ to ¾ of the span. A "square" control-line model is one with equal span and length.

Stabilizer cross sections may be flat, streamlined (symmetrical) or even cambered like an airfoil to develop lift. Flat tails are suited only

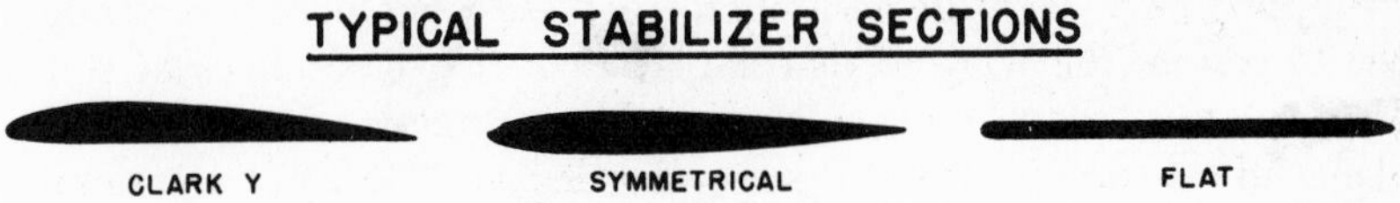

TYPICAL STABILIZER SECTIONS

CLARK Y   SYMMETRICAL   FLAT

Fig. 3–9.

to small models and warp when made too large. Which type of stabilizer cross section to use depends on the type of free-flight machine, and its size. Flat tails are useful only on small to medium-sized ships. The flat tail would be employed on simple rise-off-ground (R.O.G.) or stick jobs and would be made from sheet balsa, or built up of edges and crosspieces, perhaps using one spar. On gas or rubber fuselage jobs, the flat stabilizer can be used only when the C.G. is placed rather far forward on the wing. The symmetrical-sectioned stabilizer comes into play when the size of the plane dictates a more rigid warp-free structure than is possible from sheet balsa or a built-up flat tail consisting of edges, spar, and crosspiece ribs. This section is used on sport and flying scale gas models and radio jobs where the C.G. is forward and where none of the load is to be carried by the stabilizer. This is why you see symmetrical-sectioned stabilizers on cabin gassies but never on a pylon. The lifting stabilizer must be utilized with high-performance pylons, or cabin jobs where the profile of the cabin is such that the wing is rather highly located and wherever the C.G. falls further rearward on the wing chord than 50 per cent of the width of the wing. The lifting-type stabilizer is a must on any high-performance rubber job due to the great excess of power at the beginning of the flight (here it does the same job as it does for a fast-flying pylon) and because of the natural rearward position of the C.G. The C.G. can fall behind the wing due to the length of the heavy rubber within the fuselage. This, of course, throws some of the weight-carrying burden upon the stabilizer.

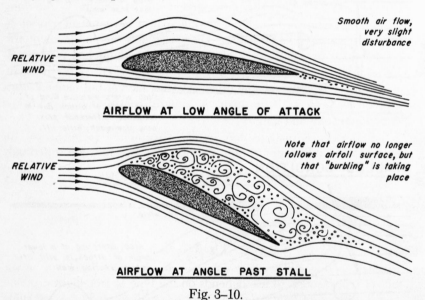

Fig. 3–10.

For maximum stability the wing is usually given a greater angle of attack (built into the structure of the model) than the stabilizer. The difference is generally 2 to 4 degrees. The explanation is this: at moderate angles of attack the airflow over the upper surface of the wing is smooth and unbroken. But as the angle of attack is increased, the airflow no longer follows the contour of the rib section but breaks

28

away from the surface nearer and nearer the leading edge, until at last air just boils turbulently over the wing, destroying lift. This condition occurs after approximately 16 degrees of angle of attack has been reached. It is called the stalling point, or burble point. Now, if the tail is set at a lesser attack, it will continue to lift after the wing has stalled, and, consequently, tend to restore the plane to a level flight position. Although you cannot see this corrective force at work, it resists the wing's increasing its angle of attack and therefore resists any approach to a stall. The average arrangement is to set the stabilizer at zero degrees and the wing at whatever angle of attack is found necessary to fly the ship. However, this angular difference between wing and tail must not be too large. If it is, the high power of a gas engine or a heavy rubber motor will either loop the model or

STEADY LEVEL FLIGHT

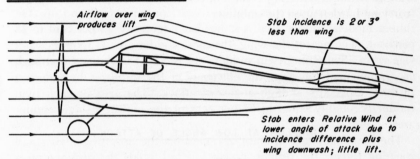

Airflow over wing produces lift

Stab incidence is 2 or 3° less than wing

Stab enters Relative Wind at lower angle of attack due to incidence difference plus wing downwash; little lift.

STALLED CONDITION

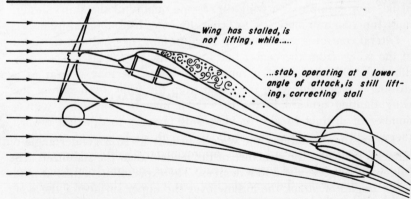

Wing has stalled, is not lifting, while.....

...stab, operating at a lower angle of attack, is still lifting, correcting stall

Fig. 3–11. Angular Difference.

carry it into a series of vicious power stalls. The term *angle of incidence* is often used. Incidence is the angular setting of the wing with respect to the thrust line and is built into the structure of the plane.

Successful planes have been flown without any apparent angular difference between wing and stabilizer. Both the wing and stabilizer were placed with their bottom surfaces on the same, or parallel, base line. However, these machines must be carefully adjusted and flown.

Stabilizers have many shapes. The trend in gas models is to make the stabilizer elliptical with an aspect ratio of approximately 3:1, or rectangular with parallel leading and trailing edges. On rubber designs the stabilizer tends to a rectangular shape like a wing and may have an aspect ratio of as high as 6:1. Rudders, including both fin and rudder surface, also vary in shape, but have an aspect ratio of approximately 1½:1. Rudder area on gas jobs ranges from 4 per cent to 10 per cent of the wing area. The former figure is possible on some pylon jobs but cabin types require from 7 or 8 per cent and up. On rubber models, rudder area is somewhat larger, say 16 per cent to 18 per cent. The nearer the wing, the more rudder area is required, and vice versa. Sometimes twin rudders are used. It is claimed that such an arrangement improves the efficiency of the stabilizer by reducing tip loss, especially at high angles of attack. The area of *each* twin rudder is roughly equal to 65 per cent of the required single rudder area.

The horizontal tail, or stabilizer, controls the upsetting diving and zooming forces; the rudder, or vertical tail, holds the airplane on a steady heading, controlling left or right turning forces. The one requirement for inherent stability is lateral (rolling) control of the airplane. For example, if a wing dips, some quality of the ship's design must function automatically to bring the wing back into position.

Lateral control is accomplished by upturning, or uptilting, the sides of the wings from the center line toward the tips. This is known as dihedral. Dihedral takes a number of forms. It may appear as a shallow V when the wing is viewed from the front, each side of the wing slanting upward to the tip. Or it may be polyhedral with a number of distinct breaks, or increasing changes in dihedral toward the wingtips. Visualize the shallow V with each side of the letter bending sharply upward again approximately halfway toward the tip. Elliptical dihedral forms a steady curve running from tip to tip. Elliptical dihedral is the most efficient, but it is also the most difficult to build. Polyhedral is most popular. The correct amount of dihedral is essential and varies with the vertical location of the wing on the

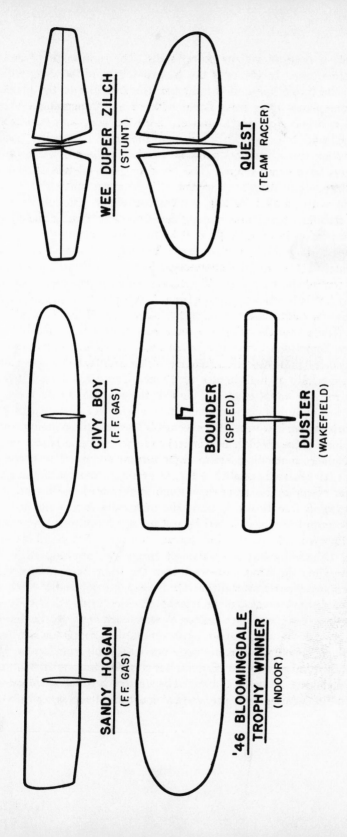

WEE DUPER ZILCH
(STUNT)

QUEST
(TEAM RACER)

CIVY BOY
(F. F. GAS)

BOUNDER
(SPEED)

DUSTER
(WAKEFIELD)

SANDY HOGAN
(F.F. GAS)

'46 BLOOMINGDALE
TROPHY WINNER
(INDOOR)

REPRESENTATIVE TAIL PLANFORMS

Fig. 3–12.

31

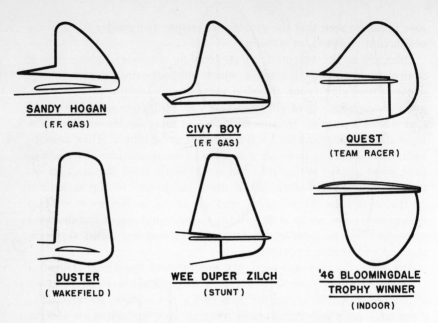

SANDY HOGAN
(F.F. GAS)

CIVY BOY
(F.F. GAS)

QUEST
(TEAM RACER)

DUSTER
(WAKEFIELD)

WEE DUPER ZILCH
(STUNT)

'46 BLOOMINGDALE
TROPHY WINNER
(INDOOR)

REPRESENTATIVE RUDDER SHAPES

Fig. 3–13.

model. Low-wing installations, for instance, require a greater dihedral angle than do high wings. Parasols need least of all. Minimum dihedral seems to be about 1 inch for every foot of wing span, although 1½ to 2 inches per foot of span are recommended to insure stability. High-powered models, contest jobs for example—especially gas jobs with relatively short wings—use as high as 3 inches of dihedral for each foot of span. This should be the maximum needed for a low-wing gas design. 2½ inches of dihedral per span foot seems adequate for most models.

Power affects dihedral this way. The propeller is nothing but a rotating wing developing thrust as its lift. The propeller blades create their own resistance in turning, causing torque, a force that tends to rotate the model in the opposite direction to the turning propeller. If the propeller turns counterclockwise, then the torque rotates the model clockwise, and vice versa. The higher the power, the greater will be the propeller's rpm; the higher the propeller's pitch, the greater will be the torque. You may have noticed that with the usual right-hand propeller on your model, flight under power tends to left-hand circles with the left wingtip low. Since dihedral prevents flying one wing

32

low, it can be seen that the greater the torque, the greater the amount of dihedral required for stability.

Dihedral is not essential on control-line airplanes, whose lateral control is assured by the wires which automatically prevent rolling. Among free-flying types, dihedral ranges from as little as 5 or 6 degrees on a radio-control job to as much as 12 degrees on a Wakefield type where a prop of perhaps 20 inches or more in diameter compels some all-out compensation for the resulting great torque. How does dihedral work? While there are a number of interpretations of its action, the correct answer is that dihedral serves to decrease the angle of attack of the higher wingtip when the plane begins to slip in a turn. At the same time the effective angle of attack in the lower wingtip is increased. The result is to add lift to the wingtip that has dropped earthward and to subtract lift from the tip that has rolled skyward; the ship will be rolled upright.

The more the dihedral used, the less efficient the plane. Dihedral sacrifices lift. For example, if the two wing panels were to be given 90 degrees dihedral—measured between a flat surface on which the wing rests and the wingtip—both wingtips would meet in an upright position overhead. Naturally, there would be no lift and the plane could not fly. The designer therefore is grudging in his use of dihedral

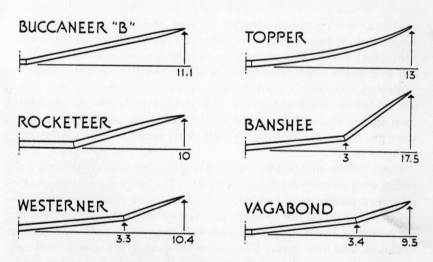

DIHEDRAL ANGLES
Figures indicate per cent of total span

Fig. 3–14.

33

because of its cost in terms of lift. He is forced, however, to allow enough dihedral to guarantee safe flight. He also knows that he must allow for windy weather. A plane that flies smoothly on a calm day may not have sufficient dihedral for a breezy day when it will develop a spiral power dive into the ground.

Still another valuable function of dihedral—particularly in polyhedral form—is to roll upright at the top of a loop any model that accidentally (through too much power while in a tail-heavy trim condition) gets into an inverted position.

The explanation of why low wings require more dihedral and high wings less dihedral reveals a cardinal principle of stability. This is aptly called *pendulum stability,* which, as the name indicates, means that the lower the C.G. relative to the C.P. of the wing, the greater the inherent stability of the airplane. Let's suppose a parasol model gets into a one-wing-low position. Then its weight, acting through the plane's C.G., tends to swing back to a vertical line running from the plane's C.P. to the earth in the same manner as the pendulum in a grandfather clock swings. This is why most have high wings. You can see that any ship with the C.G. above the C.P. would not be stable. Low wings, therefore, have severe dihedral in order to raise the C.P. of their wings above the ship's C.G.

For maximum stability, it is desirable to concentrate weight as much as possible. Weight should also be kept as close as possible to the C.G. A 1-ounce object that is 6 inches away from the C.G. has double the effect of an object of the same weight that is 3 inches away. Such an object—let's say the engine—resists sudden movements, but also acquires an inertia or tendency to keep moving, once displaced. Thus, if the plane should be forced to turn unexpectedly, the weight of the engine would tend to continue in the same direction despite the corrective force of dihedral or other features of the design. Similarly, a heavily-built tail structure is a disadvantage, or unusually heavy wings, especially when the tips are far from the C.G. Extremely long structures, as in long moment arm fuselages, or very high aspect ratio wings, tend to place weights far from the C.G. Contest fliers know that the nose of a free-flight gas job should be short. Sometimes the propeller is located even with the leading edge of a parasol wing or even behind that edge! There is only one exception to the rule of minimizing the distance between weights and the C.G. This is the desirability of placing weighty objects as low as possible—like the batteries on a radio job. By placing the objects low, the C.G. position itself is lowered with respect to the airplane. The lower C.G.

enhances pendulum stability, within reasonable limits, of course.

Spiral stability is a function of the position of the C.G. in relation to the side, or profile, area of the model. One theory is that in a banking turn, the air stream striking against the side area of the model—the fuselage side area primarily—will cause the model to bank progressively steeper if most of that side area is above the C.G. The bank will lessen automatically if enough profile area is below the C.G.

Certain conditions of model design have been found to have a bearing on spiral diving tendencies. It was already pointed out that too small an angular difference between the angles of incidence of wing and stabilizer, lowers the resistance to spiral dives. Another factor is the force of the slip stream which, twisting back from the propeller, strikes the right side of the airplane, pushing against the pylon, or a high cabin, and even the vertical tail. In a gas model this force is especially severe. First, the small, fast-turning prop concentrates the slip stream against the pylon and other vertical surfaces. Secondly, a gas job unfortunately provides such surfaces for the slip stream to react against. It is desirable, therefore, to minimize any surface which would make the propeller wash or slip stream effective. Reduce the side area of a pylon—but not to the point of structural weakness. Lower the vertical tail, perhaps using a smaller vertical tail with a couple of additional subrudders, attached to the under surface of the stabilizer. Avoid large side areas on fuselages of the cabin type. Instead of curving the top line of the fuselage outward from wing to stabilizer, bend it inward toward the thrust line. Avoid the "hatchet" type of gas job. It is apparent that the pylon gas job, for example, has a more drastic right turn and spiral dive tendency under power than does a rubber job. In the latter, the larger propeller diffuses the slip stream; moreover, the side area of the model is smaller in proportion to the diameter of the twisting slip stream.

Much discussion pro and con has been heard over the merits, or even the existence, of a center of lateral area. In the case of high-powered airplanes it is doubtful how much the relationship of the C.G. to the side area of the plane has to do with turning characteristics—forgetting for the moment the fact that side area and propeller wash create a right turn tendency. Wing warps, adjustments to the rudder, changes of propellers, propeller torque, any of these things are certainly more powerful influences which are common causes of spiral-dive crashes. Free-flying models usually have all these tendencies balanced out in the adjustments before flying so that a desired flight path is the result.

TO INSURE SPIRAL STABILITY.....

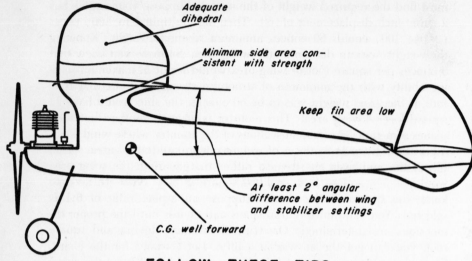

Adequate dihedral

Minimum side area consistent with strength

Keep fin area low

At least 2° angular difference between wing and stabilizer settings

C.G. well forward

FOLLOW THESE TIPS

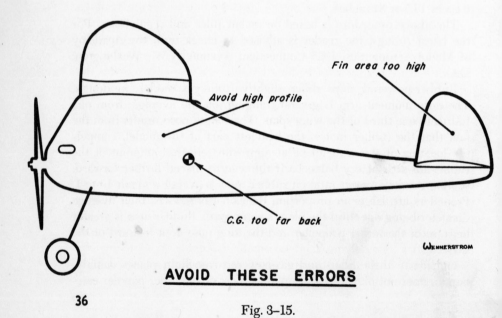

Fin area too high

Avoid high profile

C.G. too far back

WENNERSTROM

AVOID THESE ERRORS

36

Fig. 3–15.

The following is a handy method for determining the required size of a free-flight contest type machine. Rules specify a minimum loading of 100 ounces per cubic inch of engine displacement. First, we must find the required weight of the model. Suppose your engine has a cubic inch displacement of .60. Then .60 multiplied by 100 ounces (.60 × 100) equals 60 ounces minimum required weight. Knowing the weight, we can determine the wing area. Suppose you knew that 5 ounces per square foot of wing area would result in maximum soaring ability with the minimum of structural strength required. Therefore, if the gross weight was to be 60 ounces, the ship would have 12 square feet of wing area. This monster is an extreme case but such planes sometimes are seen in sections of the country where wind is not a problem. Even at 8 ounces of weight per square foot of area, which places the emphasis on strength rather than soaring, the wing area would be 7½ square feet, or 1,080 square inches. Now we need to know the span and the chord. Suppose an aspect ratio of 6:1 is selected. You can multiply trial spans and chords until the proper dimensions are determined. Or, with elementary algebra and square root, you can get the answer in a jiffy. Let C stand for the chord. Then with an aspect ratio of 6:1, the span would be $6C$ and the chord C, and the area $6C \times 6$ or $6C^2$. Since $6C^2$ equals 1,080 square inches, we have $6C^2$ equals 1,080, or C^2 equals 180. The square root of 180 is approximately 13.5 inches. If 13.5 inches is the chord, the span is 6 times 13.5 or 81 inches.

The above procedure is based on recent rules and regulations. For the latest rulings, the reader is advised to check with the Academy of Model Aeronautics, 1025 Connecticut Avenue, N.W., Washington, D.C.

Rubber-powered ships differ slightly from gas models in design. The nose moment arm is greater, ranging, on the average, from one fourth to one third of the wing span. The longer nose results from the fact that the rubber motor, the heaviest part of the model, compels the location of the wing to be at approximately the midpoint of the rubber for satisfactory balance. If the wing is placed farther forward, stalling results. Aspect ratio on rubber models averages about 10-to-1. Propellers are larger in proportion than on gas models, their average diameter being one third the plane's wing span. Rudder area is greater because of the larger propeller and the long nose area forward of the C.G.

Outside of the rubber- and gas-powered free-flight planes, aerodynamics does not play a primary part in most of the other popular cate-

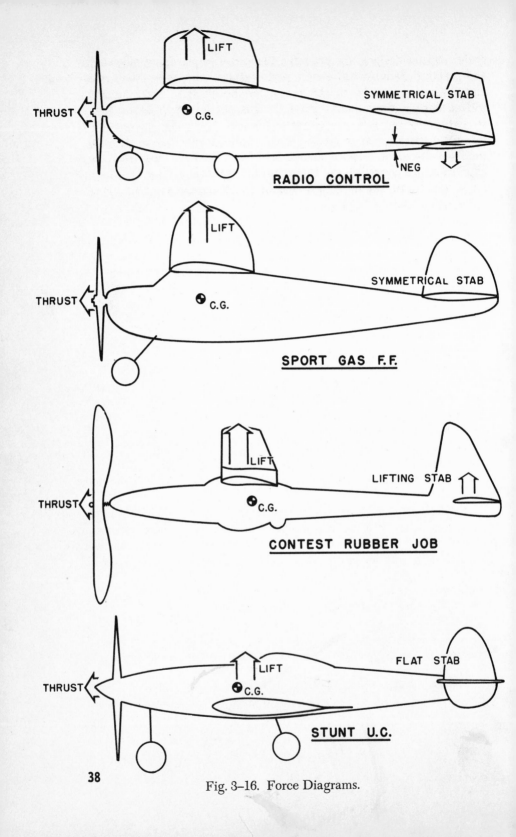

38

Fig. 3–16. Force Diagrams.

gories. Speed designs, for example, place the emphasis on efficiency and practical design with reliable performance. This necessitates cut-and-try experiments by the builder unless he elects to make already proved designs from plans. Stunt designs put an emphasis on high strength-to-weight ratios in construction with low wing loadings determining the amount of stuntability. All the reader has to do is to follow well-known rules of layout that have been evolved from the experience of hundreds if not thousands of contest fliers (see the chapter "Control-Line Models"). The indoor model stresses superlight construction and flight efficiency.

4

CONSTRUCTION

Before going into more detailed construction of various popular types of machines, let's look over the basic types of fuselages, wings, and tails, and the methods of assembling them. The figures 4–1 and 4–2 illustrate tools used and the various balsa sizes and cuts. This will enable you to pick out the proper kind of balsa wood for the parts in question.

Meanwhile, keep in mind these few tips on obtaining sound structure regardless of type. For key parts which carry heavy loads, such as wing spars, trailing edges, and longerons, select the hardest possible balsa, with the straightest possible grain (unless directions specifically tell you otherwise).

Modelers have a choice of a number of completely different ways to construct wings, tails, fuselages, and other structural parts. (See figures 4–4 and 4–5).

There are multispar wings with six to eight thin spars spaced on both the top and the bottom of the wing, single-spar wings with their balsa-sheeted leading edges, the standard two-spar wings, sparless wings with heavy leading and trailing edges to carry the load, and numerous less important types. Tail surfaces differ in the same manner.

Fuselages. The term *fuselage* refers to the body of the airplane. The most popular fuselage or body from the hobbyist's standpoint is the common box. Such a fuselage most often consists of four longerons

MODEL-MAKING TOOLS

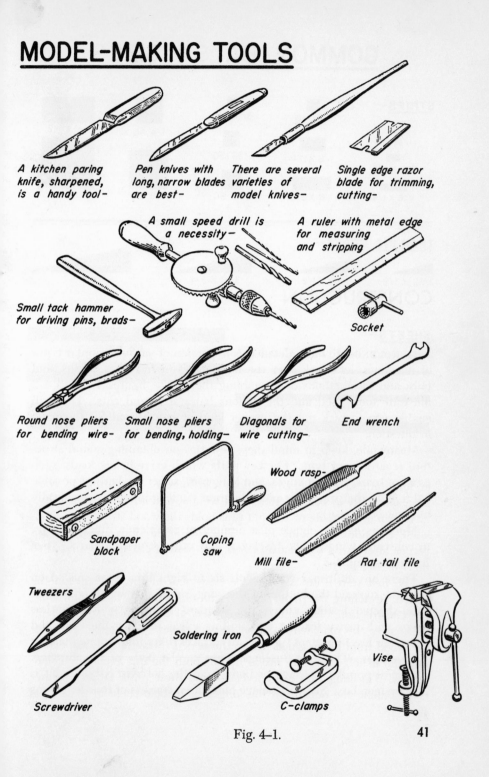

A kitchen paring knife, sharpened, is a handy tool—

Pen knives with long, narrow blades are best—

There are several varieties of model knives—

Single edge razor blade for trimming, cutting—

A small speed drill is a necessity—

A ruler with metal edge for measuring and stripping

Small tack hammer for driving pins, brads—

Socket

Round nose pliers for bending wire—

Small nose pliers for bending, holding—

Diagonals for wire cutting—

End wrench

Sandpaper block

Coping saw

Wood rasp-

Mill file-

Rat tail file

Tweezers

Screwdriver

Soldering iron

C-clamps

Vise

Fig. 4–1.

41

COMMON BALSA SIZES

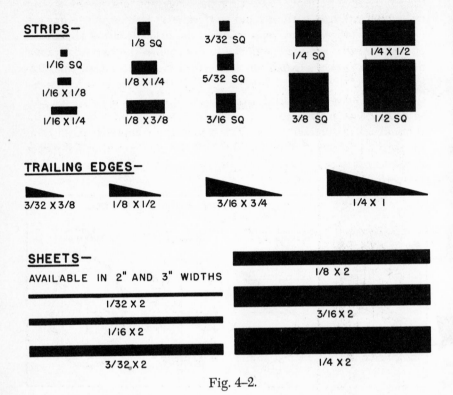

Fig. 4–2.

or longitudinal members braced by crosspieces. Box fuselages combine simplicity of construction, light weight, and adequate strength.

A form or jig made of straight pins holds the wood strips in position while the sides are being built. The completed sides are joined together afterwards by means of top and bottom crosspieces precut to their proper lengths.

The first step is to lay the side-view plan of the fuselage on the bench, stretching the paper tight to pull out wrinkles that could hamper construction. Thumbtack the corners of the plan to keep it taut; then cover the plan with a sheet of wax paper. Wax paper prevents the wood from being glued fast to the bench. Straight pins are driven into the bench along the inside line of both the top and bottom longerons. The longerons are curved around these pins. Other pins are tacked along the outside of the longerons to hold them in place. Do

42

not pierce the balsa strips with the pins. Now all the crosspieces visible on the side view of the plan are cut to an exact fit and are glued in their respective positions. Select for the longerons four pieces of strip balsa that match in hardness and in thickness. If these longerons are not matched, the stronger ones will pull the fuselage out of alignment, either when it is removed from the form or when the two side frames are joined together. Install all the vertical crosspieces first; then follow up with the diagonal braces. Cut all the crosspieces to the required size before cementing any of them in place. Construct the two side frames simultaneously, one over the other in the form. This insures identical fuselage sides. To remove the completed parts from the forms, pull out all the pins. Peel off the wax paper, and separate the two fuselage halves by sliding a two-edged razor blade between the longerons.

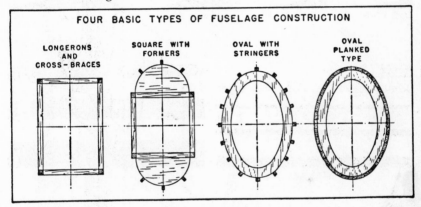

Fig. 4–3.

Assembling the two sides is the only difficult operation. First, cut the top and bottom crosspieces to their proper lengths. Attach the widest crosspieces first; then, after the cement has dried, draw together the nose and tail ends of the body as required, finally inserting the remaining crosspieces.

When joining together the side frames, attach 4 crosspieces, 2 top and 2 bottom, at the widest part of the body. To hold them in place temporarily, force 4 thin straight pins through the sides of the longerons; then, after putting a drop of cement on the end of each crosspiece, the crosspieces are stuck on the pin points flush with the inside surface of the longerons. Glue all crosspieces first to one side frame; then attach the other side frame to the loose ends of the crosspieces. The whole assembly is placed upright on the bench so that the cross-

43

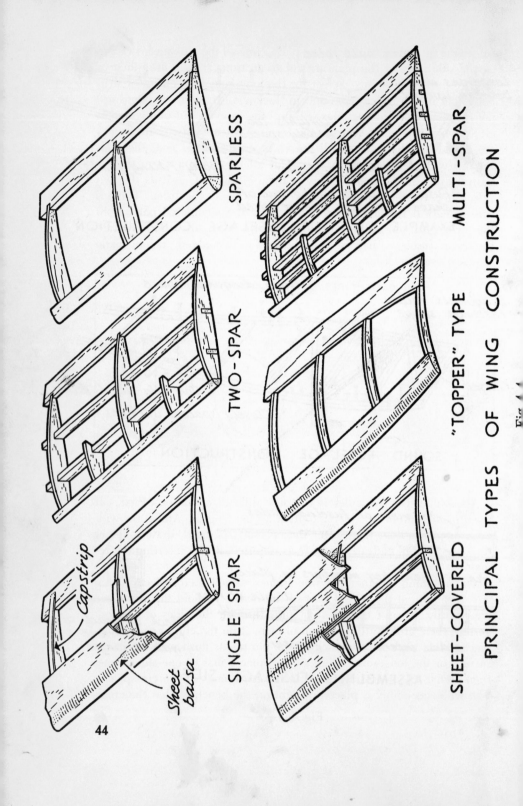

SPARLESS

MULTI-SPAR

TWO-SPAR

"TOPPER" TYPE

Capstrip

Sheet balsa

SINGLE SPAR

SHEET-COVERED

PRINCIPAL TYPES OF WING CONSTRUCTION

44

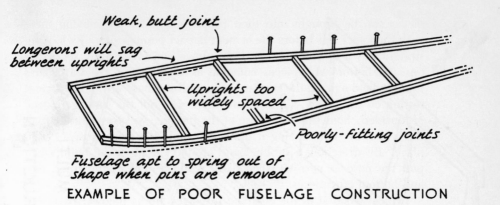

Weak, butt joint

Longerons will sag between uprights

Uprights too widely spaced

Poorly-Fitting joints

Fuselage apt to spring out of shape when pins are removed

EXAMPLE OF POOR FUSELAGE CONSTRUCTION

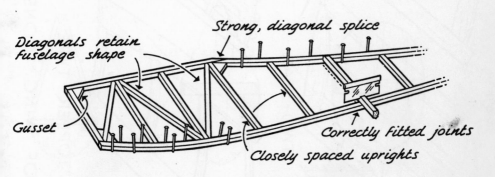

Diagonals retain fuselage shape

Strong, diagonal splice

Gusset

Correctly Fitted joints

Closely spaced uprights

SOUND FUSELAGE CONSTRUCTION

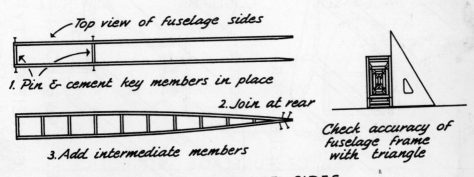

Top view of fuselage sides

1. Pin & cement key members in place

2. Join at rear

3. Add intermediate members

Check accuracy of fuselage frame with triangle

ASSEMBLING FUSELAGE SIDES

Fig. 4–5.

45

pieces can be brought into their proper alignment by moving them with the finger tips before the cement has set permanently. By looking straight down on the fuselage from above you can readily see if the top and bottom crosspieces coincide as they should. A draftsman's triangle held against the fuselage side with the base of the instrument resting on the bench will indicate whether or not the fuselage is true or lopsided. Sometimes the nose of the fuselage will be narrower than the widest section, making it difficult to glue the front crosspieces in place. By stretching a rubber band around the nose, the builder can pull the nose as narrow as he likes, while he inserts the front, top, and bottom crosspieces.

Typical wood sizes for box-type fuselages are as follows: balsa $\frac{1}{16}$

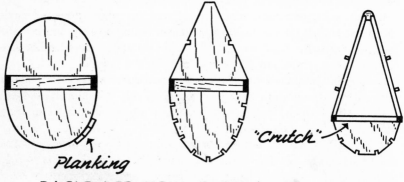

Planking

BASIC "CRUTCH" FUSELAGE TYPES

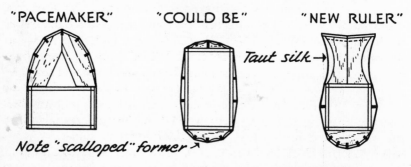

USE OF FUSELAGE STRINGERS

Fig. 4–6.

46

inch square for models having a 12- to 18-inch wing span; $\frac{3}{32}$ inch square for 18- to 24-inch wing spans; $\frac{1}{8}$ inch square for 24- to 36-inch spans; $\frac{5}{32}$ inch square for 36- to 48-inch spans; $\frac{3}{16}$ inch square for 36- or 48-inch to 48- or 60-inch spans, and $\frac{1}{4}$ inch square for spans over 60 inches. Some ships (racers) may have unusually large fuselages in proportion to their wing span and consequently require heavier wood than the sizes tabulated above. A nicely rounded nose, which could be used in connection with a propeller spinner or cone for streamlining, is not too difficult to make. Four pieces of sheet balsa or thin balsa blocks, as the size of your model may require, are glued to each of the four sides of the nose. This solid nosing should be extended back two or three or more crosspiece stations so that the wood can be carved and shaped to flow in with the fuselage outlines, at the same time forming an absolutely rounded nose.

Round and streamlined noses are common on rubber-powered models. Most free-flight gas fans forget streamlining entirely and cut the body off flat behind the motor. This arrangement is popular because of easy construction and the accessibility to the engine.

Gas-model fuselages of box construction occasionally are covered with sheet-balsa siding rather than paper or silk. Medium hard sheet balsa $\frac{1}{16}$ inch thick is correct for small gas jobs of 48-inch or so wing span, $\frac{3}{32}$ inch on larger jobs.

A second popular system of constructing flat-sided fuselages is the sheet-balsa method. This system is simple and sturdy. It is widely used for many types of planes, sport rubber, small and medium-sized contest free-flight and tow liners, sport free flight, U-control (the sheet balsa method is practically universal here), and radio-control. (On larger sizes the wood may be covered for added strength.) First, two identical sides are cut from sheet balsa and are connected together with sheet-balsa bulkheads (or plywood if called for). The sides may be assembled by the same basic methods that applied to assembling the sides of cross piece construction. The top and bottom of this fuselage may be sheet as well, or the bottom may be sheet, with the top rounded off with some blocks, formers, and stringers, or bent sheet balsa, perhaps with a cockpit cut-out. For rubber and gas free flight, the sides would be $\frac{1}{32}$ to $\frac{1}{16}$ inch thick for ships under 24 inches span; $\frac{1}{16}$ inch thick for 24 to 30 inch spans, $\frac{3}{32}$ inch for spans of 36 to 48 inches, $\frac{1}{8}$ and $\frac{3}{16}$ inch thick for spans up to 5 feet, and $\frac{1}{4}$ inch for still bigger machines.

The bulkheads should be $\frac{1}{16}$ inch thick for free-flight models of approximately 18-inch wing span, $\frac{3}{32}$ to $\frac{1}{8}$ inch thick for an 18-inch

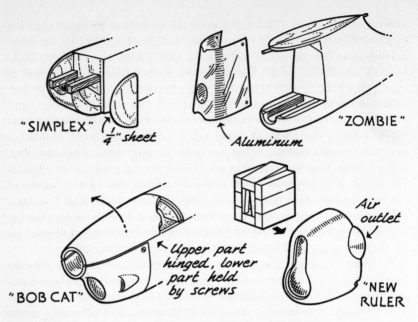

"SIMPLEX" $\frac{1}{4}$" sheet

Aluminum

"ZOMBIE"

Upper part
hinged, lower
part held
by screws

"BOB CAT"

Air
outlet

"NEW
RULER"

ENGINE COWLINGS

Fig. 4–7.

to about a 30-inch wing, $\frac{1}{8}$ to $\frac{3}{16}$ thick for spans from 48 to 54 inches and $\frac{1}{4}$ thereafter. Where internal strength is required for attaching wings and landing gears, hard plywood should be substituted for sheet-balsa bulkheads.

Box fuselages of perfectly square cross section are often mounted on edge with one corner beneath the wing, another corner at the bottom of the plane, and one corner on each side. Such a model is known as a "diamond."

Streamlined fuselages are generally of monocoque or shell construction. That is, they seldom have internal framework and are either hollowed out of a solid block of soft balsa or are built up with bulkheads or formers, with closely spaced stringers forming the surface contour, or with stringers and planking combined as the final surface.

Built-up, streamlined fuselages generally consist of bulkheads (cut to shape with templates or patterns from hard balsa) and longitudinal stringers. This construction is ticklish for any but the experienced builder. The technique is to put the two center side stringers in place on the two widest adjacent bulkheads, one stringer on the left side and one on the right. The next step is to draw these stringers together to a point at the rear, or to a small tail bulkhead or wooden tail plug, according to the particular plans being used. After this the nose bulkhead is attached, and all the intermediate bulkheads are inserted in their proper stations. Then the top and bottom stringers are installed, followed by all the remaining stringers.

Here are a few steps to facilitate construction of bulkheaded fuselages. Glue a thin strip of wood across each of the wide bulkheads near the top and bottom. This prevents splitting. Cut all notches first, using a thin-pointed sliver of a double-edged razor blade. It is possible to use a single wide keel, made by tracing the bottom curve of the fuselage on sheet balsa and cutting the keel piece about ½ inch or more wide. First mount the widest bulkheads on the keel; then install a stringer on each side and the top of the bulkheads, followed by all the remaining bulkheads and finally the other stringers.

Bulkhead fuselage designs can be simplified by making a primary framework, either a square tube made from four pieces of sheet balsa or a square built-up internal fuselage having longerons and crosspieces. This primary or foundation fuselage is then rounded off at the crosspiece stations, or the bulkhead stations as the case may be, with four formers, one former each for the top, the bottom, and the two sides. Stringers complete the job.

Planked fuselages make beautiful models. Planking consists of thin flat strips laid side by side over the entire fuselage surface. Where planking strips overlap as the fuselage frame narrows down at the ends, each plank must be shaved to a tapering fit as it is glued in place. The finished planking is sanded smooth and is then covered with silk. One piece of silk can be wrapped around the entire fuselage without wrinkling simply by stretching the cloth to make difficult bends.

Planking is begun with four planking strips, one over each of the four foundation stringers that are cemented to the outside of the bulkheads. Other planks are added one at a time to the edges of the first four. Do not complete one side of the fuselage first since it may pull out of line owing to the uneven strain. Give the body a quarter turn each time a plank is fastened in place. To speed up the cementing of the long edges of the planks, try tubes of cement instead of bottles or cans.

Bulkheads are made from $\frac{1}{32}$-, $\frac{1}{16}$-, $\frac{3}{32}$-, and $\frac{1}{8}$-inch sheet balsa. However, $\frac{1}{32}$-inch sheet is a little too flimsy for the average modeler to work without splitting. $\frac{1}{16}$ inch balsa is used for rubber-powered flying scale designs, original designs, and general contest rubber-pow-

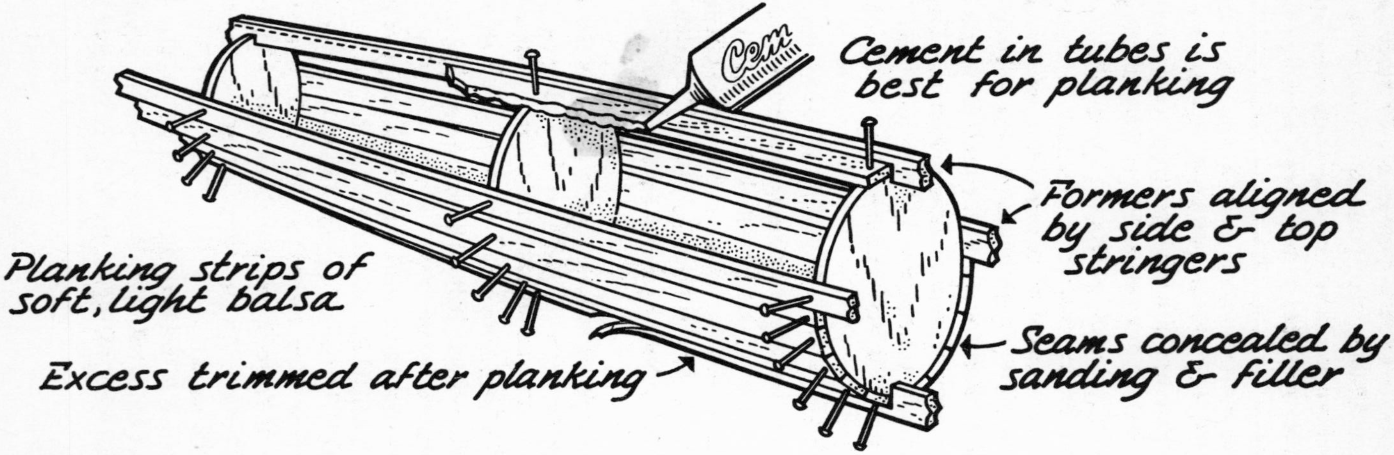

Cement in tubes is best for planking

Formers aligned by side & top stringers

Seams concealed by sanding & filler

Planking strips of soft, light balsa

Excess trimmed after planking

FUSELAGE PLANKING

Fig. 4–8.

ered jobs having up to 45- to 48-inch wing spans. In rubber-powered models having more than 30-inch wings, two-ply $\frac{1}{32}$-inch sheet balsa is recommended for bulkheads. Sheet balsa $\frac{3}{32}$ inch thick is used for this purpose on the smaller gas jobs; $\frac{1}{8}$ inch sheet is used on the larger ones. Since bulkhead or former grain is vertical, these members tend to bend and split in assembly. Cement a light crosspiece across the grain to stop splitting. On gas models, bulkheads need not be cut out for lightness or for the passage of a rubber motor. Stringers are $\frac{1}{16}$ inch square for ships having approximately a 24-inch wing span, $\frac{1}{16}$ x $\frac{1}{8}$ inch (set on edge) for 24- to 36-inch spans, $\frac{1}{8}$ x $\frac{1}{4}$ inch or even $\frac{1}{8}$ or $\frac{3}{8}$ inch on 6-foot designs. When a square fuselage is built with the intention of being rounded off or faired to a more streamlined cross section, try balsa strips $\frac{3}{32}$ inch square for the longerons when the wing span is less than 36 inches, $\frac{1}{8}$ inch square for spans of 36 to 48 inches, and $\frac{3}{16}$ or $\frac{1}{4}$ inch square for intermediate and large-sized gas jobs respectively. Planking strips are $\frac{1}{16}$ x $\frac{1}{4}$ inch, and $\frac{1}{16}$ x $\frac{3}{8}$ inch for rubber-powered models, and as heavy as $\frac{1}{8}$ x $\frac{1}{2}$ inch for gas design.

Crutch construction is a recent development, handy for gas models. A crutch is nothing but a fuselage backbone consisting of two heavy side stringers, generally $\frac{1}{8}$ to $\frac{1}{4}$ inch square or from $\frac{1}{8}$ x $\frac{1}{4}$ up to $\frac{1}{4}$ x $\frac{1}{2}$, depending on the size of the model, and connected with crosspieces. The crutch is built flat on the bench over a drawing. The upper part of the fuselage is built upon the crutch while it is still on the bench.

Wings. The greatest single variation in wing design is the number of spars. The most popular forms of built-up wing construction are: single-spar, double-spar, multispar, sparless, and solid. Built-up wings are required for free-flight gas models, towlines, and all but the smallest rubber-powered designs. Solid wings are used on speed gas models, U-control trainers and team racers. Large wings can be built entirely of balsa by covering them with sheet balsa or planking, but this is the exception. Small ships, especially hand-launched gliders and rubber-powered R.O.G.'s (rise-off-ground) and other flying-model designs of only a foot or so wing spread, are equipped in most cases with sheet-balsa wings. The exceptions are found among R.O.G. and small rubber-powered fuselage designs where a very simple form of built-up wing may also be used.

The most elemental of all is the flat sheet-balsa wing. The wing is outlined first on the sheet balsa and then is cut out with a razor blade. Dihedral, or uptilt of the wing for flying stability, is incorporated by

51

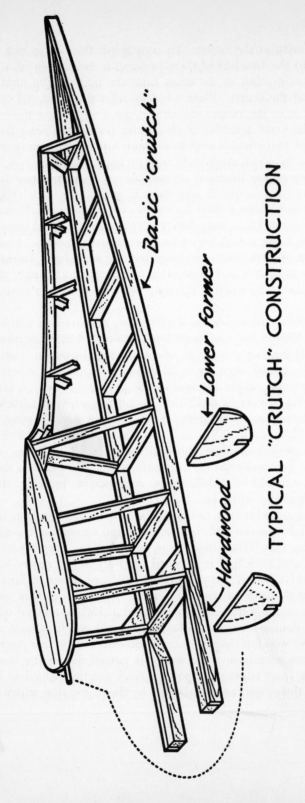

Basic "crutch"

Lower former

Hardwood

TYPICAL "CRUTCH" CONSTRUCTION

Fig. 4-9.

52

cracking the wing at the center. To accomplish this, fasten one side of the wing to the bench, and then, pressing a sharp edge of a rule down on the center line of the wing, raise the free wingtip until the wood cracks at the center. Place a block under the loose end of the wing to hold it at the proper dihedral angle, and cement the ciack copiously. The crack resulting at the center line of the wing should receive at least two coats of cement on both top and bottom overlapping the crack by a minimum of $\frac{1}{4}$ inch on each side. Flat (no camber) wood wings are practical on models up to approximately 24 inches in span. For wings of less than 12 inches, $\frac{1}{32}$-inch sheet is required; $\frac{1}{16}$-inch sheet is used for wings ranging between 12 inches and 2 feet in span. These sizes hold true for ordinary hand-launched gliders and all-balsa R.O.G.'s and small cabin-type models. Contest hand-launched gliders that are subjected to very high launching stresses make heavier wood imperative. Here $\frac{3}{32}$ to $\frac{1}{8}$ inch sheet balsa is desirable. The wood in this wing must be sanded to an airfoil cross section.

If all-balsa wings are cambered slightly, their aerodynamic efficiency is improved. This is because more lift is generated in proportion to drag. A small cambered wing of sheet-balsa construction must be fastened at the center over a soft balsa block, shaped to match the camber of the wing, and to incorporate the proper dihedral. A larger sheet-balsa wing, say of over 12-inch spread, requires an additional wing rib or so on each side of the center line. A 24-inch wing, for example, would be made of $\frac{1}{16}$-inch sheet balsa; the center block for holding the correct camber and dihedral would be 1 to 2 inches wide and flat on the bottom to rest on the fuselage top. Two $\frac{1}{8}$-inch sheet-balsa wing ribs should be added, one on each side of the wing, about 6 inches out from the center line.

The wing is assembled by fastening the ribs to the bench in their properly spaced positions and then bending and cementing the sheet balsa over these ribs. When the cement has dried, the wing is severed at the middle and each half is matched carefully to the center block for camber and dihedral. Any wing made of one sheet of balsa is known as a single-surfaced wing; one made from two sheets of wood for both a top and a bottom surface is called a double-surfaced wing.

To make a double-surfaced all-balsa wing, cut out two wing outlines from sheet wood of the necessary thickness. The bottom piece of sheet balsa (lower surface of the wing) is pinned flat on the bench. The wing ribs (and edges and spars, if any) are then glued to this sheet balsa in their positions as indicated by the plans, after which the

53

top piece of sheet balsa (upper surface of the wing) is bent over the ribs and cemented to them and to the bottom surface at both the leading and trailing edges. Sheet balsa $\frac{1}{32}$ inch thick is sufficient for double-surfaced wings on rubber-powered designs having wing spans of 24 to about 36 inches; $\frac{1}{16}$-inch balsa is used for larger sizes. For free-flight gas models, where power and higher flying speeds make weight of less importance than on rubber-powered models, $\frac{3}{32}$ to $\frac{1}{8}$ inch sheet balsa is suitable for spans of approximately 36 to 60 inches. For U-control use, $\frac{1}{16}$ to $\frac{1}{8}$ inch thick sheet is best on spans up to 30 inches. Select soft balsa. To prevent nicks in the leading edge or actual breakage, cover the leading edges of all wood wings with a band of covering tissue on small ships, silk on the larger ones. The entire surface of a wood wing should be sanded to eliminate as much roughness as possible. A few coats of sanding sealer will fill the pores in the wood and will contribute substantially to cutting down the drag due to skin friction in flight.

Heavier sheet balsa sometimes is used for solid wings on various types of U-control machines, especially team racers and profile trainers. On the team racer, $\frac{1}{4}$ inch hard sheet would be required for a span of 24 inches or so. The same applies to the trainer, except that the work of shaping is tough for a beginner. He would be better off with a prefabricated kit. Trainer wings may run to $\frac{3}{8}$ inch thickness; they are fully shaped in a kit.

Following the flat sheet-balsa wing in simplicity is the built-up, paper-covered, single-surfaced variety exemplified in baby R.O.G.'s and small stick models of from 6 to 18 inch wingspread. Such wings are generally of rectangular shape and never have spars. The leading and trailing edges carry the entire load. These wings are assembled from square strips in the same manner as a fuselage side frame. The front and rear edges are pinned to the bench while the crosspieces or ribs are cemented in place. For an 18-inch wing the only crosspieces needed are one at the center line, one at each wingtip, and one halfway out on each wing panel. Dihedral is attained by cracking the two wing edges at the center line, then cementing the cracks after the tip (or tips if polyhedral or tip dihedral are desired) has been raised to the proper elevation off the bench. The model tissue covering is applied to the top of the wing frame only Never dampen or dope this tissue since the light framework is apt to warp. The completed wing is attached to the motor stick by means of a pair of music wire clips. One clip is glued to the leading edge of the wing, the other to the trailing edge. These clips grip the motor stick and can be detached from it should it become necessary to balance the model by moving the wing fore or aft. The cambered single-surface wing is constructed in the same way as a flat wing with the exception that the curved wing ribs are cut to shape beforehand from thin sheet balsa. The covering is applied to the top of the wing only and should not be sprayed or doped. Select strips $\frac{1}{16}$ inch square for spans of less than 15 inches, $\frac{3}{32}$ inch square for wings ranging between 15 and 24 inches in span, and $\frac{1}{8}$ inch square for spans between 24 and 30 inches.

The single spar wing is popular on small and medium-sized rubber jobs, towliners, and gas free-flight models. On larger wings, there is a tendency for the wing to warp about the single spar. The single spar always should be placed well forward on the chord of the wing, usually at about the one third chord position. The spar must be deep to prevent the shrinking of the top surface covering material from warping the wing upward like a bow. Spar and edge sizes vary widely. On a small wing of, perhaps, 24 inch span, the spar would be $\frac{1}{8}$ x $\frac{1}{4}$; for 30–36 inches of span, $\frac{1}{8}$ x $\frac{3}{8}$. The leading edge for these two examples would be $\frac{3}{32}$, $\frac{1}{8}$, and $\frac{3}{16}$ inch square, if set on edge with the material fitting into a triangular slot cut in the fronts of the ribs. If the leading edge is set perpendicular, $\frac{1}{8}$ inch square would suffice for the smaller sizes, $\frac{1}{8}$ x $\frac{1}{4}$ for the other. These edge sizes, incidentally, hold true when other spar arrangements are used. On very large wings, the edge might be $\frac{1}{4}$ x $\frac{1}{2}$ or even larger. Trailing edges are triangular-cut in standard widths. Use $\frac{3}{8}$-inch wide for the 20 inch span, $\frac{1}{2}$ inch wide for 24 inches to 30 or so of span, $\frac{3}{4}$ for 30–36 to 48–54 inches or so of span.

When two spars are employed the cross section of the material is smaller. Thus, if a single spar measuring $\frac{1}{4}$ x $\frac{1}{2}$ had been used, two spars of $\frac{3}{16}$ x $\frac{3}{8}$ inch could be substituted. The combined cross section of the two spars would be greater than that of the one spar. Compare material cross-section areas when computing such substitutions. Sometimes the front spar of a two-spar wing is placed on the bottom surface, but the rear spar is on the top to help prevent warping. A lighter third spar can be put on top, near the trailing edge, when two main spars are placed normally on the bottom surface.

The first step in constructing a double-surfaced built-up wing is to cut out all the wing ribs from the proper grade of sheet balsa. Sheet balsa $\frac{1}{32}$ inch thick is proper for models of up to 24-inch wing spread, $\frac{1}{16}$ for spreads between 24 and 48 inches. Small gas jobs require sheet $\frac{1}{16}$ inch thick for ribs; intermediate gas designs, $\frac{3}{32}$ inch thick; and large gas models, $\frac{1}{8}$ inch. Magazine plans include a full-size wing-rib pattern. (Kits contain die-cut sheets of wood.) Paste this paper rib on thin stiff cardboard or aluminum, and cut it out for a template for marking the outlines of the required number of ribs on the sheet balsa. A handy tip for quick accurate work is to pin all the ribs together side by side in a bundle with straight pins. In this way all the ribs can be trimmed and sanded to a uniform outline. The spar notches should *not* be cut out until the ribs have been matched.

The next step in assembling the wing is to pin the spar (or spars if two are used) in correct position over the plan. Naturally, if the bottom of the wing is undercambered the spar will not touch the bench. In this predicament cut small balsa blocks to fit under the spar to support it above the bench. Drive the pins for the form on either side of the spar, not through it. The ribs are cemented directly over the rib stations indicated on the drawings; then come the leading and trailing edges. With undercambered ribs, it may be necessary to jack up the front of the trailing edge with slivers of wood. The curved wingtips are cut to shape from pieces of sheet balsa, generally at least two pieces to a tip. If you use but one piece of sheet balsa for a wingtip, it will warp and twist out of shape on any but the smallest of models. The segments of each tip are butted and cemented together cross grain to form one piece which is in turn pinned in place on the wing frame until the cement takes hold.

Sheet balsa used in wingtip construction varies from $\frac{1}{16}$ inch for 12 to 18-inch spans, to $\frac{1}{8}$ inch for 30 to 48-inch spans for rubber-powered models; $\frac{1}{8}$ inch and $\frac{1}{4}$ inch are used for free-flight gas models of intermediate and large sizes. Sheet balsa can be laminated for greater thickness or strength. Squared tips, *à la* Messerschmitt, may be shaped from soft balsa blocks, hollowed for lightness. Sparless wings, popular in small free-flight gas models and U-control stunt models, depend on their sturdy leading and trailing edges to carry the load. The leading edge is a thick piece of balsa shaped to flow into the rib contour. The trailing edge is carved to a sharp edge. A 40-inch wing for a rubber-powered model calls for approximately a $\frac{1}{2}$ x $\frac{3}{4}$ inch leading edge and a $\frac{1}{4}$ x $\frac{3}{4}$ inch trailing edge.

The multispar wing is assembled flat on the bench like any other built-up wing, except that if undercamber is used construction cannot be completed until the wing is taken from the form in a semi-finished condition and inverted for the finishing touches. First of all, the positions of the spars on the wing ribs determine the procedure in assembly. Since rubber-powered contest-model designs often have undercambered wing ribs, it is probable that most, if not all, of the

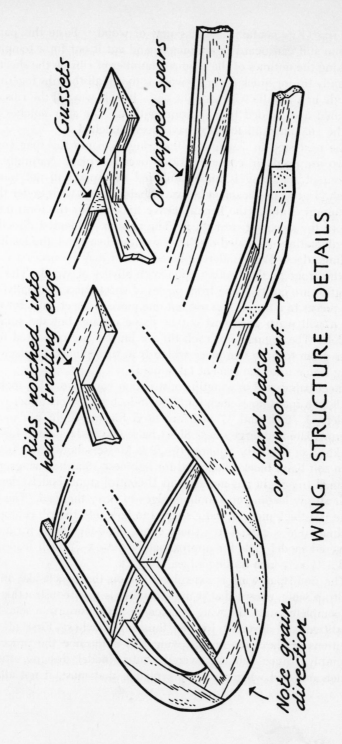

Gussets

Overlapped spars

Ribs notched into heavy trailing edge

Hard balsa or plywood reinf. →

Note grain direction

WING STRUCTURE DETAILS

Fig. 4-10.

57

spars for the bottom surface of the wing will not touch the bench when they are fastened in place in their proper notches cut into the ribs.

Therefore, to facilitate assembly it is advisable to design your model so that at least one bottom spar is located on the deepest bulge on the lower surface of the ribs, insuring that the spar will rest flat on the bench. If this is done, all the ribs can be cemented in position right on the spar. The spar itself can be pinned to the bench. The trailing edge should be shaped and pinned in place before anything else is done. By cementing the ribs both to the spar and to the trailing edge, they can be held in perfect alignment. The leading edge comes next, followed by all the top spars and finally by the wingtips. Now comes the novel part of the procedure. Remove all the pins from the form and invert the wing. The remaining bottom spars are now glued in place.

The multispar wing popularized by the Cleveland contest model builders is most often used on rubber-powered contest models of 36 to 54 inch wing span. The ribs are cut from $\frac{1}{16}$ inch sheet balsa, the spars are balsa $\frac{1}{16}$ inch square, the leading edge is $\frac{1}{8}$ inch square set on edge "diamond" fashion, and the trailing edge is $\frac{1}{8}$ x $\frac{3}{8}$ inch or $\frac{1}{8}$ x $\frac{1}{2}$ inch triangle stock. Six to eight spars are used, half on the top surface and half on the bottom. Larger gas models may use three to five spars of deep cross section, all placed on the bottom surface or inserted through holes in the ribs. The latter makes for a strong, warp-free structure.

Modelers have two reasons for covering the leading edge section of their wings with thin sheet balsa. One reason is that a more accurate wing-rib contour can be made with wood than with paper, which can, and does, sag between the ribs. The other reason is to gain sufficient strength to withstand collisions of the leading edges with branches or sharp objects that would cut through the wing. This sheet balsa is applied by cementing one edge of the wood to the slanted side of the leading edge (most leading edges are set diagonally in the fronts of the wing ribs) and then by bending the sheet down and over the ribs. A $\frac{1}{8}$ inch square strip should be countersunk across the tops of all the ribs from tip to tip, providing a foundation for the rear edge of the balsa sheeting. Usually, wood sheeting of the leading edge extends back about $\frac{1}{3}$ of the chord of the wing (to the spar on a single-spar wing, to the front spar on a two-spar wing). Sheet $\frac{1}{32}$ of an inch thick is used for small gas-powered models and large rubber-powered ships; $\frac{1}{16}$ inch sheet is used for gas jobs of intermediate and large sizes.

False ribs can be substituted for sheet-balsa covering of the leading edge. False ribs are nothing but the abbreviated or cut-off noses of the regular ribs. They are cemented in place between spar and leading edge and serve to keep the covering from sagging badly between the full-length ribs.

On large rubber-powered designs and all gas models it is advisable to sink the rear edges of the wing ribs into notches cut in the trailing edges. The ribs should be cut about $\frac{1}{16}$ to $\frac{1}{4}$ inch in length, depending on size. Never force tight fits as warps will result.

Dihedral imposes some pretty problems in making wing-spar joints

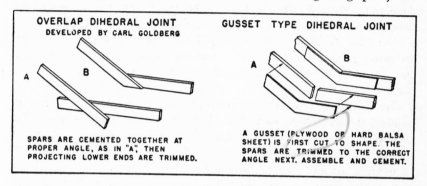

Fig. 4–11.

for gas models. There are two popular methods for reinforcing the spliced spar joints. The builder may slant the edges of the spar sections to piece them together neatly and then "box" the joint by cementing to each of its sides (the front and the rear faces) flat pieces of hard sheet balsa or possibly veneer. Or the spar sections can be so placed in each wing panel that their ends will overlap when joined.

On smaller Half-A free-flight models, a single thickness of $\frac{1}{8}$ inch sheet—butt-jointed for added width if necessary—is sturdy enough for the pylon-deck support. For bigger Half-A's, laminate two thicknesses of $\frac{1}{8}$ inch sheet. On Class A free-flights, it is advisable to laminate two thicknesses of $\frac{3}{16}$ inch sheet. The best construction for crutch type ships is to build the central pylon frame of, say, $\frac{1}{4}$ inch thick strips and pieces of sheet, as part of the fuselage backbone. This backbone is propped upright on the crutch, and the crutch and backbone are further assembled together with bulkheads or formers. Finally, the pylon frame can be covered over with $\frac{1}{8}$ inch sheet or whatever thickness sheet the builder feels is necessary. The sizes just given suit a Class A model. On very large free-flights, it is suggested that the pylon be given a wide, streamlined cross section, using formers and paper or silk covering.

Tails. Tail surfaces can be considered in almost all instances as small wings. Construction is similar but lighter. Stabilizers with flat cross sections generally consist of one square spar, rectangular edges, and square crosspieces. The leading edges are rounded after assembly, with the trailing edges shaved to a point. Spars and crosspieces vary as follows: $\frac{1}{16}$ inch square for 12 to 18 inch wing spans, $\frac{1}{8}$ inch square for 24 to 30 or 36 inch spans, $\frac{1}{4}$ inch square for medium-sized gas models. Leading edges for tails are, on the average, of the same thickness as the crosspieces, but twice as wide. For the above spar and crosspiece sizes, leading edges would vary from $\frac{1}{16}$ x $\frac{1}{8}$ inch to $\frac{1}{4}$ x $\frac{1}{2}$ inch. Trailing edges should be approximately three times as wide as the spar and crosspiece thickness, ranging in the cases cited from $\frac{1}{16}$ x $\frac{3}{16}$ inch to $\frac{1}{4}$ x $\frac{3}{4}$ inch. Sometimes, for lightness, stabilizer and rudder crosspieces are of the same depth as the spar but only half as thick. Thus with a $\frac{1}{8}$ inch square spar, $\frac{1}{16}$ x $\frac{1}{8}$ inch crosspieces would be used. For small rubber models a single sheet of either $\frac{1}{32}$ or $\frac{1}{16}$ inch balsa serves as a simple tail. Sheet balsa tails should be quartergrained; otherwise thin stiffener strips must be glued across the tail to prevent warping.

Streamlined and lifting-type stabilizers may be sparless (just a leading and trailing edge) or may have one or two heavy spars, or any number of light spars. Sometimes two thin sheets of balsa are used with ribs placed in between. Although lifting-type tails very often are built up with spars and ribs like a wing, they can also be satisfactorily constructed by using one sheet of balsa, curved to an airfoil shape over a single heavy center rib and held at the proper camber by twin rudders cemented to the tips. Sheet $\frac{1}{32}$ inch thick is adequate for small rubber jobs; $\frac{1}{16}$-inch sheet for large rubber jobs and small gas models; and $\frac{3}{32}$ inch sheet for large gas models.

Rudders, too, have infinite varieties. However, rudders having flat and streamlined cross sections are the most popular. Sheet balsa is most commonly used, $\frac{1}{16}$ inch thick for Half-A size, $\frac{1}{8}$ for Class A, and so on. Coat the wood with dope that has been plasticized with about eight drops of castor oil to the ounce of dope. This prevents warping.

Rudders and stabilizers are assembled in a form with straight pins in the same manner as built-up wing frames.

Now let's see how these systems of construction are applied to everyday airplanes, control-line, for instance. Both team racers and stunt ships go in heavily for sheet-sided fuselages. But here, there is an innovation. Since such planes take abuse, "doublers" are used. A doubler is an added thickness of material cemented to the inside front of the fuselage side. It usually extends to the rear ends of the motor mounts or to the trailing edge of the wing. In the team racer, it may be sheet balsa. In stunt models it should be plywood. Team jobs generally are of a shoulder or low-wing layout. Stunters are mid-wing or low-wing. In all cases, slots are cut through the fuselage to match the wing contours. These big cut-outs are one reason doublers are needed. Nose impacts due to flying errors are the other reason. Solid wood wings for team ships have been mentioned. Stunt frameworks must be light and tough, hence the use of lightweight built-up wings. These wings usually have a top and bottom spar—such as $\frac{1}{4}$ inch square on a 40-inch span, with wide trailing edge and a D-section leading edge. This D is formed by covering the front of the wing, both top and bottom with $\frac{1}{16}$ sheet balsa, spanwise grain. The sheet butts against both top and bottom spar. If vertical pieces of scrap are inserted between the ribs against the rear faces of the spars, truly tremendous strength results.

The speed plane uses a variation of the hollow-block fuselage, plus the solid wing. However, the block fuselage should be in two halves, upper and lower, hollowed to a wall thickness of perhaps $\frac{3}{8}$ inch. Also, pine should be used and even this wood is of doubtful strength for lower shells. Hence these shells are cast of magnesium and aluminum. The double-sheeted wing principle might also be used but the material would be one-piece sheet aluminum, wrapped around a metal spar and flush riveted along the only seam at the trailing edge. The solid wing would be shaped like that of the team racer but again pine would be utilized for maximum strength. Also, the leadouts must run through the wing for minimum air resistance and consequently long grooves are cut in the under surface of the wing. Metal tubing is placed in the grooves, the leadouts running through the tubing. The grooves are covered over so carefully that close inspection will not reveal them. Tail surfaces are flat, solid surfaces: plywood for speed models, sheet balsa for stunt and team designs. It is advisable to make vertical tails of ply to avoid damage from turn-over accidents.

With the exception of the long Wakefield rubber jobs, construction in this category is the same as it has been for a generation. The extreme length of the Wakefields, coupled with the need of ultralight weight, has taught the boys some tricks over the last year or two. Crosspieces have only half the cross section they used to have; a $\frac{1}{8}$ inch square crosspiece to match a $\frac{1}{8}$ inch square longeron is now $\frac{1}{16}$ x $\frac{1}{8}$ inch. These crosspieces are not vertical but are placed in a series of continuous V's from nose to tail.

5

LANDING GEARS AND PONTOONS

LANDING GEARS may employ a single wheel, two wheels, or even a tricycle arrangement of one nose wheel and two larger rear wheels. Landing gears may be permanently located or retractable.

Retracting mechanisms usually consist of a rubber-band-loaded or spring-loaded single wire landing-gear strut that is held open by the weight of the plane, retracting, therefore, as soon as the plane lifts into the air. Sometimes a dethermalizer type fuse is used to keep the gear from retracting until the plane is safely airborne. Single wheels are swung rearward and upward into a slot in the fuselage bottom.

When two wheels are used, one on each side of the body, it is impossible to swing them straight back for retracting in any practical manner. Why, then, do not all free-flight models employ a single-wheeled chassis? Because the monowheel chassis has its drawbacks too. Unless the model is especially designed for its monowheel gear, it won't stand upright on the ground. Sometimes two additional fins are placed beneath the stabilizer to serve as twin tail skids, keeping the model on an even keel when on the ground. Or twin rudders may be used, one on each end of the stabilizer, having a large underslung portion to rest on the ground to serve as a tail skid. The stabilizer may be given reverse dihedral (cathedral) so that the tips rest on the ground.

Three-wheeled arrangements are uncommon on model airplanes. Such landing gears are usually found on radio models. The wise gas-

LANDING GEAR DESIGN AND CONSTRUCTION —

★ FOR RUBBER MODELS —

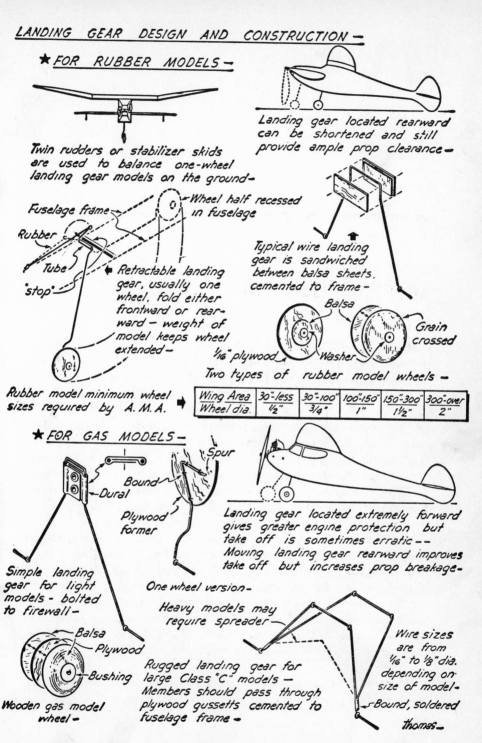

Twin rudders or stabilizer skids are used to balance one-wheel landing gear models on the ground —

Landing gear located rearward can be shortened and still provide ample prop clearance —

Fuselage frame

Rubber

Tube

"stop"

Wheel half recessed in fuselage

Retractable landing gear, usually one wheel, fold either frontward or rearward — weight of model keeps wheel extended —

Typical wire landing gear is sandwiched between balsa sheets, cemented to frame —

Balsa

Grain crossed

1/16" plywood   Washer

Two types of rubber model wheels —

Rubber model minimum wheel sizes required by A.M.A. ➡

Wing Area	30"-less	30"-100"	100"-150"	150"-300"	300"-over
Wheel dia.	1/2"	3/4"	1"	1 1/2"	2"

★ FOR GAS MODELS —

Spur

Bound

Dural

Plywood former

Landing gear located extremely forward gives greater engine protection but take off is sometimes erratic — — Moving landing gear rearward improves take off but increases prop breakage —

Simple landing gear for light models - bolted to firewall —

One wheel version —

Heavy models may require spreader —

Wire sizes are from 1/16" to 1/8" dia. depending on size of model —

Balsa

Plywood

Bushing

Wooden gas model wheel —

Rugged landing gear for large Class "C" models — Members should pass through plywood gussetts cemented to fuselage frame —

Bound, soldered

thomas —

Fig. 5–1.

model builder locates his wire landing gear so far forward that the wheels sometimes are actually beneath the propeller, if not slightly in front of it. But on very large ships having tricycle landing gears the weight-supporting wheels are generally farther back beneath the fuselage, giving a better take-off run.

The ordinary two-wheeled gear, unfortunately, has a tendency to ground loop. It is important to place the rear wheels of a tricycle gear just slightly aft of the C.G.

Music wire is the favorite landing-gear material. Its flexibility and strength make it superior to other materials. On fuselage designs, a portion of the wire is clamped between two pieces of hard sheet wood with another piece of hard sheet balsa inserted into the crevice between the outer layers inside the U of the wire chassis. In effect, this is nothing but a sandwich, the two outer pieces enclosing the wire U and the sheet-balsa filler piece. On gas jobs, the U is held against a plywood bulkhead (firewall) by a metal strap fitting, bolted in place over the wire.

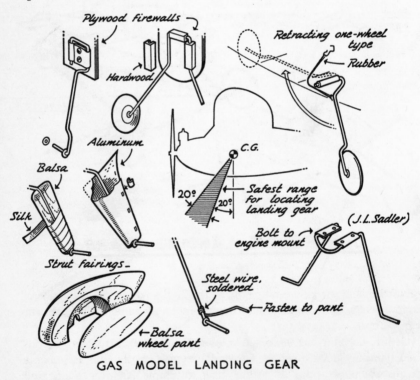

GAS MODEL LANDING GEAR

Fig. 5–2.

Scale-model landing gears are most often made from streamlined balsa strips. These strips are shaped by selecting wood with a rectangular cross section, ⅛ x ¼ inch for instance, and rounding the front edge and tapering the rear edge to a point. When sanded smooth, strips so shaped make excellent streamlined struts. If the scale struts are not wide enough to provide sufficient strength to take the landing shock, strengthen them with music wire, bamboo, or dowel

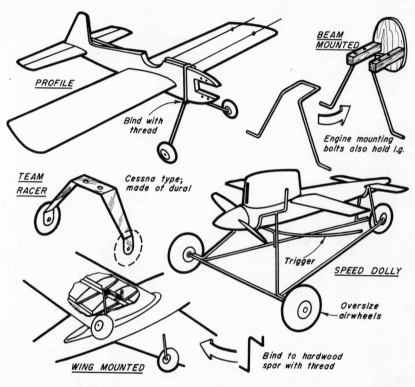

PROFILE

Bind with thread

BEAM MOUNTED

Engine mounting bolts also hold l.g.

TEAM RACER

Cessna type; made of dural

Trigger

SPEED DOLLY

Oversize airwheels

WING MOUNTED

Bind to hardwood spar with thread

CONTROLINE LANDING GEARS

Fig. 5–3.

reinforcement strips, countersunk in the balsa wood. Struts made of combinations of material should be covered with paper or other covering material.

So far, nothing has been said about the U-control models. In this field, landing gears must be extremely rugged, as flexible as possible to absorb blows (and to spring back to shape instantly), and well mounted in the machine. In general, the wire selected should be heavier than on free-flights. For example, a Half-A job would use $\frac{1}{16}$ inch diameter wire for the landing gear, although its wing span might be 12 to 18 inches. A 2-foot job could well use $\frac{3}{32}$ inch wire, and a 3 to 4 foot plane, $\frac{1}{8}$ inch wire. In almost all cases, the wire is in one piece, running continuously from wheel to wheel, through the fuselage. It may be attached, free-flight fashion, to a firewall but using heavy strap fittings, or the U-shaped top of the bent landing gear wire (the part that ordinarily fits into a sandwich mount on most types of planes) can be made extra deep, and then bent back at right angles to be fastened in place by strap fittings and bolts. When gears are attached to the wings, the wire may go up to the wing, back to the spar, cross-ship to the other side, and thence down to the other wheel. The portion running along the spar should be well bound and cemented to the wood.

Control-line plane designers take advantage of any heavy structural members for tying in the landing gear. The familiar hardwood beam mounts in the box-fuselage stunter are ideal for attaching landing gear wire. The wire may be diverted back along one mount, across to the other, then forward again, and down to the other wheel. The wire should be well bound to the wood. Or a heavy plywood plate should be well glued to the bottom surface of the bearers and a large U, bent in the wire, should be fastened with strap fittings and bolts to the plywood. In the case of a heavy profile fuselage, the wire should be bent with a narrow but deep U to fit over the profile. A slight groove

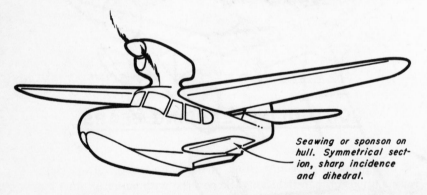

Seawing or sponson on hull. Symmetrical section, sharp incidence and dihedral.

FLYING BOAT WITH SPONSONS

Fig. 5–4.

at the proper place on each side of the profile would help countersink the wire into the wood. Another type of gear frequently seen on team racing types is the dural, sheet metal leg.

Turning to hydro models, there are two types: flying boats and pontoon or float planes. The former have a single boatlike hull, especially shaped for easy take-off and stability when resting or taxiing on the water. Sea wings or sponsons jut from the sides of the hull to hold the ship upright. Sometimes small tip floats are used—pontoons mounted beneath the wingtips to touch the surface of the water whenever the model tilts to one side. Pontoon models may have one, two, or three floats. Several kinds of float arrangements have proved practical. First, there is the familiar two float scheme as seen on real aircraft. Two long, thin floats are required. These may be of scale or semi-scale design. Such arrangements are seen mostly on scale or semi-scale sport jobs where realism is desirable, but are not often seen

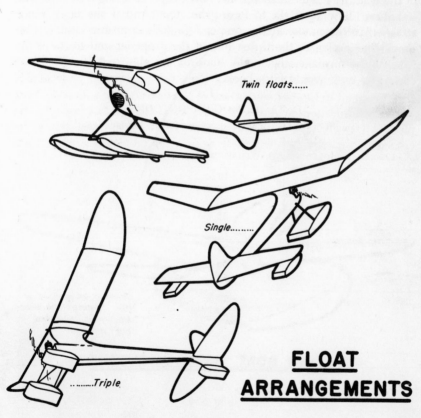

Twin floats......

Single.........

.........Triple

FLOAT
ARRANGEMENTS

Fig. 5–5.

on contest planes. On contest free-flight gas models one large forward float is centered beneath the fuselage, with two smaller, but ample, floats at the rear, one at each tip of the stabilizer. Still another popular arrangement for the same kind of flying calls for two medium sized floats paired forward, with a fairly large float in the tail skid position.

There are two basic kinds of floats used on model airplanes. First, there is the rounded-top variety with the V bottom, the "semi-scale" type. These are long and thin by comparison with the second type, the "sea-sled" design. As the name implies, sea-sled floats are flat-bottomed, shaped like the common sea-sled speed boats seen on any lake. In fact, these floats have flat tops and sides as well as flat bottoms.

On model planes, proper float design probably is more difficult than the model itself. The designer must know the size of float required for any given size and weight of model. He must know the proportions of the float, how wide it should be, how deep, what angle to make the V bottom, how far back to locate the step. And if the float is not attached to the model at the proper fore-and-aft position and at the proper inclination to the thrust line of the propeller and to the flight path of the airplane, the model may not be able to take off. Float design by itself would fill a book.

DATA ON MODEL PONTOONS
(Length of float is equal to 70 per cent of the fuselage length)

LENGTH OF MODEL	WEIGHT OF MODEL	REQUIRED WIDTH OF FLOAT
20 in.	16 oz.	3.37 in.
	18	3.50
	20	3.62
	22	3.87
25 in.	18 oz.	3.25 in.
	21	3.50
	24	3.75
	27	4.00
30 in.	20 oz.	3.25 in.
	24	3.50
	28	3.75
	32	4.00
35 in.	24 oz.	3.25 in.
	28	3.37
	32	3.62
	36	3.87

(Length of float is equal to 70 per cent of the fuselage length)

LENGTH OF MODEL	WEIGHT OF MODEL	REQUIRED WIDTH OF FLOAT
40 in.	28 oz.	3.25 in.
	33	3.50
	38	3.75
	43	3.87
45 in.	33 oz.	3.37 in.
	38	3.62
	43	3.75
	48	4.00
50 in.	40 oz.	3.50 in.
	45	3.75
	50	4.00
	55	4.25
55 in.	43 oz.	3.50 in.
	48	3.75
	53	4.00
	58	4.25
60 in.	50 oz.	3.62 in.
	55	3.87
	60	4.00
	65	4.12
65 in.	53 oz.	3.62 in.
	58	3.87
	63	4.00
	68	4.12
70 in.	60 oz.	3.62 in.
	66	3.87
	72	4.00
	78	4.12
75 in.	66 oz.	3.62 in.
	74	3.87
	82	4.12
	90	4.37

Alan Booton, the noted model designer, developed over a period of years the most successful semi-scale float design to date. His data are boiled down into a full-page drawing illustrating this chapter.

The accompanying table lists pertinent data for any size and weight of model you may desire to equip with pontoons.

For best results, twin floats should each be 70 per cent of the model's

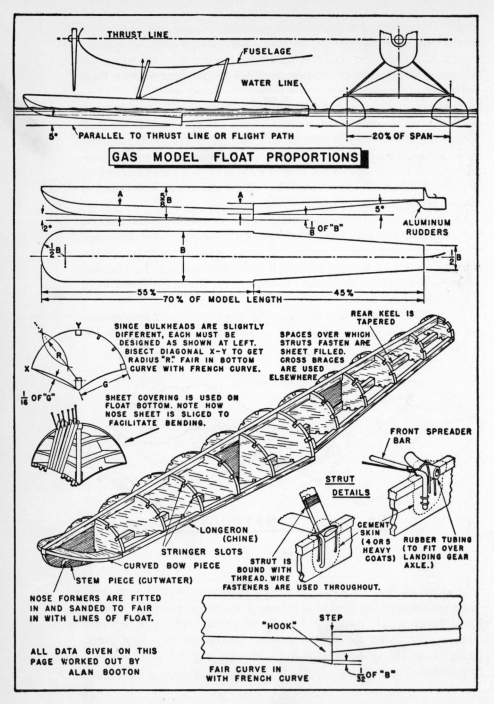

THRUST LINE

FUSELAGE

WATER LINE

5° — PARALLEL TO THRUST LINE OR FLIGHT PATH

20% OF SPAN

GAS MODEL FLOAT PROPORTIONS

A

B

5°

ALUMINUM RUDDERS

2°

⅛ OF "B"

½ B

B

½ B

55%

70% OF MODEL LENGTH

45%

REAR KEEL IS TAPERED

SINCE BULKHEADS ARE SLIGHTLY DIFFERENT, EACH MUST BE DESIGNED AS SHOWN AT LEFT. BISECT DIAGONAL X-Y TO GET RADIUS "R." FAIR IN BOTTOM CURVE WITH FRENCH CURVE.

SPACES OVER WHICH STRUTS FASTEN ARE SHEET FILLED. CROSS BRACES ARE USED ELSEWHERE

Y

R

X

G

⅟16 OF "G"

SHEET COVERING IS USED ON FLOAT BOTTOM. NOTE HOW NOSE SHEET IS SLICED TO FACILITATE BENDING.

FRONT SPREADER BAR

STRUT DETAILS

LONGERON (CHINE)

STRINGER SLOTS

CURVED BOW PIECE

STEM PIECE (CUTWATER)

STRUT IS BOUND WITH THREAD. WIRE FASTENERS ARE USED THROUGHOUT.

CEMENT SKIN (4 OR 5 HEAVY COATS)

RUBBER TUBING (TO FIT OVER LANDING GEAR AXLE.)

NOSE FORMERS ARE FITTED IN AND SANDED TO FAIR IN WITH LINES OF FLOAT.

ALL DATA GIVEN ON THIS PAGE WORKED OUT BY ALAN BOOTON

"HOOK"

STEP

FAIR CURVE IN WITH FRENCH CURVE

⅟32 OF "B"

Fig. 5–6. Booton Floats.

length. The step in the float bottom should be 55 per cent of the float length back from the nose of the float. Each float should be approximately ⅝ times as deep as it is wide, and the depth of the triangular bottom should be approximately one fifth of the float width. Twin floats should be spaced apart one fifth of the wing span.

Blunt- or round-nosed floats prevent "digging in." Never use a pointed float. A downward curve or hook incorporated in the float bottom directly in front of the step aids take-off and prevents fore-and-aft rocking during the take-off, known as "porpoising." A small aluminum rudder is required at the rear of each float to prevent circling on the water when making a take-off run. These aluminum water rudders can be bent for adjustments.

Thoroughly dope the entire surface of the model. Dope the internal framework of the pontoons. Waterproof the ignition, coil, batteries, wires, etc., with a coat of hot liquid wax. Leave no openings in the covering of the plane. The ship should resist soakage for the few minutes necessary for the builder to retrieve it. Mount the motor high. If possible do not invert it.

The proper installation of floats on the model is of vital importance. For instance, the float step must lie two to five per cent ahead of the ship's C.G.

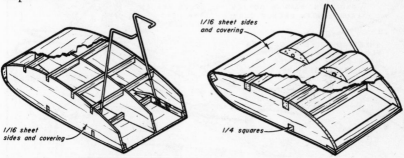

1/16 sheet sides and covering

1/16 sheet sides and covering

1/4 squares

SEA SLED CONSTRUCTION

Fig. 5–7.

Sea-sled floats seem simpler to design and construct. Fortunately, complete data for this kind of float have been compiled by the Virginia Brain Busters. The sea-sled float is interchangeable with wheeled landing gear. After the contest builder flies his job as a land plane, he slides out the wheeled gear and snaps the proper type of sea sled in position.

A typical sea-sled float for an A-Class gassie measures about 6 inches long, 4 inches wide and about 2 inches deep. The smaller stabilizer floats should be from one half to two thirds the size of the main float. The cubic inch capacity of sea-sled floats should be three for every ounce of model weight. Thus, 40-ounce craft requires a minimum float content of 120 cubic inches. You can figure a set of floats for your own plane. On a 40-ounce ship, the front floats would be approximately 10 inches long, with 7-inch rear floats. Seating these floats at the proper angle to the fuselage is important. They have proved satisfactory when nosed up ten degrees. Sometimes the float angle is measured relative to the thrust line. Five degrees, with the float line meeting the thrust line extension forward of the nose, is considered good practice. Floats that are too large hinder flying and, due to the increase in drag and its effect on trim, may interfere with the flying characteristics of the plane.

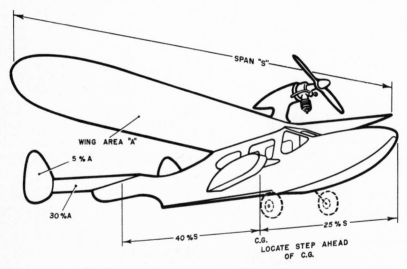

FLYING BOAT PROPORTIONS

Fig. 5–8.

A sea-sled float is easy to construct. For a rubber-powered plane, use $\frac{1}{16}$ inch sheet balsa. The framework consists of two sides and a few crosspieces, with paper, silk, or sheet balsa covering. A good all-wood float can be made if the wood is well doped a couple of times, then covered with paper, and given several more coats of dope. Be sure that all seams of the covering material overlap. For the average gas model, $\frac{1}{8}$ inch sheet balsa is substituted for the thinner sheet of the rubber design. For really large floats, three side pieces are made, rather than two. The third piece is placed in the middle, somewhat as wing ribs are placed on the wing spars. Three or four crosspieces, one or two on the top surface and two on the bottom, plus bow and stern pieces (nose and tail) will make the float amply strong.

The usual method of mounting the floats is to attach float-wide pieces of metal tubing to the top of the crosspieces and then to slide the landing gear wire (the wheel having been removed) into the tubing. An auxiliary strut to help maintain alignment is bound to the single main strut of the ship with the other and extending into the tubing further back on the top of the float. Floats should be mounted well forward with their noses slightly ahead of the prop position.

6

PROPELLERS

FOR ANY given model design there is a propeller that will perform better than all others. Rubber-powered models, particularly, require the precise combination of correct propeller diameter (distance from tip to tip), pitch (the distance the propeller will travel forward in one complete revolution), and blade area. On gas models, pitch and diameter are the most important factors. The engine manufacturer specifies the required propeller diameters for his engine. Propeller manufacturers turn out such excellent products that very few builders will take the time and trouble to carve their own gas-model propellers.

Model builders have evolved a rule-of-thumb technique for choosing propeller specifications for any size and type of rubber-powered model. They have discovered the ratio between pitch and diameter that automatically indicates the blade area for any propeller. Pitch-diameter ratios vary from 1:1 to 2:1. Low pitch makes for fast climb. Contest endurance-type rubber-powered models use from 1½:1 to 2:1 ratios. A handy thing to bear in mind is that the pitch is always proportional to the thickness of the propeller block while the diameter is proportional to the width of the propeller block. Thus, knowing the diameter and pitch of his required propeller, the designer can figure the width and depth of his block. To start with, he knows that the average fuselage endurance model has a propeller diameter equal to approximately 40 per cent of the wing span.

Dick Korda, the former Wakefield champion and one of the world's most famous designers of rubber-powered models, says: "By endless testing with different types of props, it was found that one carved from a 2x2x18 inch block was best suited for a ship of approximately 200 square inches of wing area, with a 40- to 45-inch wing span." A check of many designs indicated that blocks of 18-inch diameter vary principally from 1¼ x 2 and 1½ x 2 inches through 1¾ x 2 to the 2 x 2 size recommended by Dick Korda.

So the informed builder, knowing the rough proportions of his block, makes use of a universal layout method. The propeller block is marked into quarters by drawing pencil lines across the widest face. Diagonals are drawn in, running from the ends of the halfway mark on each blade to the opposite corners of the same mark on the other blade

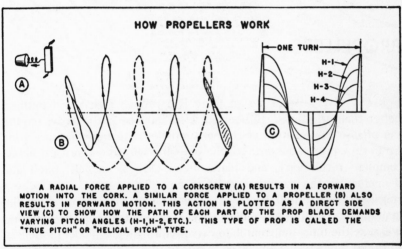

HOW PROPELLERS WORK

A RADIAL FORCE APPLIED TO A CORKSCREW (A) RESULTS IN A FORWARD MOTION INTO THE CORK. A SIMILAR FORCE APPLIED TO A PROPELLER (B) ALSO RESULTS IN FORWARD MOTION. THIS ACTION IS PLOTTED AS A DIRECT SIDE VIEW (C) TO SHOW HOW THE PATH OF EACH PART OF THE PROP BLADE DEMANDS VARYING PITCH ANGLES (H-1, H-2, ETC.). THIS TYPE OF PROP IS CALLED THE "TRUE PITCH" OR "HELICAL PITCH" TYPE.

Fig. 6–1.

(the propeller hub is filled in about ⅜ inch wide). The propeller tips are tapered in thickness from the halfway mark to the tip, the tip proper being just half the depth of the block at the halfway mark. The hub, likewise, is tapered in thickness to just half the original thickness.

In constructing a prop, select a good block of medium variety, firm and white with the straightest grain possible and even texture throughout. When you carve a prop from a block that varies in texture, you must lighten the heavier blade by sanding it thinner than the other. This causes an uneven airfoil section. Despite balancing, the prop will still vibrate when turning under power.

After the block has been laid out, drill a hole for the shaft, keeping it as straight as possible. Shape the block by cutting along the outline of the side view first, then the top. When the block is finished, sand the edges and the hub. Carve the tip outline drawn on the top view.

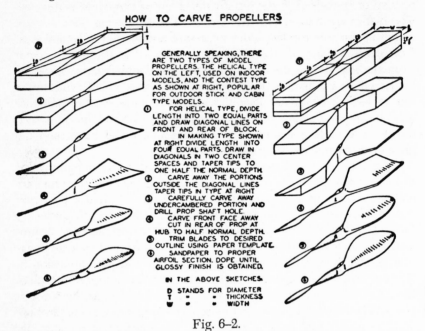

HOW TO CARVE PROPELLERS

GENERALLY SPEAKING, THERE ARE TWO TYPES OF MODEL PROPELLERS. THE HELICAL TYPE ON THE LEFT, USED ON INDOOR MODELS, AND THE CONTEST TYPE AS SHOWN AT RIGHT, POPULAR FOR OUTDOOR STICK AND CABIN TYPE MODELS.
① FOR HELICAL TYPE, DIVIDE LENGTH INTO TWO EQUAL PARTS AND DRAW DIAGONAL LINES ON FRONT AND REAR OF BLOCK.
IN MAKING TYPE SHOWN AT RIGHT DIVIDE LENGTH INTO FOUR EQUAL PARTS. DRAW IN DIAGONALS IN TWO CENTER SPACES AND TAPER TIPS TO ONE HALF THE NORMAL DEPTH.
② CARVE AWAY THE PORTIONS OUTSIDE THE DIAGONAL LINES TAPER TIPS IN TYPE AT RIGHT
③ CAREFULLY CARVE AWAY UNDERCAMBERED PORTION AND DRILL PROP SHAFT HOLE.
④ CARVE FRONT FACE AWAY CUT IN REAR OF PROP AT HUB TO HALF NORMAL DEPTH.
⑤ TRIM BLADES TO DESIRED OUTLINE USING PAPER TEMPLATE.
⑥ SANDPAPER TO PROPER AIRFOIL SECTION. DOPE UNTIL GLOSSY FINISH IS OBTAINED.

IN THE ABOVE SKETCHES.
D STANDS FOR DIAMETER
T " " THICKNESS
W " " WIDTH

Fig. 6–2.

Begin carving by hollowing the inside of the blade first, cambering it about $\frac{3}{16}$ inch at the widest part, fading out as you reach the tip. Excessive camber will not improve performance.

Finish one blade with medium sandpaper; too coarse a paper will leave cuts that are very hard to remove. Carve the other blade as much like the first as possible. Uneven blades bring on vibration. The most difficult part to carve is the inside of the blade. Carve as close as you safely may, then use plenty of sandpaper.

When shaving down the top of the blade, be careful not to come too close to the edges. Also watch the thickness of the blade. Thickness should taper from about $\frac{1}{4}$ inch near the hub to $\frac{1}{16}$ inch at the tip. Sand to a smooth, even finish with fine paper, and balance. Use several coats of clear dope, sanding between coats with the finest paper obtainable. These directions apply to diameters of 16–20 inches; camber should be decreased for smaller diameters.

For an efficient glide, drag must be reduced to a minimum. Freewheeling and folding props are essential in contest competition. Freewheeling props cut drag by means of a small catch—various freewheeling devices are illustrated in figure 6-3—that disengages the prop from the shaft after the rubber has unwound, thus permitting the prop to revolve or freewheel in the air stream. Folding props are better still. The blades are hinged near the hub so they can swing back at right angles against the fuselage sides to present a minimum of frontal area. Centrifugal force holds the blades in position while the rubber motor is unwinding. When the motor has stopped, the air stream blows the blades backward against the fuselage. This arrangement, while superior to freewheeling, has its difficulties. For instance, the propeller must be stopped at one particular position on every flight. If it isn't, the delicate glide adjustments will be thrown out of kilter, and the glide path cannot be controlled properly.

Rubber tensioners have been adopted to control the stopping point of folding propellers. In principle, a coil spring between the propeller and the nose plug, or between the front of the hub and a bent-over right angle extension of the front end of the shaft, moves the propeller forward as the rubber motor unwinds and loses its tension. A projection, usually an L-shaped piece of music wire formed by a continuation of the shaft rubber hook—see figure 6-3 and the discussion in "Rubber Models"—engages a stop in the rear face of the nose plug. Usually this stop is a wood screw firmly embedded in the wooden plug. When the L-catch strikes the stop, the propeller locks in position, and the blades fold back in the wind. The location of the stop determines the position of the propeller when the blades fold.

One-bladed propellers are apparently most efficient. The one-bladed propeller's superiority is said to result from the fact that, with two or more blades, each blade is revolving in the turbulent wake of the blade before it.

One-bladed props require counterweights for balancing. The usual counterweight consists of a lump of solder attached to the end of a short piece of music wire, connected to the propeller hub opposite the single wooden blade. This wire attachment has its end bent at right angles and embedded in the hub. Thread binding and cement prevent it from coming loose. The counterweight is made by pouring molten lead into the empty metal top of a pencil held in a small wood block. The wire attachment piece is held in the pencil top while the lead solidifies.

It is interesting to note that wise builders slant their propeller-blade hinges so that the blades fold back and fit flat against the fuselage.

FITTINGS AND PARTS –

Round nose pliers are ideal for bending wire parts–

Bend end first, then large loop.

Distance from end determines size of loop–

Equip hook with "spaghetti" tubing to protect rubber–

A TYPICAL FOLDING PROP AND RUBBER TENSIONER–

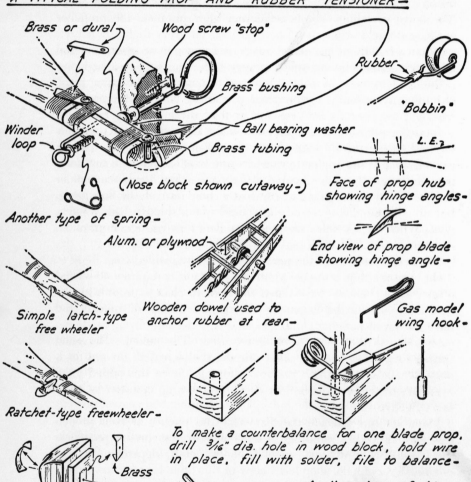

Brass or dural

Wood screw "stop"

Rubber

Brass bushing

"Bobbin"

Winder loop

Ball bearing washer

Brass tubing

L.E.

(Nose block shown cutaway–)

Face of prop hub showing hinge angles–

Another type of spring–

End view of prop blade showing hinge angle–

Alum. or plywood

Simple latch-type free wheeler

Wooden dowel used to anchor rubber at rear–

Gas model wing hook–

Ratchet-type freewheeler–

To make a counterbalance for one blade prop. drill 3/16" dia. hole in wood block, hold wire in place, fill with solder, file to balance–

Brass

Another type of hinge for folding prop – Always finish hinges completely before cutting blades apart–

Nose blocks are usually made of crossed grain sheet balsa to prevent splitting – plug is pine–

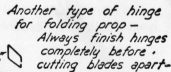

Thomas–

Fig. 6–3. Typical Folding Prop.

Passing on to gas jobs, we find many excellent manufactured prop designs. These are made from gumwood, basswood, birch, mahogany, and walnut. For two reasons metal propellers are not often used: they increase the likelihood of crankshaft damage in bad landings and, when revolving, they are hazardous to fingers. Folding propellers are sometimes used for gas or free-flight models. Folders boost gliding efficiency, especially on small gas ships where the propeller is fairly large in relation to the model. Folding gas-model propellers must be built with care. Centrifugal force will "throw" a blade if the hinges are not strong enough or if the workmanship is not of a high order. The newer glow plug engines attain such high rpm figures that a folder is too much of a risk.

When a free-flight gas model hangs on its prop in an almost vertical climb, its actual forward speed is very little, and a low-pitched propeller is at its best. A control-line speed model, on the other hand, requires an unusually high-pitched propeller. Here the propeller is hard put to screw its way forward as fast as the model is traveling.

Propeller pitch for free-flight contest machines should vary according to the type of climb. An almost straight-up flight indicates a lower pitch to enable the engine to exert its power effectively and not dissipate its thrust through slippage. If, on the other hand, the builder favors a wide, circling kind of climb at a comparatively shallow angle, but at a higher flying speed, he should use a slightly higher pitch. Among the Half-A ships there is a tendency to use stock props no matter what, with builders favoring 3½ or 4 inches of pitch.

In the case of a cargo clipper, where weight is added from flight to flight until the ship is unable to remain aloft for its required 40-second official flight, builders have noted the need to change props with the load increases. In the beginning, the plane will take off quickly and have a form of hanging climb. As load is added, the flying angle becomes less so that more pitch is required. The model is traveling further forward to gain the same altitude; the increased forward tendency demands more pitch to avoid slipping. Since this added pitch overloads the engine, the builder decreases the prop diameter to maintain effective rpm's.

Manufacturers indicate the diameters and pitches of their propellers. Top Flite has published a table which gives proper propellers for free-flight, stunt, and speed U-control craft, depending on the engine. Every model shop has a copy of this table for your inspection.

In general U-control practice, selection of the propeller is comparatively simple. The diameter is known. While pitches are given in the table, the correct pitch for a given plane may vary according to the weight and drag of the machine itself. Too low a pitch will produce plenty of engine noise but a very poor forward speed, the plane seeming to hang with a very small margin of reserve speed. Too high a pitch will hinder take-off and hold down rpm's noticeably.

Propellers for indoor models are notable for their large diameter (about half the wing span) and large blade area. Needless to say, they must be featherweight, since weight reduces flight endurance. Indoor-model propellers are sometimes carved from soft balsa (which weighs about 4 pounds per cubic foot) to a paper-thin state, tapering from $\frac{1}{16}$ inch at the hub to $\frac{1}{64}$ at the tip. More often these props are built up like a wing, the edges being bent from a continuous piece of $\frac{1}{32}$-inch sheet balsa with very thin ribs cut from $\frac{1}{64}$-inch sheet. Built-up propellers are covered with microfilm.

7

COVERING

COVERING MATERIALS vary according to the size of the model and its purpose. (See figure 7–1 for tools and materials used in covering.) Generally, small rubber-powered ships are covered with some such light tissue as Silkspan or Skysail. Paper usually comes in at least two grades of weight and strength. Small gas designs are also covered with light tissue. Large gas models are covered throughout with paper, silk, or nylon, or sometimes with silk or nylon on the fuselage and paper on the wings and tail.

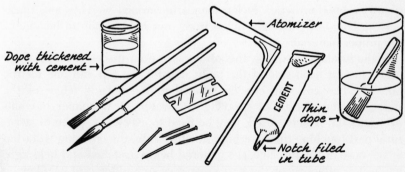

TOOLS & MATERIALS FOR COVERING

Fig. 7–1.

Wet-or-dry tissues are the latest thing on the market. This paper can be soaked in water, wrung out, and placed on the framework. Where streamlined fuselages or difficult curved fillets are to be covered, wet covering saves a lot of headaches. Ordinary model tissues will wrinkle when covering double curvatures. Wet papers can be stretched with the greatest of ease around almost impossible curves. Clear dope is used as the paper adhesive; it will stick to the paper despite its wetness. Model tissues come in numerous colors.

When using the wet method, it is advisable to dope those portions of the framework which will be in contact with the covering material. This is good practice whether the plane is to be covered wet or dry because it insures a firm contact of material and framework, minimizes damage from tears and greatly adds to the strength of the ship. Also it is difficult to fix any covering to untreated wood because the dope for fixing the material will enter the wood. In the use of wet covering, there is a further advantage in first doping the wood surface. Not only will the covering adhere better: its moisture cannot cause the wide, thin trailing edges of the wings to warp or bow.

Silk is one of the strongest of all coverings. However, its weight limits its use to gas models, and chiefly large ones. Gas models of medium size may have silk on their fuselages, but their wings are usually paper-covered. For really large gas jobs, the added cost of silk covering is justified by the increased strength of the model. Silk may be applied either wet or dry.

Nylon is stronger than silk. Like silk, it may be applied wet or dry. When wet, it dries rapidly. If the covering dries before it is completely applied, it may be wet again, as many times as necessary. Nylon has no grain as silk does. It may therefore be applied either spanwise or chordwise. Nylon comes in various weights and thicknesses. Obtain lightweight nylon from your hobby shop to be sure of the proper material.

If the fuselage is square, the job is easy. Four pieces of material are used, one for each side of the body, one for the top and one for the bottom. The covering can be applied to the outside edges of the frame and shrunk tight by spraying with water. Or the paper, or whatever material is being used, may be fixed to every crosspiece or structural part touching the covering. In either case, the covering is started at the nose of the fuselage, the material being stretched and held tight while it is attached to the rear crosspiece or rudder post. Following this, the covering is doped to one longeron and finally to the other longeron, while the paper is worked as tight as possible without

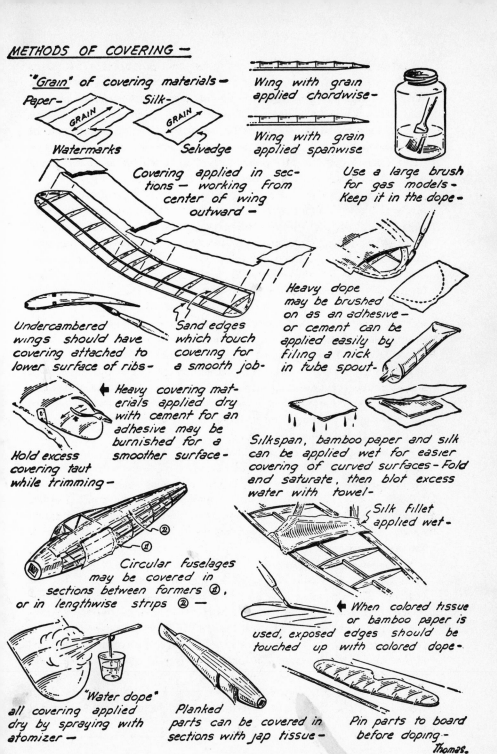

"Grain" of covering materials —

Paper —   Silk —

GRAIN   GRAIN

Watermarks   Selvedge

Wing with grain applied chordwise —

Wing with grain applied spanwise

Covering applied in sections — working from center of wing outward —

Use a large brush for gas models — Keep it in the dope —

Undercambered wings should have covering attached to lower surface of ribs —

Sand edges which touch covering for a smooth job —

Heavy dope may be brushed on as an adhesive — or cement can be applied easily by filing a nick in tube spout —

Heavy covering materials applied dry with cement for an adhesive may be burnished for a smoother surface —

Hold excess covering taut while trimming —

Silkspan, bamboo paper and silk can be applied wet for easier covering of curved surfaces — Fold and saturate, then blot excess water with towel —

Silk fillet applied wet —

Circular fuselages may be covered in sections between formers ①, or in lengthwise strips ② —

← When colored tissue or bamboo paper is used, exposed edges should be touched up with colored dope —

"Water dope" all covering applied dry by spraying with atomizer —

Planked parts can be covered in sections with jap tissue —

Pin parts to board before doping —

Thomas.

Fig. 7-2.

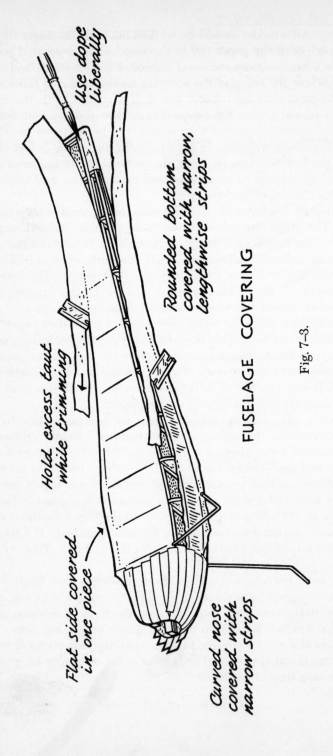

Use dope liberally

Hold excess taut while trimming

Rounded bottom covered with narrow, lengthwise strips

Flat side covered in one piece

Curved nose covered with narrow strips

FUSELAGE COVERING

Fig. 7-3.

84

wrinkling. All wrinkles should be worked out with the finger tips before the edges of the paper dry to the wood. The dope used for the adhesive is brushed onto the wood surface of the longerons and crosspieces. Where the edges of the covering touch the doped framework, the covering should be rubbed into a firm contact with the wood. The two fuselage sides are covered first, then the top and bottom.

Silk and nylon, because of their weave, can be stretched in any direction to pull out wrinkles. In covering with silk, nylon, or wet-or-dry papers, the best adhesive for fixing the material to the framework is a half-and-half mixture of clear dope and cement. The final doping is done with thinned clear dope only.

Streamlined fuselages of all kinds may be covered with strips of tissue. The strips are made as wide as possible without causing wrinkles. Again, silk or nylon may be applied in large sheets. Any faired or streamlined fuselage should have the surfaces of all bulkheads sanded away in a shallow curve between all stringers. The covering should not touch the bulkheads but should rest on the stringers only, except, of course, at the very nose and tail of the fuselage.

Silk and nylon will take many more coats of dope than paper will. A wing that is not thoroughly doped actually develops a leakage of air pressure from the bottom surface through to the top. Either paper or cloth requires at least six coats of dope thinned to half strength with thinner. If you use Sta or Aerogloss, remember that you must also use the same type of thinner and sanding sealer.

Of course, silk or nylon should be used only on planes that have a rugged framework to withstand their tautness. Small, lightweight planes covered with paper may also warp. This action—it occurs only on wings and tails—can be minimized by a process known as plasticizing. This means that several drops of castor oil are stirred into an ounce of dope. The slight amount of castor oil will prevent further pulling, and will add a certain flexibility to the paper (without making it loose) so that it will not so easily tear or puncture. If a total of three coats is used, use plasticized dope for the final one. Two of each, if you use four coats, and so on.

There are a few simple tricks in covering wings. (See figure 7–4.) First, any wing will have dihedral, dividing the wing into two or more panels or straight sections, depending on the form of dihedral used. V dihedral has two panels; tip dihedral, three; polyhedral, four. The top surface of a wing is covered with as many separate pieces of tissue as there are dihedral panels. The bottom of the wing may be covered with one long strip of tissue.

85

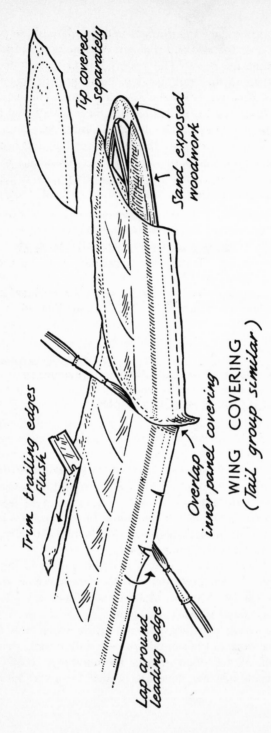

Tip covered separately

Sand exposed woodwork

Trim trailing edges
Flush

Overlap inner panel covering

Lap around leading edge

WING COVERING
(Tail group similar)

Fig. 7-4.

86

The wing covering is attached to the four outside edges of the panel to be covered; that is, to the two end ribs and the leading and trailing edges. Run the grain spanwise. The material is first stuck to the leading edge and then to the trailing edge, being pulled tight with the fingers until the adhesive holds the covering tight. The material is then doped, first to one end rib, then to the other, again being held tight while the adhesive dries. Some builders prefer to attach the material to the end ribs first and only then to the leading and trailing edges. Wings having undercamber must have the covering material applied to the bottom of *every* rib. This is done with the wing inverted and small weights resting on the covering to hold it tight to the ribs.

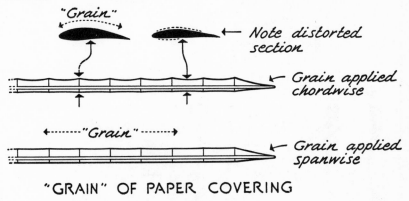

"GRAIN" OF PAPER COVERING

Fig. 7–5.

Regardless of the material used, all dry-covered wings should have their covering sprayed with water to pull the covering to drumlike tautness. If you have tried this and had your wing warp, you did not do it properly. Only one panel of a wing should be sprayed at a time and this panel should be pinned tightly to the bench until dry. It will not stick to the bench when pinned down.

Cover wingtips with a separate piece of material, precut to the required pattern. Sand all cemented joints so that one piece of wood fits flush with its neighbor. See that dried cement does not jut out to snag the covering. Sand down every joint.

Sometimes silk or nylon may not pull up tightly when it is first doped. Exposing the work to the sun will usually do the trick. It will be found that use of colored dope reduces the number of coats. If, for example, eight coats of clear dope are needed for a certain silk-

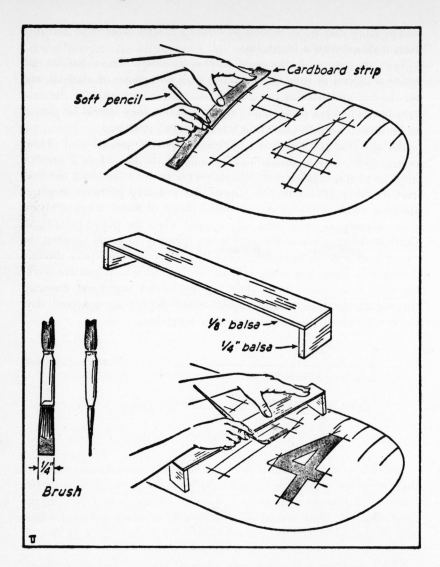

Fig. 7–6. Lettering of Wing Covering.

covered framework, perhaps four coats of clear plus two of colored will have the same effect. Another useful fact concerning nylon is that if wrinkles appear before doping, they can be removed by placing dope on an adjacent edge of the covering to loosen it, after which the wrinkles can be pulled out and the edge doped down again.

Always use a new razor blade for trimming. The thin frayed edge

88

that remains may be smoothed by wetting it with clear dope and rubbing it down with a finger tip.

Tails are covered in the same manner as wings. The usual flat tail, either stabilizer or rudder, is covered with two pieces of material, one for the top and one for the bottom or one for each side, as the case may be. When tail surfaces are water-sprayed, they should be pinned to the bench until the covering has dried and stretched.

For spraying purposes, any household sprayer can be used. However, a paint sprayer is desirable because of the fine vapor it creates. Most paint sprayers have an adjustable nozzle for controlling the fineness of the particles in the vapor. An ordinary perfume atomizer makes a handy sprayer. Avoid actual *drops* of water when spraying your covering as small tears may appear when the paper pulls tight. Don't stand too close to the part being sprayed—to avoid blowing the paper hard enough to damage it—and don't point the spray directly downward. Stand the wing, tail, or fuselage on which you are working against a nearby wall. Don't worry about water-wet covering sticking to the bench. If possible, avoid doping on a humid day. Dope will "blush," leaving large white splotches.

8

MINIATURE GAS ENGINES

PRACTICALLY ALL gas engines for model airplane usage operate on the two-cycle principle. This means that the power stroke (when the vaporized fuel-air mixture is fired within the cylinder) is delivered on every second stroke of the piston (the down stroke).

There is a great deal of difference between two- and four-cycle engines. The four-cycle engine has four movements of the piston, two up and two down, for every power stroke. On the first stroke, the piston travels downward creating a partial vacuum in the top of the cylinder, thus drawing in through the open intake valve the charge of vaporized gas. On the second stroke, the piston travels upward, compressing the gas mixture in the top of the cylinder, intake and exhaust valves now being closed. The timer now causes the spark plug to fire, exploding the gas-air mixture. This is the power stroke, the explosion driving the piston down, transmitting the force of the explosion through the crankshaft to the propeller (or flywheel). The piston now travels up again, forcing the burned gases through the open exhaust valve. Then as the piston goes down again, a fresh charge of fuel is sucked in through the open intake valve, and the cycle repeats. Because of its mechanically operated valves four-cycle gas engines are seldom used as model airplane power plants. They are complicated and costly.

In the two-cycle engine the fuel-air mixture is admitted directly into

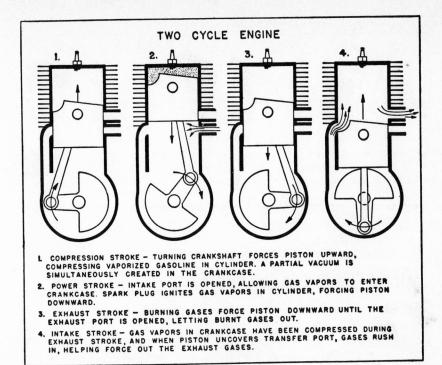

TWO CYCLE ENGINE

1. COMPRESSION STROKE – TURNING CRANKSHAFT FORCES PISTON UPWARD, COMPRESSING VAPORIZED GASOLINE IN CYLINDER. A PARTIAL VACUUM IS SIMULTANEOUSLY CREATED IN THE CRANKCASE.

2. POWER STROKE – INTAKE PORT IS OPENED, ALLOWING GAS VAPORS TO ENTER CRANKCASE. SPARK PLUG IGNITES GAS VAPORS IN CYLINDER, FORCING PISTON DOWNWARD.

3. EXHAUST STROKE – BURNING GASES FORCE PISTON DOWNWARD UNTIL THE EXHAUST PORT IS OPENED, LETTING BURNT GASES OUT.

4. INTAKE STROKE – GAS VAPORS IN CRANKCASE HAVE BEEN COMPRESSED DURING EXHAUST STROKE, AND WHEN PISTON UNCOVERS TRANSFER PORT, GASES RUSH IN, HELPING FORCE OUT THE EXHAUST GASES.

Fig. 8–1.

the crankcase chamber. The crankcase is hermetically sealed. On the first stroke, the piston travels upward, compressing the gas vapor in the cylinder and causing a partial vacuum in the crankcase. In moving upward, the piston uncovers the intake port so that the partial vacuum in the crankcase causes a fresh charge of fuel to be sucked into the crankcase. When the plug ignites the fuel mixture in the cylinder, the piston is driven downward for its second stroke. When the piston reaches its lowest point, it simultaneously uncovers both the exhaust port in the cylinder wall and, on the opposite side of the cylinder, the bypass from the crankcase to the cylinder, permitting the fuel vapor in the crankcase to rush up into the cylinder. The pressure of the fuel in the cylinder helps push the exhaust gases out the open exhaust port. A baffle, or raised ridge, on the piston top prevents the fresh vaporized fuel mixture from racing directly across the cylinder and out the exhaust port on the opposite side. The baffle deflects the mixture upward.

In the ignition motor, a properly timed spark fires the fuel vapor. This spark is made possible by means of batteries which supply the

SEVERAL TYPES OF MOTOR MOUNTS-

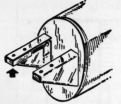

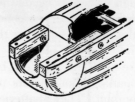

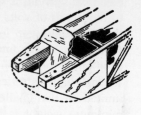

Metal motor mounts are bolted to firewall-wooden blocks absorb vibration-

A simple type in which bolted bearers can be easily replaced-

Thin plywood sides, tacked and cemented to blocks makes a firm mount-

CUTAWAY SKETCH OF TYPICAL TWO-CYCLE MODEL ENGINE

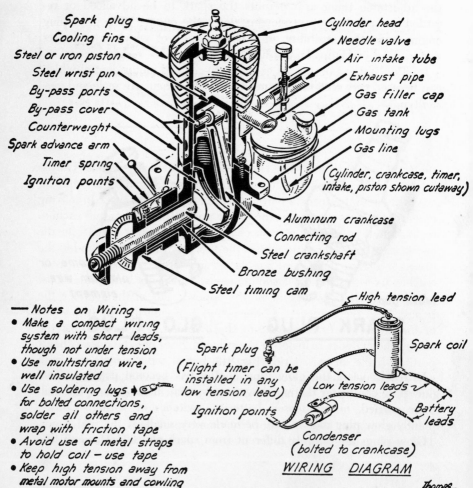

Spark plug
Cooling Fins
Steel or iron piston
Steel wrist pin
By-pass ports
By-pass cover
Counterweight
Spark advance arm
Timer spring
Ignition points

Cylinder head
Needle valve
Air intake tube
Exhaust pipe
Gas Filler cap
Gas tank
Mounting lugs
Gas line

(Cylinder, crankcase, timer, intake, piston shown cutaway)

Aluminum crankcase
Connecting rod
Steel crankshaft
Bronze bushing
Steel timing cam

— Notes on Wiring —
• Make a compact wiring system with short leads, though not under tension
• Use multistrand wire, well insulated
• Use soldering lugs ✦ ⊙ for bolted connections, solder all others and wrap with friction tape
• Avoid use of metal straps to hold coil — use tape
• Keep high tension away from metal motor mounts and cowling

High tension lead

Spark plug
(Flight timer can be installed in any low tension lead)

Ignition points

Spark coil

Low tension leads

Battery leads

Condenser
(bolted to crankcase)

WIRING DIAGRAM

Thomas—

92

Fig. 8–2. Ignition Engine.

electrical current, a spark coil which steps the voltage from three up to thousands of volts (high voltage is needed to make the spark jump the spark-plug gap inside the cylinder), a condenser, a timing device (the points, built into the motor) for firing the spark at the proper position of the piston, and the spark plug.

Flash light batteries are used. All sizes can be used, pen cells being limited to the smaller spark-ignition motors powering planes where minimum weight is important. These batteries are used in pairs to give three volts.

Ignition engines continue to have certain special uses. In general, they develop less power than glow plug engines. This makes the ignition engine desirable for radio models where flexibility of power control is desirable. Some builders prefer ignition engines because the adjustable timer arm permits the spark to be advanced or retarded, so speeding up or slowing down the engine. The glow plug engine lacks this flexibility, one disadvantage of which is a greater incidence of crack-ups on test flights.

Ignition systems permit an excellent two-speed motor control which can be used very well on U-control models, particularly scale and carrier types.

Spark gap

SPARK PLUG

Nichrome or platinum wire element

GLO PLUG

Fig. 8–3.

In recent years the glow plug engine has become popular. The glow plug eliminates the entire ignition system; there is no spark coil to be carried, no condenser, batteries, switches or wiring. Consequently glow plug motors may be made very small.

Glow plugs are entirely different from spark plugs. Instead of the regular spark plug's electrodes, the glow plug features a small platinum-tipped wire coil which fits into the hollow interior of the plug in such manner that it is exposed at the lower end to the interior of the cylinder. This coil is heated by attaching outside booster batteries (usually two doorbell batteries wired to give 1½ volts); the engine is started while the batteries are still connected. The heated coil in the glow plug causes the fuel mixture to explode. As soon as the engine revs up sufficiently, the booster attachment wires or leads are withdrawn and the engine continues to run until it exhausts the fuel supply. Special fuels are required.

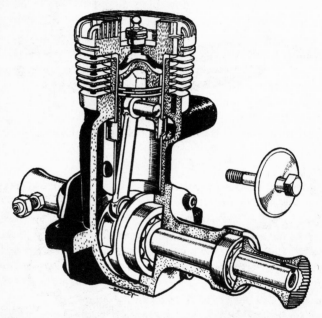

Fig. 8–4. Glow Engine.

When used for ignition, the booster batteries are wired to give three volts; glow plugs usually require but 1½ volts.

Whereas the spark engine operates on a mixture of from 2 up to 4 parts white gas to 1 part S.A.E. oil, the glow plug uses a basic mixture of nitro methane, methanol, and degummed castor oil.

Most engines have lapped pistons. Lap is a term that describes a machine shop practice by which a piston is fitted closely to the cylinder within which it rides. Other engines have piston rings. In such an engine, the piston does not fit the cylinder as closely as does the piston in the lapped engine but the rings, which fit into grooves in the piston,

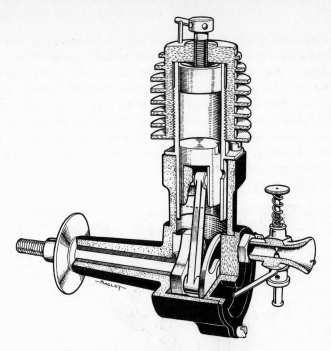

Fig. 8–5. Diesel Engine.

press tightly against the cylinder wall. When the engine wears and loses compression, the rings are easily replaced.

The Diesel engine is distinguished from the gas engine, either ignition or glow, by much higher compression ratios and the elimination of any form of ignition, either spark or glow. A fuel mixture is used which insures the necessary explosion whenever the engine is flipped over smartly. Inside the Diesel cylinder the sudden and very high compression of the fuel mixture causes it to ignite.

An odd feature of Diesels is a method of varying the compression by means of a lever or screw on top of the cylinder head. When this control is screwed in, it slightly lowers a fixed piston within the cylinder. There is now less space between the fixed and moving pistons. This has the effect of raising the compression ratio. When the "contra" or top piston is withdrawn slightly, it increases the space between the pistons and so lowers the compression ratio. This variation enables the flier to adjust the compression ratio for easy starting, then fast running and maximum power, or to allow for various fuel mixtures, even while the engine is running. When the head is screwed down and the needle valve closed down to provide less fuel, the engine runs on a lean or economical mixture.

Fuel for the Diesel is a mixture of ether, kerosene, and degummed castor oil, mineral oil, or motor oil. Most engine manufacturers recommend a mixture of equal parts ether, kerosene, and oil, but more ether is needed in cold weather.

Fuel must be mixed with air and admitted to an engine as a vapor. Everyone knows the tremendous explosive qualities of gasoline vapor; other fuel vapors are similarly powerful. Second, the amount of fuel, once it is vaporized, must be controlled to suit the speed at which the engine is being run.

PARALLEL   SERIES

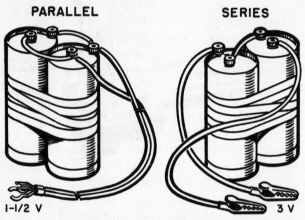

I-I/2 V   3 V

BOOSTERS

Fig. 8–6. One- and Three-Volt Wiring.

Both vaporization and amount of fuel are controlled by a needle valve. This is nothing but a long pointed rodlike piece of metal that screws into a long tube. Imagine a piece of metal tubing. To the one end, the fuel line is connected; to the other, the needle valve. In the middle is a tiny hole. When the needle is screwed all the way into the tube, it covers this small hole. No fuel can pass. As the needle is unscrewed, fuel flows from the fuel line out the hole. The needle can be delicately adjusted to close more or less of the hole as necessary.

How does the fuel become vapor? When you flip the propeller to start the engine, fuel is sucked through the hole in the needle valve and, once the engine begins to run, the fuel becomes mixed with the air that rushes through the venturi. The relationship of the small hole in the needle valve body and the venturi is very important.

As we have already seen, the upward movement of the piston inside the cylinder causes a partial vacuum in the crankcase. Thus, when the intake valve opens, the rush of air through the venturi causes the liquid fuel to be blended with air—to be vaporized. The action is similar to that of a perfume atomizer.

A common way to attach booster leads is by means of alligator clips which, as the name suggests, have serrated jaws for grasping terminals, etc. If you use such clips be sure you get small ones for model work from your hobby shop. Large ones grip too tightly and will loosen the center portion of the glow plug. Slip-on connections are better. There are two types, depending on the type of glow plug being used. Ask your dealer for the proper connection for your particular brand of plug. The connection slides over the plug, automatically making all necessary electrical connections without risk of short circuits. Once the engine starts, the slip-on is easily pulled off.

A prop wrench is essential because props frequently come loose in starting or may break on contact with the ground when landing or taking off, requiring replacement. The use of pliers on prop nuts will quickly round their corners, making it difficult to tighten or loosen the nut. Many makes of engines are shipped with such a wrench in the box. It will be found that this wrench is cleverly designed to perform many special purposes, frequently fitting, in one way or another, every removable part on the motor, including the back crankcase cover plate.

For bench testing, any motor can be operated on the fuel tank that is attached to it when purchased. A larger tank must be purchased for control-line flying. Inasmuch as the position of the tank in the plane with respect to the needle-valve level of the engine and the direction of turn in flight is vitally important, it is urged that both the engine and tank manufacturers' directions be carefully followed. If your engine is new, it may require breaking in before full-throttle operation for an extended run is possible. Therefore, it is recommended procedure to let the engine run off a few tanks of fuel at reduced throttle. This is done by screwing out the needle valve, after starting, until the engine runs with a rich mixture, indicated by a smoky exhaust and slower running. Well-made engines, particularly the bigger ones, may consume a couple of cans of fuel in this process. New engines should be operated at first on sport, not racing, fuel. Sport fuel does not permit the high rpm of more potent mixtures so that the engine does not heat up as much. If you have only a powerful fuel at hand, add 5 to 10 per cent of its volume in castor oil. For the duration of the break-in period use a prop slightly smaller than the recommended size for the particular engine.

How do you know when the engine is broken in? Turn or screw in the needle valve while the engine is running (to lean out the mixture) until the engine reaches its obvious maximum number of rpm. The smoky exhaust will disappear and the radical change in sound will be easily detected. Now, if the engine continues to run steadily, holding a constant rpm until the fuel is exhausted, it is ready for flying. If, on the other hand, the engine seems to run up and down hill, alternately slowing and speeding, it requires more breaking in. It is good practice not to run the engine for more than 30 seconds the first time you try it.

Here is a foolproof method for starting glow engines:

1. After selecting the desired propeller, position it on the crankshaft. If you face the motor from the front, and turn the shaft to the left with your fingers, you will feel the piston come up against compression inside the cylinder. The prop then should be on the shaft diagonally in such a manner that the tip to your right is slanted upwards in the two o'clock position. This position minimizes breakage when the ship lands. It also makes for easy and natural flipping and minimizes the number of times the prop will kick free.

2. After filling the tank with fuel, some raw fuel must be gotten up to and into the engine. Some builders prefer the choke method. This means that a finger is placed over the open end of the venturi while the prop is turned until fuel is observed to flow through the fuel line up to the needle valve. A couple of extra flips at this point induces enough fuel vapor into the cylinder to give a pop and perhaps a start. Other builders prefer to prime. This means that a jet of fuel is squirt-gunned into the exhaust port. The prime.should be small, consisting of a few drops; anything more should be run off by tipping the engine and blowing away the excess. When priming, it is still necessary to choke slightly in order to fill the fuel line, otherwise the engine will start, run off the prime, and then strike an air space in the fuel line before the raw fuel reaches the needle valve.

Squirt the prime against the piston through the port; the piston prevents an excess of fuel getting into the cylinder. Flip the prop a few times before attaching the booster leads. Should an engine become flooded, remove the glow plug (with the proper wrench, never with pliers) and invert the engine, at the same time holding in the lowest position the venturi. The excess fuel will drain out the various openings. Spin the prop with the finger to make sure that extra fuel is ejected through the glow plug hole. Lower the piston by turning the shaft and blow through the exhaust ports. Blow excess fuel off the glow plug filament.

98

3. Once the engine is primed and fuel has been drawn into the line ready to run, attach the booster slip-on connections and flip the propeller smartly in a counterclockwise direction. If the prop stops with a loud bang or smack, you have over primed the motor. Remove the booster leads, check the prop for looseness and change in position, then flip it over several more times, attach the leads once more and attempt to start. If the prop does not stop short again with a bang, continue to flip up to a dozen times or until the engine begins to run. If there is no action prime again, lightly, and flip again.

Sometimes you will hear a very mild pop, perhaps the instant you flip the prop, then maybe another pop. This means that the engine is on the verge of starting so continue flipping until it runs. There is a slight excess of fuel in the engine but not enough to cause flooding.

4. When the engine starts abruptly and runs for only a second or two at extremely high rpm—just a brief scream—the fuel mixture is too lean. The engine merely ran off the prime. Open the needle valve one quarter turn and repeat the starting procedure. If the engine now runs at high rpm but stops within seconds, open the needle valve another quarter turn, and so on until the engine runs satisfactorily.

If the engine runs but does so at a very low and faltering number of rpm, with a smoky exhaust, the needle valve is open too far and must be shut down one quarter turn at a time. If the engine continues to run but slows down—but without the telltale smoky exhaust that indicates a rich mixture—the mixture is just a trifle lean. Open the valve only a notch or two (listen for the clicks of the knurled knob that holds the needle valve steady). When the engine runs well but with an irritating, raspy sound, the mixture is slightly rich and the needle valve should be turned in a click or two until the running smooths out.

Two things are likely to happen before you get ideal adjustment. If the mixture is still lean, the engine will scream in flight and then stop abruptly or; if the mixture is too rich, the motor will continue to run, but at reduced rpm and with heavily smoking exhaust. To correct the lean mixture, open the valve a click at a time; for rich mixture correction, turn in the valve a click at a time. After this, if the engine cannot be kept running in flight, or even sometimes on the bench, it means that the tank is either in the wrong position or too far from the engine. Generally speaking, the tank top should be level with the needle valve in free flight, though it may rise as much as half the tank above the needle valve level. In control-line flying, the fuel line at point of exit from the tank should be on the level with the needle

valve body. Keep all tanks as close as possible to the engine to minimize the distance the engine has to suck fuel. An engine with poor
crankcase compression may not be able to pull fuel more than a few
inches.

Should the engine refuse to start—assuming it is not old and worn-
out with leaky bearings which permit crankcase compression to leak
past the bearing—check your battery voltage. You must have at least
$1\frac{1}{4}$ volts. Also check the battery connections, making sure the knobs
that hold down the wires are not loose. Remove the glow plug, attach
the leads, and see if it lights with a good glow.

When an engine which is known for its easy starting and good
running, suddenly develops trouble without explanation, try these
hints:

1. Is the fuel line clogged? Sometimes flecks of dirt may be seen
through the transparent neoprene fuel line at the point of attachment
of the needle valve body. This probably means that there is dirt in
the tank as well, perhaps even closing off the tiny hole in the needle
valve itself.

Remove the flexible line from the needle valve body and squirt fuel
through it. Tanks have three openings: one for the fuel line, one for
filling, and one for the vent which allows air to escape when you fill
the tank. Hold your finger over this vent, attach the squirt gun to
the filler tube, and squirt fuel through the tank and out the opening to
which the fuel line attaches. Swish the fuel around the tank and blow
through the filler opening while holding the vent closed. The pressure
will jet a stream of fuel out the fuel line tube.

Remove the needle valve body and, if the hole is clogged, work out
the dirt with the point of a pin. Attach the spray gun to one end of
the body and squirt fuel through it. Then close the far end with the
finger so that the force of the fuel under pressure is directed out the
tiny hole. Replace the valve body, being sure that the small hole is in
its original position which usually is downwards, out of sight, facing
the shaft, or inwards, facing the crankcase, in rear valve motors.

2. As directed above, make sure the hole in the needle valve is
properly placed. If the engine has been disassembled, the needle
valve body may have been improperly replaced, or it may have been
turned accidentally.

3. The glow plug may be weak. If this is the case, the engine will
start with booster batteries connected but will stop when the booster
lead is disconnected. Or the engine may always stop within a few
seconds after the leads have been disconnected. Replace the plug. A

further check is to see if the motor will keep running with the boosters connected.

4. If the engine has been run extensively and has given lots of service, it may have developed a loose fitting bearing, permitting crankcase compression to be lost. This can be detected by a wobbling crankshaft. Ordinarily, the crankshaft will not wobble but if, on picking up the motor and bending the prop in a fore-and-aft direction, you can feel play in the bearing, then it probably needs replacement.

5. Glow plugs may be loose or damaged, permitting head compression to be lost. Such compression may leak around the base of the plug or up through the center piece where the insulated material separates the contact from the outside of the plug. If the plug is loose, tighten it, but if the core piece is loose, replace the plug.

6. If the engine gradually slows down after minutes in the air, and it is known to be thoroughly broken in, but is still fairly new, a less powerful, cooler running fuel may be required. Or some oil may be added to the hot fuel mixture. Be sure, also, that your needle valve is not set a hair too lean. On long engine runs there is a tendency for the engine to lean out toward the end of the run; this is due to the fact that, as fuel is consumed, there is less weight of fuel to create pressure at the needle valve—or the level of fuel may have dropped to the point where pressure has disappeared and the engine must depend entirely on suction to make the fuel flow. So open the needle valve a notch or two and note the results on subsequent test flights.

7. A widespread cause of improper engine running lies in the size of the venturi intake. The engine that runs on the bench or in a stationary plane may stop as soon as the plane is launched. Such a rush of air passes through the venturi that the fuel mixture goes too lean to support combustion and the engine conks. The cure is to make a hard wood plug that will shut off from one third to one half the venturi opening. Push this plug into the venturi and leave it there. Engines that seem addicted to leaning out in the air, regardless of adjustments, usually will function properly with the addition of a restrictor or plug.

Diesels appear to tolerate more choking than glow engines, probably because there is no plug to get fouled up. Further, if flooded, the compression ratio can be reduced on the Diesel by unscrewing the contra-piston lever in the cylinder head. The partly flooded engine can be started with less compression. After the flood is burned off, the compression ratio should be restored to normal for another starting attempt.

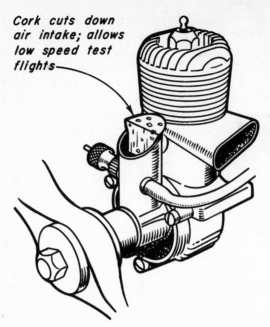

Cork cuts down
air intake; allows
low speed test
flights—

VENTURI RESTRICTION

Fig. 8–7.

About three turns open on the needle valve is correct for the average Diesel. Having opened the valve, set the contra piston. That is, screw it in a quarter turn at a time until the engine feels somewhat hard to flip over. You may discover that the engine is beginning to jam and that the prop cannot be flipped over in the normal manner. Then back off the contra piston a full turn. When the engine has about the feel of the familiar glow plug engine, flip the prop two or three times while choking the engine to bring fuel through the line up to the engine. Prime through the exhaust stack with a few drops of fuel. Now flip the prop smartly.

After a few fast flips the engine should give a pop. If the pop is mild and you can easily keep spinning the prop, do so, and the engine probably will start. But if after the first pop, the engine suddenly becomes hard to turn over, back off the contra piston until the prop again flips easily. Continue to spin the prop and the engine should run off the flooded condition. After this brief run, reset the contra piston to normal.

There is one sure way to start a Diesel, assuming it is properly primed and choked. This is to screw out the contra piston until the prop turns rather easily then begin to flip smartly, all the while moving the contra piston in about an eighth of a turn at a time. Sooner or later, you will hit the point where the engine will run.

How do you tell rich and lean mixtures on a Diesel? Most Diesels will run with a spitting sound if lean. A short-stroke high-speed Diesel will run very ragged when lean, throwing out a dirty exhaust. If the mixture is too rich the Diesel will run with a heavy smoky exhaust, throwing out a great amount of unburned oil. It will continue to run but at reduced rpm, and with a periodic "zinging" noise. Simply screw in the needle valve until the speed picks up; keep turning the needle valve slowly until the engine runs lean, then back off to some point in between the two settings.

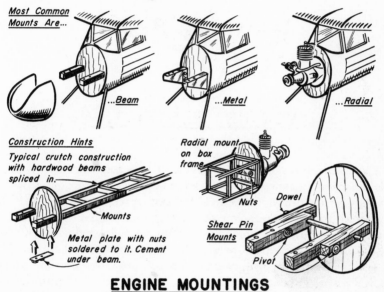

Most Common Mounts Are...

...Beam

...Metal

...Radial

Construction Hints

Typical crutch construction with hardwood beams spliced in.

Mounts

Metal plate with nuts soldered to it. Cement under beam.

Radial mount on box frame

Nuts

Shear Pin Mounts

Dowel

Pivot

ENGINE MOUNTINGS

Fig. 8–8.

The basic thing to remember when adjusting head and needle valve is that you need higher compression when using less fuel, lower compression when using more fuel. At some one point the two settings will give consistent, clean, powerful running.

The Diesel has a number of real advantages. It will turn a larger diameter propeller for a given displacement. Even in baby engines the diameter may be an inch bigger with a Diesel than with a glow. The Diesel is noted for steady running and exceptional fuel economy.

9

TANKS

LET'S FIRST discuss the fuel feed and tank problems posed by the typical high-powered contest free-flight airplane. Even though the engine may have to run but 20 seconds, it is difficult to avoid having the motor lean out after a few seconds, cutting down power or causing failure. Leaning out means that the proportion of air in the fuel mixture is increased; running rich means the opposite. It is important to maintain as constant a fuel pressure as possible throughout the engine run. Since the consumption of fuel necessarily reduces the fuel level, it follows that pressure must vary, depth of fuel in the tank being one of the factors. There are several ways the builder can minimize these fuel pressure changes and then adjust his needle valve to handle whatever change remains.

The two principal factors that bear on fuel pressure in the free-flight machine are the distance of the tank from the engine's needle valve, and the vertical location of the tank in relation to the needle valve. The further the tank is mounted from the engine, the greater the draw or distance that the engine must suck the fuel. The ability to draw fuel varies widely from engine to engine, depending on crankcase compression and other factors. Even if the engine can run with a long draw, it may be difficult to start, and to keep running. Obviously, the tank should be located as near as possible to the engine.

The relation of the tank to the needle valve, meaning whether the

FREE FLIGHT TANKS

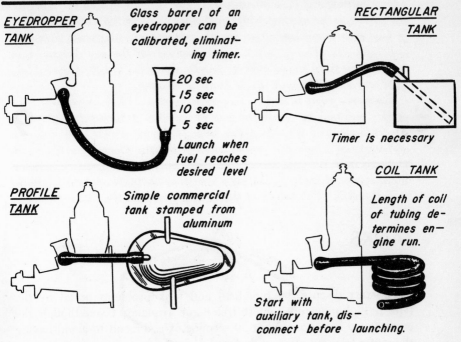

EYEDROPPER TANK

Glass barrel of an eyedropper can be calibrated, eliminating timer.

20 sec
15 sec
10 sec
5 sec

Launch when fuel reaches desired level

RECTANGULAR TANK

Timer is necessary

PROFILE TANK

Simple commercial tank stamped from aluminum

COIL TANK

Length of coil of tubing determines engine run.

Start with auxiliary tank, disconnect before launching.

Fig. 9–1.

tank is located high or low within the plane, must be precise for reliable operation. If the tank is placed high above the motor, the fuel flows downhill of its own accord and floods the engine. On the other hand, if the tank is positioned much below the needle valve, the motor will have to pull fuel against gravity. The tendency would be to run lean. Therefore, it is customary to place the top of the standard free-flight tank at the needle valve level. The free-flight tank may be a cube or it may be a cylinder, but its three main dimensions are roughly similar. A long tank is bad for a free-flying model due to the surge of fuel to the back of the tank upon launching. There is a trend in the small Half-A free-flights to use eye droppers for tanks.

The glass dropper is held to the side of the plane close to the engine with a metal strap and tiny screws, or simply clasped by a strip of pinking tape cemented (then fuelproofed) over the glass and to the ship. A piece of neoprene fuel line runs from the lower extremity of the glass tube up to the needle valve. The reasons for using such a tank include the ease of estimating the amount of fuel for a flight— the tube may be marked with small lines to show the various amounts of fuel that result in certain length motor runs—simplicity, economy, and lightness. The proper vertical position for the eye dropper tank is from one third to one half its length above the needle valve. Make tests and move the tank up or down accordingly.

For many years it was customary to mount a timer separately from engine and tank to cut off the flow of fuel and so limit the engine run. An improvement was the timer tank, a device which held a supply of fuel from which the proper amount for the desired run could be metered once the valve mechanism was operated. Ingenious modelers improved on this one by coiling a length of neoprene and simply filling it as the tank. The length of the tubing governed the motor run.

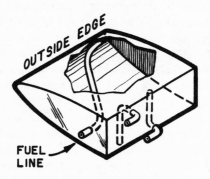

STUNT TANK

Fig. 9–2. Wedge Tank.

In the control-line field, an ingenious experimenter developed the wedge tank. The point of the wedge was placed toward the side of the plane that would be on the outside of the flying circle. Centrifugal force would push the fuel into the point of the wedge. The fuel line tube was carried to the rear, outer corner of the tank, or rear tip of the wedge. Since fuel tended to be pushed back by acceleration and outward by centrifugal force, this fuel line literally was good to the last drop. Nor did the inventor's cleverness stop here. The normal air vent tube at the top of the tank was extended to reach but not touch, the inner bottom surface. Another vent tube was attached to the bottom surface, extending up through the tank almost to the top inside surface. When the plane flipped over on its back, the bottom vent became the top vent, and the former top vent now admitted air. In other words, this tank operated equally well whether right side up or upside down. But the wedge tank was not suited for speed models. Here, centrifugal force is extremely severe. The wider a tank, the more fuel presses against the side of the tank on the outside of the circle. And the wedge tank is a wide tank. The answer for speed flying proved to be a long, high, narrow tank. Because of cramped quarters in the speed model and the interference of various parts with the tank location, all sorts of weird tank contours are resorted to. Speed builders invariably construct their own tanks.

Jim Walker developed the Walker pressure tank which is particularly useful in control-line stunt and radio work. His system consists of a neoprene tank shaped like a miniature hot water bottle, and a small regulator about the diameter of a nickel, only several times as thick. The tank (consider it as a balloon) is filled through a check valve which admits fuel from the squirt gun but does not permit the fuel to escape. The tank is mounted between two thin pieces of plywood, around which about a half dozen rubber bands are stretched. The bands squeeze the tank. The regulator, which is placed in the fuel line between tank and motor, contains a special diaphragm which is moved in and out by suction from the engine when it is turned over or started. When the engine demands more fuel, the diaphragm is moved, causing a ball valve to open and fuel rushes through from the pressure tank. When the engine needs less fuel, the diaphragm returns to its original position, shutting the ball valve, and cutting off fuel until more is needed. This type of tank is easy to use—its position is not important since it puts the fuel under sufficient pressure to reach the engine—but the builder must observe some simple requirements. The regulator must be placed on the center line of the plane, not outboard of the engine, for best results. The tank must be bled of air bubbles before starting the engine. This is done by elevating the nose of the ship and turning over the prop while choking the motor. When solid fuel fills the neoprene line the tank has been bled of air. It is common practice to insert a small sliver of wood in the air vent to poke the diaphragm in order to open the ball valve to let air escape, but this procedure is no longer recommended by the manufacturer. Gas and oil or Diesel mixtures cannot be run through the regulator because the diaphragm will swell and become inoperative. The list of permissible fuels is given in the literature accompanying the regulator.

Walker also invented the balloon tank which is used on American

Junior ready-to-fly Firebaby models. The balloon is ideally simple for most forms of U-control flying. The flexible fuel line is inserted in the mouth of a small rubber balloon and pushed to the far end, after which a rubber band wrapped around the throat of the balloon holds the tubing tightly enough to prevent leaks. To fill the tank, detach the fuel line from the needle valve and pump fuel through the line into the tank.

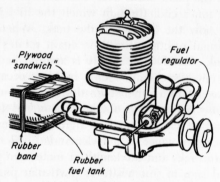

Plywood "sandwich"

Fuel regulator

Rubber band

Rubber fuel tank

BALLOON TANK

Fig. 9–3. Balloon Tank.

In control-line planes, tank position is even more critical than on free-flight jobs. In addition to any normal tendency to lean out, or richen up, the position of the tank may determine whether or not a stunt job will run as steadily on its back as when upright. The feed line must be exactly on a level with the needle valve body on stunt machines. If the feed line is higher—even $\frac{1}{16}$ inch—than the valve body, the engine will run rich when the plane is right side up, but will go lean or even quit when the ship is inverted. Or, if the tank is placed low so that the fuel line is beneath the level of the needle valve body, the engine will run lean when the plane is right side up but will richen up and lose power when the machine is put on its back. It is also essential on acrobatic control-line designs to get the tank exactly level, not tilted up or down at one end, for this, too, will interfere with normal fuel feeding.

With the development of stunt flying and the wedge tank that made it possible, it was first thought that only a wedge could be used. Some builders now claim that a square tank can be used with equal success. As a matter of fact, today we have tanks of many shapes: square, round, wedge, high rectangle, diamond, and even a combination of square and wedge.

Some tanks employ a baffle inside the tank to stop surge. Surging of fuel results from sudden accelerations and is particularly noticed in long tanks. Another interesting development is the clank tank, a home-made proposition used by many experts. The metal tubing that connects to the fuel line extends through a short piece of larger metal tubing soldered to the inside bottom of the tank. The first piece is free to rotate. As the plane turns over, the inner piece of tubing will rotate so that its inner end, through which the fuel is sucked, falls down to what is now the bottom of the tank. When the ship half loops back to normal position, the tube again rotates to the normal bottom of the tank. Steady fuel supply is assured because the inner end of the tube never sucks air. Some builders occasionally find it necessary to make a tank of their own design. The material used is shim brass or tin. Tin may be obtained from old fuel cans. Tin, though thicker and heavier, is quite all right for normal flying where the absolute top performance is not demanded. First, from experience with standard tanks and the length of motor run you desire, you sketch out your design to suit whatever particular purpose you have in mind. Next, prepare accurate patterns on thin, stiff cardboard and use them to scribe on the tin or brass the outlines of the parts you will cut out with tin snips. Allow appropriate overlapping edges for soldering and bending. Mark and drill the holes for the vents and fuel line before beginning to cut the metal. The cut, flat pieces of metal may be bent over a sharp-cornered hardwood block with a small hammer. Small flaps or flanges may be bent with needle nosed pliers. Soldering should be done with a hot, clean iron and resin-core solder. In assembling the feed tube and vents, be sure that the inner ends are in the desired positions, at the rear of the tank or some corner, as the case may be.

A common error made by the beginning tank builder on free-flight tanks, is not to run the feed line to the back of the tank. If the feed tube does not reach the rear of the tank, the fuel will surge away from it when the plane is launched. Another mistake is to forget to clean out the tank or not to be sure that it is leakproof! The tank can be cleaned by shaking it well with fuel inside, and then emptying. To pressure test the tank for leaks, put a long piece of neoprene over one of the vents or the fuel line connection, then close off the other two openings, and submerge the tank in a bowl of water. Blow through the neoprene and watch for bubbles.

10

RUBBER MODELS

THE SIMPLEST and the smallest rubber model is the baby R.O.G., or Rise-Off-Ground. Twenty years ago, every hobbyist built at least one of these cute little airplanes. Perhaps nine inches or a foot across the wing, they could be built in an evening and were loads of fun when flown indoors in a parlor or a gymnasium. The fuselage was a short piece of $\frac{1}{8}$ inch square balsa. The wing might be framed with $\frac{1}{16}$ inch square balsa with cross pieces at the tip, at the center, and, perhaps, at the midpoint of each wing panel. Sometimes the wing would be built upon a single span with a crosspiece at each tip, like the top of the letter T. There would be no edges or perhaps just a thread for a wing outline. The stabilizer outline would be the same. Wheels were made of paper: two cones for each wheel, cemented together around their circumferences. A single piece of wire comprised the landing gear. A steam-bent sheet-balsa prop made the little ships putt-putt in fine style. It was a short step from here to still bigger stick and fuselage type machines. The former utilized tubular motor-sticks made of steamed balsa, dried to shape on a form in an oven; or a built-up fuselage of longerons and cross pieces, or assembled from four sheet balsa sides with a few internal formers or bulkheads. Cabin jobs used the same wings and tail but a deeper, wider fuselage.

Since its purpose is to obtain a flyable airplane with a minimum of fuss, the small fuselage job is of the easiest possible construction. The fuselage almost always is a box and the wing is squared off with parallel leading and trailing edges with blunted tips of sheet balsa or block. When the wing span is less than 15 or 16 inches, sheet-balsa construction is advisable throughout. The fuselage sides are easily cut out and put together by means of a few key formers. The wing can be flat sheet balsa up to approximately 12 inches of span, cambered for greater strength and lift. Camber may be imparted by putting several strips of dope cross wise to the wood on one side. Or the wood may be dampened. If held in position on the bench over a few sheet balsa ribs, it will hold the desired shape when dry. After 18 inches of span, it is better to build up the wing with spars, edges, and ribs. Sheet balsa may be used on wings up to 24 inches in span, or even larger, when special attention is given to structural design, but in these larger sizes it tends to be much heavier than tissue-covered wings. Sheet can be used, however, for any sized fuselage.

The most popular size for sport rubber craft is 20-24 inches, with about 30 inches the practical limit. Hard $3/32$ inch square longerons, or medium hard $1/8$ inch square longerons make fuselages that will stand any amount of banging around. A one-spar wing is adequate, although the builder may also use two spars or multispars.

Because the weight of the rubber motor is distributed over most of the length of the fuselage, this type of model must always have a very long nose in order to balance that weight at the correct C.G. Roughly speaking, there is almost as much rubber in front of the wing as there is behind it. On the 2 to $2\frac{1}{2}$ foot wing span job, the trailing edge of the wing will rest about $\frac{1}{2}$ to 1 inch behind the point where the ship balances without the wing in place. From the chapter "Aerodynamics and Proportions," it will be recalled that the distance between the mid-chord point of the wing and the same point on the stabilizer is called the tail moment arm. Also, that rubber jobs run to higher aspect ratios than gas models. In the sizes we are now discussing, an 8:1 aspect ratio wing—a higher ratio would reduce the chord to an inefficient dimension—would result in a 3 or $3\frac{3}{4}$ inch chord. A moment arm of 50 per cent of the span would provide a fairly long fuselage. For example, 50 per cent of 24 inches would provide a 12 inch distance between the two mid-chord points. In figuring up the total fuselage length, this would leave one half the wing chord to be added, also one half the stabilizer chord, plus whatever the nose length happened to be. Half the wing chord would be $1\frac{1}{2}$ inches, half the stabilizer chord, possibly 1 inch, thus giving $2\frac{1}{2}$ additional inches, or 12 plus $2\frac{1}{2}$ inches, or $14\frac{1}{2}$ inches without the nose. The nose length, not

111

counting the actual nose block and propeller, should be at least half the tail moment arm for an average sport type rubber job. This would make another 6 inches, or a new total of 20½ inches overall length. From this it may be seen that an approximation of minimum length may be made as 75 per cent of the wing span.

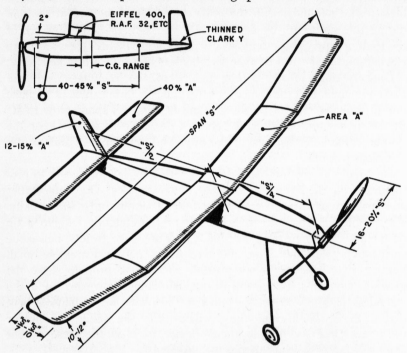

RUBBER MODEL PROPORTIONS

Fig. 10–1.

What features should you include in a rubber-powered plane? First, a knock-off wing which may be held to the fuselage with a couple of loops of ⅛ inch wide rubber. It is not advisable to allow a flat spot on top of the fuselage if this spot is only as long as the wing is wide. If you should have to shift the location of the wing in order to balance the ship, you then would be in a bad predicament. So allow room, another inch or so, both fore and aft of the expected wing position. The landing gear should be fixed, although retractable types are sometimes desirable on high-performance designs. The gear can be bent to shape from a single piece of music wire—1⁄16 inch diameter is plenty on this size of ship.

112

Key to rubber model performance is the propeller. There are several types, each with special advantages and disadvantages. First, the two-blade propeller that does not feature either a freewheeling device or folding blades. Second, the two-bladed type with a freewheeling device added. Then there is the two-blader with hinged blades which fold back in the glide, but which are held in position during the motor run by centrifugal force. One-bladed props are of the folding type. These require a lead counterweight. They are more efficient and easier to fold than two-bladers but are slightly heavier.

On very small jobs of a foot span or so, the freewheeler will not make too much of a difference and the folder is rather difficult to make due to the smallness of the hinges and fittings. As spans grow to 20, 24, 30 inches and beyond, it becomes desirable to use at least the simple freewheeler because of the improved performance and greater durations possible.

On small and medium size designs with long landing gears to protect the prop, the freewheeler will give good service. On contest types and larger designs in general, the extralong landing gear is a penalty. The problem is that the freewheeling prop frequently catches a tip on the ground when the plane lands and breakage results, hence the stilty-looking landing gear. Folding props permit extremely small landing gears since it is not possible for such a prop to strike the ground. One must be careful during launching, however, for if the extended blade tip strikes the runway, the blade hinges may be bent or torn loose. With either the freewheeler or the folder, the builder must use some sort of tensioning device to keep the loose rubber from shifting or sagging within the fuselage.

Rubber length has a direct effect on flight duration. Small jobs like baby R.O.G.'s and little fuselage or cabin machines which do not have tensioning devices can be given only slight slack in the rubber. Slack is the surplus length of the rubber, as measured between the shaft hook and the rear rubber support. When tensioning devices are employed, it is common to use rubber motors that are roughly double the required length. The tensioning prevents the motor from unwinding completely, so it remains taut between hooks at all times. The extra length allows many more motor turns. When the rubber is stretched out and wound with a winder, at least triple the normal number of turns may be put in without breakage. The baby R.O.G. or stick types can have their rubber detached from the rear hook for stretch winding. Make a small S hook which passes through the rubber loops and engages the wire hook which is built into the plane. In the cabin type fuselage, a hardwood dowel is inserted through the rear of the fuselage. This dowel can be pulled out when it is necessary to replace rubber motors. When a freewheeling or a folding prop is used, the shaft is bent to form a winding loop in front of the prop. To wind the plane, one person serves as anchor while the other pulls out the prop and nose block assembly from the front. The winding hook goes through the loop on the prop hub.

The experienced hobbyist knows a trick or two about the proper installation of a rubber motor. For consistent results he knows that the thrust line must not change position from flight to flight; otherwise the flight pattern will vary, perhaps disastrously. On a small job, he will run the direction of the grain in the nose block fore and aft, never side to side. By running the grain lengthwise, the block is better able to resist crushing. He follows a routine in carving the block. First, he marks it out and squares it off to the outside dimensions. Then he draws diagonal lines from corner to corner—or as necessary—to locate the shaft hole. This hole is drilled before the block is carved, insuring trueness. Two opposite sides of the block are then carved, followed by the other two sides, after which the corners may be rounded off. The under side of the block is carved first. When a removable nose block is used, an additional layer of wood is cut to fit snugly into the nose opening of the fuselage. This wood is cemented to the rear face of the nose block and serves as a key to prevent movement of the block when in position after winding of the motor. Many builders make the mistake of using soft wood for this key. On small models it should be rock-hard balsa; on big ones it can be of pine, plywood, or balsa, provided the four faces that bear against the insides of the crosspieces at the nose of the fuselage are finished with thin plywood. In small ships which may not have a rubber tensioning device, a small notch is cut on the front of the nose block just above the shaft hole Two light wire hooks are cemented to the bottom of the fuselage near the nose. A thin rubber band is then stretched from hook to hook, around the nose block, via the notch. This keeps the nose block and propeller from hanging loose when the rubber is wound down. The nose bearing should be of durable material, well-anchored against turning or crushing. Nose blocks of very large rubber-powered contest models may be laminated of numerous plies of hard balsa sheeting, each ply being placed crossgrain to the next. Or a hollowed hardwood block may have its rear face covered over with hard wood.

Too many builders take care of the front end properly and pay scant attention to the rear rubber anchor. The accepted method today is to insert a piece of birch dowel crossways through the fuselage.

114

Sheet balsa of the same thickness as the longerons is filled in between the crosspieces on the sides of the fuselage, between which the dowel will extend. On small planes of less than 24 inches span, a $\frac{1}{8}$ inch dowel is suitable. Use $\frac{3}{16}$ inch for up to 36 inch span and $\frac{1}{4}$ inch dowel for larger machines. Two large but light fiber or aluminum washers are cemented to the inside of this sheet balsa fill-in —the holes are the same size as the diameter of the dowel—to help anchor the dowel and to prevent it crushing the fill-in. Grain of the fill-in is fore and aft, not up and down. The dowel should fit snugly enough not to slide out, but loosely enough that it can be removed without much pressure. To assist the helper holding the plane for stretch-winding, the dowel is allowed to extend out from either side of the plane at least $\frac{1}{2}$ inch on a big ship. On larger contest planes, dural metal tubing is sometimes used. When it comes time to wind the plane, the helper simply slips a stiff metal rod through the tubing and then is able to retain a firm hold. As the rubber begins to wear, it will stretch and become longer. To prevent rubber loops sliding off hooks from this cause, the loops may be slipped over a rod held in a vise, or any other handy projection. Grasp the rubber close to this rod or peg and stretch it out a few inches. Have someone wrap a thin piece of rubber around the rubber-motor at this point and tie it tightly. A small loop will result in the end of the motor when you let it snap back to normal length. Such a loop makes it easy to slide the rear rubber dowel in and out of the motor.

A tensioner makes a radical difference. A small coil spring is placed on the propeller shaft, either in front of the prop or between the prop and the nose block, in such fashion that the spring moves the propeller forward from the nose block as the rubber winds down. Fully wound, the pull of the rubber overcomes the spring and holds the prop tight against the thrust washer. A short wood screw is inserted into the key, or back face of the nose block, fairly close to the shaft. The shaft itself is special. After the rubber hook portion is bent, the wire doubles back on itself for $\frac{1}{2}$ inch or so, then turns at right angles and juts out from the shaft. This short projection is long enough to engage the wood screw. However, when the motor is wound and the prop is in the rear position, the projection on the shaft misses the screw; as the rubber unwinds, the projection gradually works forward due to the spring tension. Suddenly it engages the screw, stopping rotation. The dimensions of the shaft and the length of the screw govern the point at which this action takes place. The screw can be turned in or out to adjust the timing.

The rubber itself must have a few tensioning turns put in it before

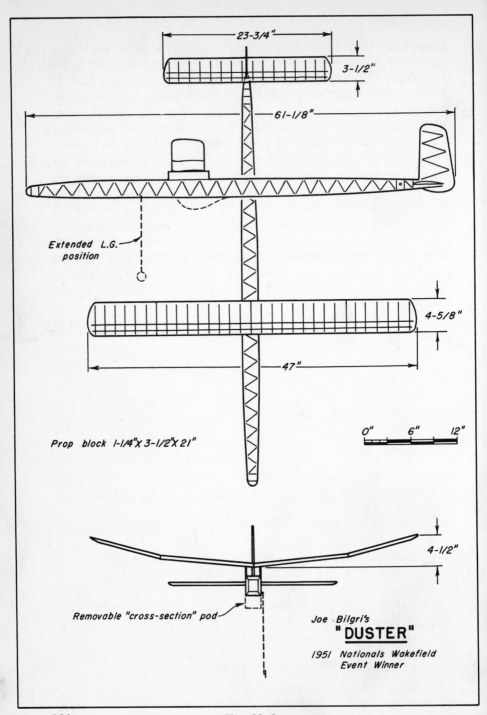

23-3/4"

3-1/2"

61-1/8"

Extended L.G.
position

4-5/8"

47"

0"   6"   12"

Prop block 1-1/4"X 3-1/2"X 21"

4-1/2"

Removable "cross-section" pod

Joe Bilgri's
"DUSTER"
1951 Nationals Wakefield
Event Winner

116

Fig. 10–2.

being placed in the plane. One method is to loop the end of the rubber motor over a doorknob, then to stretch the motor out for eight or ten feet. The strands are then divided into three portions. If you have 12 strands, for instance, there will be 4 in each group. Approximately 35 winder turns are wound into each group of strands separately. As the winder is passed from one group to the next, a wood peg or perhaps a clothespin is inserted through the winder end of each group. A helper then holds that finished group at the same stretched out point. After all groups are partially wound in this manner, they are braided together into one motor. This is done by means of the pegs or clothespins which give a convenient grip. A helper can use his fingers to slide the braids along evenly as they are made. After the entire motor is braided, it is allowed to return to its original length. When installed in the plane, it will take a few more turns for sufficient tensioning. A certain school of thought charges that braiding uses up a good many potential turns of rubber and therefore dissipates its own advantage.

Don't forget to lubricate your motor and keep it clean. Store it in a cool, dark place between flying sessions.

11

CONTROL-LINE MODELS

THE TERM control-line means that a ship is attached by means of steel wires to a small handle—usually U-shaped—which is held in the flier's hand. Small planes may be equipped with fishline or dacron control cords, rather than the heavier steel wires. Many of the plastic ready-to-fly planes are so equipped. The model is captive in that it is limited to flying a circle around the pilot. Movements of the control handle are transmitted through a bellcrank arrangement inside the plane to its elevators. When the handle is tilted back, the elevators move up; when tilted forward, the elevators move down. In this way, the plane can be caused to take off, fly inverted, perform loops and other intricate maneuvers, and then land. Probably the simplest method for flying a captive airplane is to attach a single line to it which is connected to a pylon or pole. When the plane is released, it flies a steady circular path. The draw-back to this arrangement is that the pilot can exercise no control over the plane. The idea applies best to very small Half-A powered jobs which, in this case, frequently are of all-balsa construction with a profile type fuselage and sheet balsa wings and tail. For them, light fishline or .008 or .010 wire is suitable. It is essential that this type of round-the-pylon model be balanced or trimmed very much nose heavy, even if the C.G. falls well in front of the wing. An eyelet is screwed into the side of the fuselage at the C.G. position and the line is fastened to the eyelet. A piece of wood, or wire, or any other material that will serve as a guide, juts forward from the leading edge of the wing (on the side of the plane to which the line is attached), holding the

118

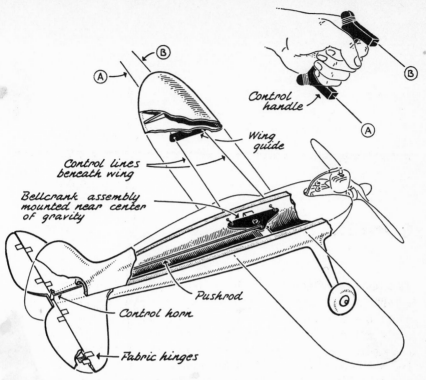

Fig. 11–1. Control-Line Model.

control-line in its proper position. The line also may be attached to end of a fishpole held in the flier's hands.

Control-line planes come in many types and sizes. For the beginner there is the primary trainer, usually an all-balsa profile creation of extreme stability, strength, and simplicity. As a rule, the trainer is able to perform nothing more violent than a wing over or simple loop. Profile means that the fuselage is a very thick piece of balsa. Most of the plastic ready-to-fly planes are copied after real plane configurations. Such models are packaged with motor in place, and include control handle, control cords, etc.

After the trainer comes the stunt model. Here, more wing area is included and construction is much lighter. In many cases, the entire airplane, excepting the tail surfaces, is of built-up construction. Greater power, lighter weight, more area, and more violent control surface movement insures top maneuverability. In many cases, profile fuselage construction is combined with a built-up paper, silk or nylon-covered wing. Many advanced stunt airplanes have wing flaps, which are hinged surfaces attached to the trailing edge of the wing. These

CONTROL SYSTEMS

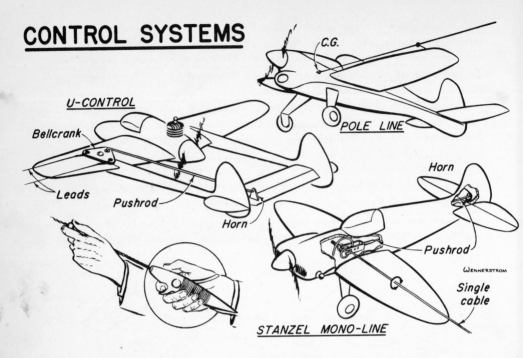

U-CONTROL

Bellcrank

Leads

Pushrod

Horn

C.G.

POLE LINE

Horn

Pushrod

WENNERSTROM

Single cable

STANZEL MONO-LINE

Fig. 11–2.

flaps are connected to the control-moving linkage in such manner that the flaps tilt up when the elevators tilt down, and vice versa. When the flaps tilt down, they tend to increase the lift of the wing, helpful when the plane performs an abrupt change in direction. It matters little whether the stunt model is upright or inverted in flight. The wing has a symmetrical section—in other words, no top or bottom aerodynamically speaking—and the control movement is precisely the same either right side up or upside down. The trainer generally is slim and long to insure steady flight; the stunter is very short to permit quick maneuvers. Accordingly, the stunter is sensitive on the controls and reacts with a bang.

A relatively new type of control-line model is the combat plane. These are highly maneuverable, very fast stunt ships, refined to the ultimate in simple, speedy construction and light weight. The combat model must turn on a dime and must be considered expendable because of the frequent collisions during heat of competition. Briefly, two, sometimes more, planes are flown simultaneously against each other. Each trails a crepe-paper streamer. The object is to cut, or remove, the enemy's streamer, while protecting one's own streamer.

120

Points are given for the number of attacking passes, the amount of streamer removed, etc. Loss of the streamer amounts to a "kill." Most combat ships are profile jobs with lightly built, paper-covered wings. To save weight, landing gears are usually dispensed with. The models then have to be launched by hand.

The most exquisite miniature planes imaginable can be built and flown by the U-control method. Some of these planes take many months to build and duplicate an infinite amount of detail found on the real craft, such as rockets, lights, retractable landing gears, working wing flaps, instrument panels, seats, seat belts, make-believe controls, and accurately scaled engines and paint schemes. In most cases, the scale plane has very limited performance, being capable of straight and level flight, wing overs, and, at most, a mild loop. However, skillful fliers with large, lightly built, powerful scale jobs, have been

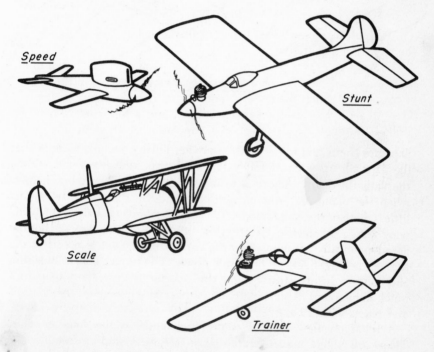

RELATIVE SIZES OF VARIOUS
CONTROLINE TYPES

Fig. 11–3.

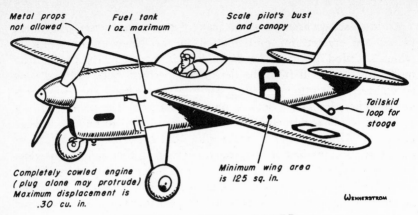

Metal props
not allowed

Fuel tank
1 oz. maximum

Scale pilot's bust
and canopy

Tailskid
loop for
stooge

Completely cowled engine
(plug alone may protrude)
Maximum displacement is
.30 cu. in.

Minimum wing area
is 125 sq. in.

WENNERSTROM

TYPICAL TEAM RACER

Fig. 11–4.

able to put these fine craft through all the maneuvers called for in the stunt flight pattern.

The team racer was developed in California and was intended to be flown in actual races with two, three, four or more fliers in the center of the circle. Such planes are required to have cockpits, a limited wing area (125 square inches maximum), and a top displacement of .299 in the engine. An interesting stipulation is that the fuel tank may have a capacity of only one ounce. When the plane runs out of fuel, it must land. A "pit crew" refuels it and starts the motor again, after which the pilot takes it off and rejoins the race.

To begin the race, the planes are staggered one behind the other, at different distances from the center of the circle. When all engines are running and the fliers signify readiness, the starter waves a green flag for each plane to take off. They follow each other at split-second intervals. Sometimes, a mechanical stooge retains all models in starting position, while helpers leave the circle; then, upon signal, the starter pulls a lanyard to release all planes simultaneously. All planes must have a means of engine cut-off. This is usually done by a fuel shut-off device attached to the bellcrank in such fashion that a sudden extreme forward movement of the bellcrank actuates the shut-off.

Mixed construction is utilized. Most popular is a hollowed balsa block fuselage with solid balsa wings and tail. Sometimes the wing is built up with ribs and spars as in stunt types. Fuselages, too, can be built up from sheet balsa sides and bulkheads or formers of sheet balsa. Engines are fully cowled excepting the glow plug which juts out for easy access in starting.

122

An interesting variation of the scale model is the carrier job. These planes are created for participation in the Navy carrier event in which a scaled-down carrier flight deck is placed in the circle. The model must take off from the deck, then perform both fast and slow speed runs, and attempt a deck landing. Sand bags and stop cords are stretched across the deck as on a real carrier. The plane carries a tail hook which is retractable. Since it is important to be able to vary power in flight in order to make slow and high speed runs, carrier planes are equipped with two-speed engines. Either ignition or glow two-speed systems are used. Their control is accomplished by a third control line or by means of enamel-coated control wires through which an electrical current can be passed (the pilot carrying batteries in his pocket) to operate a relay mounted inside the plane. The Walker U-Reely handle is used. The relay either selects a low-speed set of points on the ignition engine, adjusts a throttle, or richens the mixture on the glow engine.

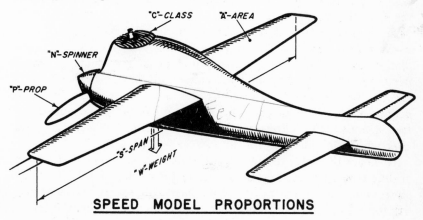

SPEED MODEL PROPORTIONS

Fig. 11–5.

Probably the most advanced of all U-control ships is the speed model. Competition is divided into four classes: Class AA, up to .05 cubic inch displacement; Class A, up to .199; Class B, from .20 to .299; Class C from .30 to .60. These hornets are extremely small in all classes. They are very heavily built in order to stand the engine vibration and the wear and tear of skid landings on concrete runways. No landing gears are employed. Take-off is from a dolly, usually a wire cradle having three huge air wheels. Classes AA and A usually hand launch due to small size. When the plane picks up sufficient speed to fly it lifts from the dolly and is on its own. A speed job is timed over a certain number of laps, which are averaged to show the maximum speed attained. This may be faster than 160 mph in Class C. High speed engines are used, as are special hot fuels, and small high-pitch props.

Construction favors hardwood, although hardwood, metal, balsa, and plywood are sometimes combined. The fuselage invariably consists of two shells, an upper and a lower. The engine, tank, and usually the control system are mounted inside the bottom shell. The top shell lifts off for easy access to the interior. The bottom shell may be of hard wood or metal, the top shell hard wood or balsa. Cast magnesium bottoms are on the market. These afford better engine mounting and cooling, hence higher rpm and greater speeds. They also stand up better under the battering of high speed landings. Wings are either shaped from solid hardwood, like pine, or are made up of a sturdy metal spar wrapped with thin aluminum sheeting to form a top and bottom surface. This metal sheeting is flush riveted along

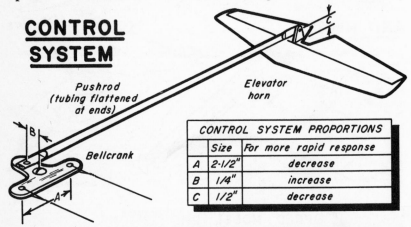

CONTROL SYSTEM

Pushrod
(tubing flattened
at ends)

Elevator
horn

Bellcrank

CONTROL SYSTEM PROPORTIONS		
	Size	For more rapid response
A	2-1/2"	decrease
B	1/4"	increase
C	1/2"	decrease

Fig. 11–6. Bellcrank and Linkage.

the trailing edge. Tail surfaces are usually plywood, although metal can be used. Speed engines usually are started by means of an electric motor starter operated from an old car battery.

Sponsored by Pan American World Airways is a new event, control-line endurance. As a stunt a gas model was flown continuously more than 24 hours. The ship was refueled in flight by pumping fuel through a neoprene tube to the big tank inside the machine.

Heart of the Walker invention control system is the bellcrank which is securely mounted inside the fuselage or upon the wing close to the fuselage. The bellcrank is pivoted at the center; small holes at the ends of the two long arms provide for the attachment of the leadouts,

124

which are music wire pieces running through the wing, over it, or under it, depending on the configuration of the plane. The other end of each leadout terminates in a loop to which the actual control lines are attached. A heavy music wire pushrod extends back from the bell-crank to the control horn affixed to the elevator or elevator spar.

Extremely simple in principle, the control system must be prop-

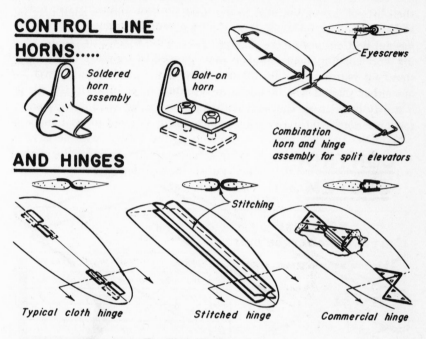

CONTROL LINE HORNS.....

Soldered horn assembly

Bolt-on horn

Eyescrews

Combination horn and hinge assembly for split elevators

AND HINGES

Stitching

Typical cloth hinge

Stitched hinge

Commercial hinge

Fig. 11-7. Hinges and Horns.

erly installed for safe, reliable flying. The first requirement is to suit the strength of the system and the size of its components to the size, weight, and speed of the aircraft. A Half-A sport-flying job may be flown on dacron lines (a thin cord manufactured by Sullivan Products from a DuPont material) or other sturdy lines like lightweight fish line or thin music wire. Wire should be .008 to .010 in diameter. Flexible wire is advisable for these small craft. The line may attach directly to the bellcrank (only in small jobs) or to music wire leadouts running from the bellcrank to a point outside the guide plate near the wingtip. These leadouts can be of some such diameter as .022, .024, and so on. The pushrod can be of $\frac{3}{64}$ or even $\frac{1}{16}$ music wire. The bellcrank may be made of thin plywood or aluminum or may be bought finished from a hobby shop. The horn may be purchased or made from thin music wire with a loop, through which the bent-over end of the pushrod is inserted.

The Walker control system basically is a two-line system. The second most popular system is Mono-Line, which is a single-line system. At the present writing, Mono-Line is used to a small extent for stunting (but its popularity will increase) and has all but taken over the speed events. The big advantage of Mono-Line is the drastic reduction in air drag resulting from the elimination of one control wire. Even though the equivalent Mono-Line wire is required to be of a greater diameter, it still has less drag, as well as weight, than the normal two wires. The illustrations show the control handle used for Mono-Line flying and the elevator-actuating mechanism in the plane. The handle is grasped in one hand, and the sliding knob, which moves back and forth on the twisted wire actuator connected to the handle, is worked by the free hand. Movements of the knob cause the twisted wire actuator to rotate and, as the actuator rotates, so must the control wire running out to the plane. Pulled toward the operator, the knob imparts "up" to the plane, and vice versa.

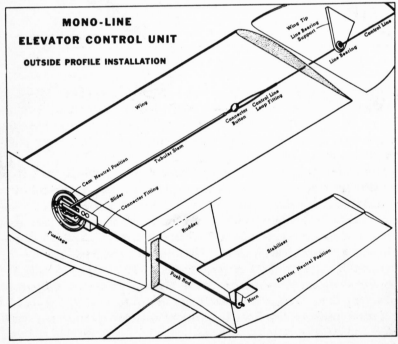

Fig. 11–8.

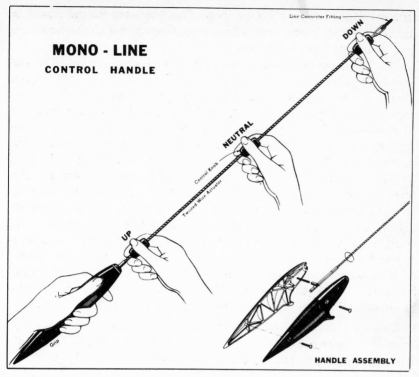

Fig. 11–9.

Mounted within the wing, or upon the fuselage (figure 11–8) is another actuator which looks like a coiled spring. This spring converts the rotary or twisting motion of the control wire that runs from the handle to the plane, into a linear or back-and-forth motion of the push-rod that connects the coiled spring to the elevators.

Mono-Line flying has some unique advantages. Unlike U-control, or the two-line system, the plane is not dependent upon centrifugal force to maintain line tension. In the two-line system, any loss of line tension results in the plane sliding in toward the flier, especially in a wind, and may cause a crack-up. When the lines go slack, it becomes impossible to work the elevators. The one-line system will operate the elevators even when the line is quite slack. This ability to work the elevators with small line tension means that the plane can be flown on extra-long line. Thus, when planes are limited to, say, 30 feet and 70 feet respectively on two lines, the same planes may operate at as much as 50 and 100 feet or more with one line. The apparent disadvantage is the unnaturalness of the sliding control knob, as compared with the simple up-and-down movements of the control handle that is used for two-line systems. This, probably, is a matter of what we have been used to.

Stanzel, who markets Mono-Line, also makes available for contest speed fliers a special machined cam and bellcrank suitable for the kind of control and heavier loads normal to such flying.

In larger models, it is imperative to use sturdy components firmly installed in the plane. AMA rules specify certain line diameters for each class or size of ship. Planes entered in actual competition must be submitted to pull tests before they are allowed to fly. The pull test is performed by having one man hold or anchor the model while the other holds the handle and pulls heavily on the end of the lines.

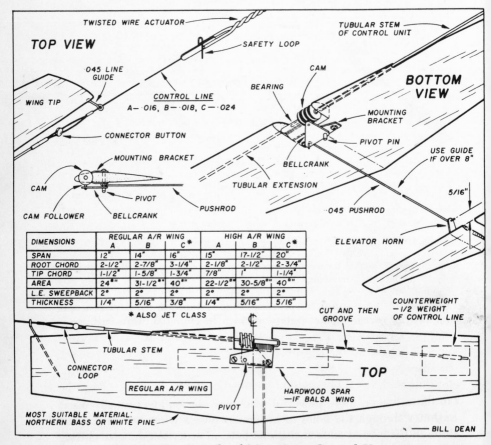

Fig. 11–10. Details of Mono-Line Control Unit.

A scale is attached between the lines and the handle. A certain number of pounds pull is specified as the minimum that guarantees safety for each size plane. These tests insure that the control system is strongly installed within the ship and cannot break loose, and that no wires or joints will break under stress of high-speed flight. The test for the larger size control liner calls for as much as 20 times the weight of the model, which indicates how strong you should make your airplane. Line diameters and line lengths are as follows:

CLASS	LINE DIAMETER		LINE LENGTH
	One Line	Two Lines	
A	.016	.010	35 feet
AA	.010	.006	52½
B	.018	.012	60
C	.024	.016	70

Control-Line Jet

one only	.024 minimum	.016 minimum	70

Control-Line Endurance

one only	.020	.014	52½ to 70

Team Racing

one only	.018	.012	60 minimum

Control-Line Aerobatics

A	.016	.010	all classes
B	.018	.012	52½ to 70
C below .400	.020	.014	
C above .400	.024	.016	

Control-Line Flying Scale

Line diameters same as control-line speed for models weighing less than 4 pounds; 4 to 10 pounds, .016 minimum for two lines, or .020 for single line; models over 10 pounds, .020 for two lines and .028 for single line.

Line length 52½ to 70 feet except when engine is less than .10 displacement or where largest engine on multimotored model is less than .05, when lines are 35 feet long.

Control-Line Combat

one Class	.020	.014	59½ to 60½

On these bigger, more powerful machines, the builders usually insert bushings through the holes in bellcranks where wires will attach and through the looped ends of the lead outs, in order to minimize cutting effects of the part on the wire during long service.

129

The length of line used depends on the size of the ship and size of the flying site. Too long a set of lines on too small or underpowered a plane will result in inadequate control and the ship coming in on the lines, especially in a wind. Too short a set of lines on too fast and powerful a machine will make the plane hard to fly and almost impossible to stunt. The ship would circle the flier too quickly. For sport flying, therefore, common sense dictates the line length. As a rule, Half-A jobs are flown on 35 foot lines if they are light and fast, otherwise, shorter lines must be tried until the plane seems to perform satisfactorily. For general flying of planes equipped with .19's to .29's, but where performance is not on the hot side, 50 to 60 foot lines are proper. Stunting is done on 50 or 60 or even 70 foot lines, the latter if the ship is fast and powerful. As a rule, lines come in 35, 52½, 60, and 70 foot lengths.

Anchor a bellcrank firmly. The pivot bolt should pass through thick plywood or a wood block faced with ply, and the whole unit should be mounted between ribs in the wing center section (for example) so that the entire assembly cannot pull sideways. Support the pushrod at one or more points along its length—more on big jobs—so that it cannot bend or buckle under load. Very often the pushrod will bow when the flier applies down elevator, which puts the rod under compression instead of tension. Secure the control horn on the elevator, covering over the cement joint with a piece of pinking tape or cloth cemented in place. On larger ships, control horns should have holes through which small bolts can be inserted to hold the horn rigidly in place.

On all control-line ships larger than Half-A it is advisable to provide some method of preventing control pushrods pulling out of control horns or from wing flap horns. A washer should be soldered over the end of the wire after it has passed through the hole in question.

If you design and build your own, consider these requirements (this applies to the kits as well). You will not want abrupt or erratic control responses. Starting with the handle, the lines should not be attached at the widest spacing (many handles have two or more sets of holes to vary the line spacing) as this gives maximum elevator movement. On the bellcrank, the pushrod should be attached at the hole nearest to the pivot. Later, when you become more adept, the pushrod may be inserted through the hole farthest from the pivot.

The end of the control pushrod that attaches to the elevator control horn should be inserted through the hole nearest the outer end of the horn. The nearer to the elevator the pushrod is mounted on the horn, the greater will be the elevator travel and hence its reaction. Elevator

130

area on the trainer generally is somewhat less than 50 per cent of the horizontal tail area. Control area on the speed job is about one third the total horizontal area. On stunt, it may run as high as two thirds with 50 per cent the average.

Reels and handles vary widely in price and quality. An adjustable handle is a nice thing to have. Very often when you attach your lines to the ship for the first time, you will find that the elevator is either slightly up or down when you hold the handle in neutral position. If you tilt the handle to put the elevators in neutral, then the handle

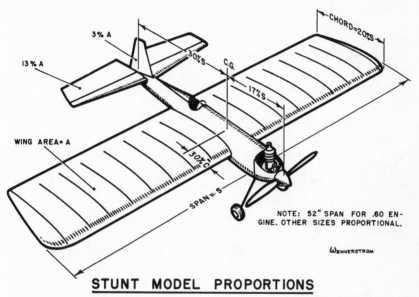

STUNT MODEL PROPORTIONS

Fig. 11–11.

must always be held in that position between maneuvers. Adjustable handles have a set screw which can be loosened while an adjustment is made, then tightened again. Some reels are designed to serve as handles.

As far as the control system is concerned, this leaves the bellcrank, leadouts, pushrod, control horn, and elevator hinges. Bellcranks come in a variety of forms. The simplest is a triangular piece of fairly thick dural with holes bored for attachment of the lines, pushrod, and for the pivot. The more expensive ones have pivot bearings. Some even have the leadouts in place. For small planes, a 2-inch bellcrank is correct; for larger ships a 2½ or 3-inch. Elevator hinges take many forms. The most popular consists of thin strips of linen or pinking

131

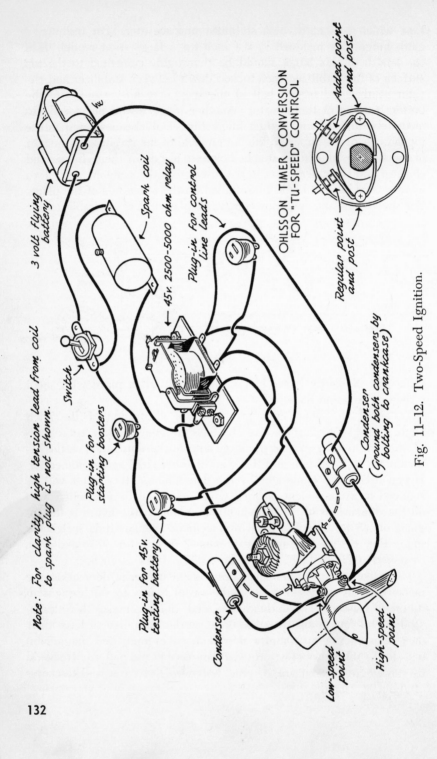

OHLSSON TIMER CONVERSION FOR "TU-SPEED" CONTROL

Added point and post

Regular point and post

3 volt flying battery

Spark coil

45 v. 2500-5000 ohm relay

Plug-in for control line leads

Switch

Plug-in for starting boosters

Plug-in for 45 v. testing battery

Condenser

Condenser (Ground both condensers by bolting to crankcase)

Low-speed point

High-speed point

Note: For clarity, high tension lead from coil to spark plug is not shown.

Fig. 11–12. Two-Speed Ignition.

tape which cement to both stabilizer and elevator. For instance, a cloth hinge may measure ½ x 1 inch for a large stunt model. Half the length of this hinge should be thoroughly cemented to the top surface of the stabilizer, then tucked down between stabilizer and elevator so that the second half of the strip may be cemented to the bottom surface of the elevator. Another hinge would be placed immediately adjacent to the first hinge but would be cemented to the top side of the elevator and the bottom side of the stabilizer. One pair of these hinges should be attached close to the tip of the stabilizer and elevator and the other closer to the fuselage in the same manner. Two more sets of hinges should be installed on the other side of the plane. For speed jobs and high-powered stunt planes, it is advisable to use

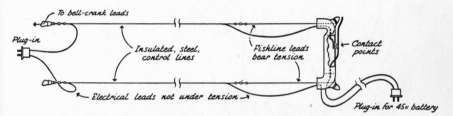

Fig. 11–13. Two-Speed Lines.

some sort of sturdy metal hinge which is fixed in place with small screws or nuts and bolts.

To adapt the dimensions given in the illustration of the Zilch (figure 11–11) to various size stunters suitable for different classes of engines, use the span of the large ship in the illustration as the denominator in a fraction and the span of other sizes as the numerator. If you divide the numerator by the denominator, this factor will be reduced to a convenient decimal which can then be multiplied with all the dimensions of the drawing. The plane in the figure is for engines of .45 to .60 cubic inch displacement and has a 52 inch wing span. For .19's to .35's, make the span 42 inches; for .075's and .09's, 34 inches; .049's and .065's, 24 inches; .035's, .045's, 20 inches.

Very few speed model kits exist. Some concerns do market the metal bottoms or speed pans in the various sizes to suit designs in different classes. The individual speed builder makes his design around the proper size pan. Some enthusiasts arrange to have their own pans cast. Any foundry that pours aluminum and magnesium will do the job reasonably, provided you supply the pattern. It should be carved from mahogany or pine, hollowed to have a wall thickness of about 3/32 inch.

The following table will enable the reader to adapt a standard tank design (figure 11–14) to whatever size ship he has in mind. Note that the dimensions are given in letter form and that these letters are repeated in the table.

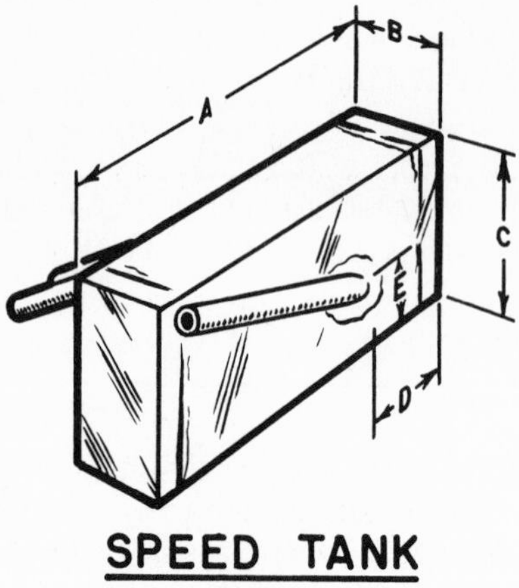

Fig. 11–14.

SPEED TANK TABLE

ENGINE	*A*	*B*	*C*	*D*	*E*
.19	2	½	1	½	⅜
.29	3	½	1⅛	¾	⅜
.49	3½	⅝	1¼	1	½
.60	4½	⅝	1¼	1¼	½

Among the accidents that have caused death by electrocution, has been an occasional mishap with a control-line type of model striking high-tension lines. Do not fly near such power lines. A fatality may result even though neither the model nor its control wires come in contact with the power lines, for the electrical charge in high-voltage lines can jump a considerable distance to a grounded control line.

The specifications of all control-line models, the line diameters and lengths for various events, and so on are set forth in great detail in the *Rules Book* published by the Academy of Model Aeronautics, 1025 Connecticut Avenue, Washington, D.C. Available at ten cents a copy, the book is a good outline of competitive modeling types and how they are operated in competition.

12

JET MODELS

THE PULSE JET ENGINE has a single moving part, a thin sheet-metal valve. To fire up this engine, a pump, such as an ordinary bicycle pump, is used to start the flow of air. As in the ordinary gas engine the flow of air through the venturi tube sucks in a certain amount of fuel—gasoline in this case. The spark plug fires the atomized mixture. The force of the explosion closes the leaves of the valve and, at the same time, tends to drive the unit forward. After the explosion has taken place, the next blast of air opens the valve, pulling in fuel, and the cycle is repeated. Usually, a few pumps of air results in loud pops from the engine which begins to operate by itself with a continuous roar. The valve opens and shuts at such a high rate that the sound of individual pulses is almost lost.

The foremost example of the model pulse jet engine is the Dynajet, which has been in use for many years. This engine is 21 inches long, 2½ in diameter, weighs 16 ounces, and develops 4½ pounds of thrust.

The operating characteristics of the miniature pulse jet have so far rather limited its application. It becomes very hot, turning cherry red around the combustion chamber. The heat dissipation problem limits the engine to placement outside the fuselage. It is usually mounted above the body and wing with a sheet of asbestos between it and the wood to prevent burning. A few ambitious builders have mounted the engine inside the fuselage in scale type planes but this is a difficult feat, involving lining the inside wall of the fuselage with insulating and fireproof material, and leaving adequate air space between the jet and the fuselage wall for a flow of cooling air.

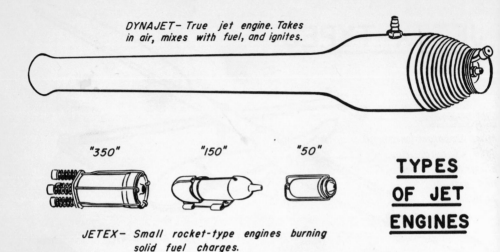

DYNAJET– True jet engine. Takes in air, mixes with fuel, and ignites.

"350"   "150"   "50"

TYPES
OF JET
ENGINES

JETEX– Small rocket-type engines burning solid fuel charges.

Fig. 12–1

The pulse jet is now widely used by contest fliers. It may attain velocities in excess of 150-160 mph. Such planes are flown on .016 wire, 70 feet long, and develop a large amount of pull on the control handle. A jet scale plane has a span in the neighborhood of 3 feet and weighs several pounds.

The English firm of Wilmot, Mansour, Ltd., following a different avenue of development, eventually produced a much smaller power plant known as Jetex. Jetex is satisfactory for free-flying models of both original and scale design. It is suited to small and medium sized ships and it may be used successfully in such spectacular planes as the Mig-15, the Sabre, the Starfire, Thunderjet, and Vampire. It can be placed on simple hand gliders or built-up paper-covered airplanes, or all-wood types. Jetex runs quietly with a gentle hissing noise. Technically, Jetex falls into the rocket category since it uses a solid fuel. In principle, the Jetex power plant is a small cylinder, closed at one end, with a removable cap at the other, or rear, end. This cap is pierced in the center. The charge of fuel is inserted in the cylinder, the cap is put in place, and a lighted wick running through the hole in the cap is used to ignite the fuel. When the fuel burns, the exhaust gases squirt through the hole in the cap under high pressure, driving the unit forward.

Jetex units may be obtained in this country in four different sizes: the 50, 150, 200, and 350. The fuel is cylindrical in shape and perhaps

136

JETEX TYPES

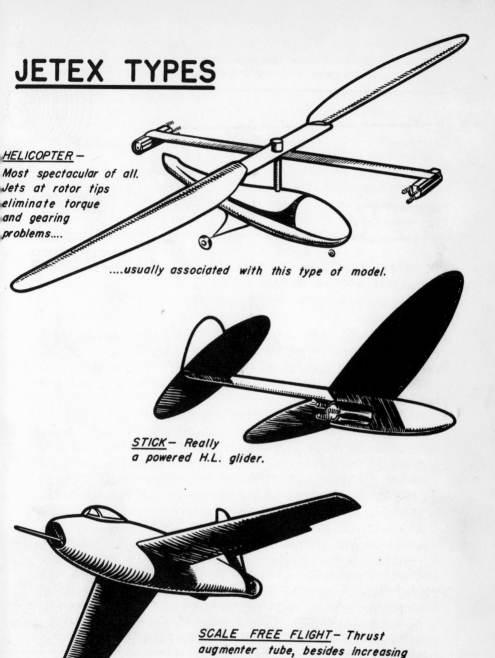

HELICOPTER –
Most spectacular of all.
Jets at rotor tips
eliminate torque
and gearing
problems....

.....usually associated with this type of model.

STICK – Really
a powered H.L. glider.

SCALE FREE FLIGHT – Thrust
augmenter tube, besides Increasing
power, permits buried engine installation for true scale appearance

Fig. 12–2.

137

half an inch long. It is brown in color and has a slightly retarded rate of burning which means that it is incapable of accidental explosion. The largest Jetex motor, the 350, will take one, two, or three charges. One charge burns for 12 seconds, two for 24 seconds. Three charges can put a jet out of sight!

Most popular of the three engine sizes is the little Jetex 50. It measures $1\frac{5}{8}$ inches long, $1\frac{1}{16}$ in diameter. Its weight is .4 of an ounce and the thrust developed is .6 of an ounce. Half the weight is made up of the fuel charge. The engine is suitable for models having a wing span of 12 to 20 inches. The 100 is $2\frac{1}{4}$ inches long, 1 inch in diameter, weighs .88 of an ounce and develops a thrust of 1.2 ounces. The 200 measures $2\frac{7}{8} \times 1\frac{5}{32}$, weighs .3 of an ounce and has 2.3 ounces thrust. The 350 measures $3\frac{3}{4} \times 1\frac{3}{8}$, weighs 2.9 ounces and develops a thrust of 4 ounces. The 100 is suitable for planes of 18 to 30 inches wing spread, the 200 for 24 to 36 inches, and the 350 for ships between 32 and 54 inches, which means a large jet model indeed.

It is advisable to start with the simplest and sturdiest airplane design possible. This should be an all-balsa hand-launched type of glider with the power plant attached either under the body or on a sheet-wood pylon well above the wing. Not having a prop, the Jetex model has no torque and no slip stream. The only thing tending to make it turn is your adjustment (make it delicate!) or warps in construction. Effect of warps on the Jetex plane is drastic.

After the fuel charge begins spewing an audible but tiny jet of exhaust gas, the flier continues to hold the plane for a few seconds until the engine has begun to put out full power. At this point the model is moved forward in a mild launch, just as if you were hand-launching a balsa glider on its very first test. For a second or two the plane seems barely to move but it quickly accelerates until it fairly hurtles skyward. It is this wide variation in speed that makes it important not to have warps or crooked construction. For example, we know that a slight positive angle in a wingtip will cause that tip to exert more lifting force than the other tip. With a varying speed, varying amounts of lift would develop. The plane would roll at high speed.

Other points of importance on the all-balsa jet are light weight and smooth finish. Firm $\frac{1}{16}$ inch sheet balsa is sufficient for a small Jetex 50 design. $\frac{3}{32}$ stock would be suitable if given an airfoil section by means of a sanding block. This thicker wood ought to be of medium soft texture. For the 100 and comparable power plant sizes, use $\frac{3}{32}$ to $\frac{1}{8}$ inch stock. The completed plane should be sanded as smooth as possible, using several coats of sanding sealer or clear dope.

138

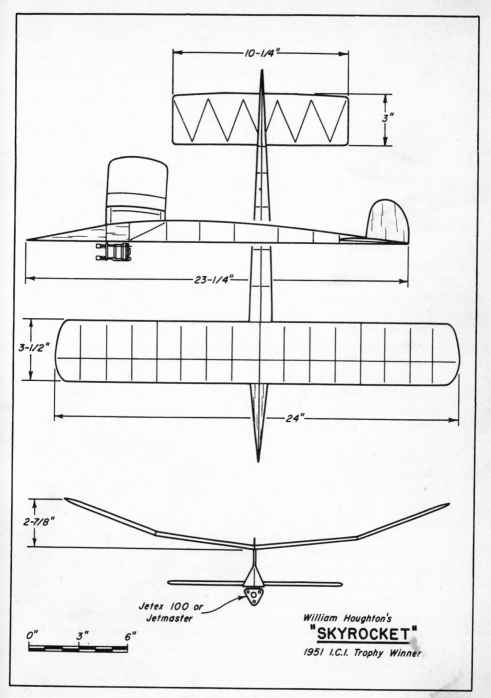

10-1/4"

3"

23-1/4"

3-1/2"

24"

2-7/8"

Jetex 100 or Jetmaster

William Houghton's
"SKYROCKET"
1951 I.C.I. Trophy Winner

0"   3"   6"

Fig. 12–3. English Jetex.

With the Jetex 100 and larger power units, the built-up type of construction offers advantages. Lighter weight relative to area is one; this means a superior glide and greater duration. Small, lightweight rubber jobs can be converted successfully. Any such construction is desirable for jet flying.

Where paper covering is utilized, it is advisable to protect any covering adjacent to the power unit from fire, particularly if the unit is close to the surface of the model. A thin piece of asbestos or a section of thin sheet aluminum can be attached to the surface. Sometimes sparks fall from the fuse when it is first ignited, so extend the protective material beneath the fuse area.

Since realistic scale ships are flown free-flight, their construction should be patterned after rubber-powered and Half-A engine-powered flying scale designs. Construction should be made as light as possible without the covering material bowing or warping any of the structural members. Choose good grades of wood. Thin the dope and plasticize it with castor oil to prevent excessive paper pull. Another important aspect of designing a scale job for Jetex power is the accessibility and placement of the power plant. The engine should be located at approximately the C.G. This undoubtedly will be amidship at the widest point of the fuselage. A small platform of $\frac{1}{16}$ inch plywood can be glued to some appropriate internal structure. The metal brackets that hold the engine are screwed to this platform just as they ordinarily would be screwed to the wood surface of the glider type of plane. Arrange a hatch of generous area which can be lifted off in order to remove the detachable chamber of the motor from its clips in order to refuel. Be sure you have provided an exit tunnel at the tail for the exhaust gases and that all bulkheads or formers between the power plant and the tail have large cut-out holes for the same purpose. With the engine mounted internally some means must be used to prevent the covering catching fire. The interior of the plane aft of the engine may be coated with waterglass, a fireproof glue obtainable at a drugstore. A protective tube may be made by coating a piece of writing paper with waterglass, then rolling the paper to the desired diameter. The tube should be of a diameter and length to match the round lightening holes cut in the formers. Thin asbestos sheeting may be rolled into a tube. Jetex also manufactures an augmeter tube. Made of thin metal, this tube is bell-shaped at one end to fit over the Jetex engine. It is so designed that air is sucked in between the edge of the tube and the engine, with the result that power may be increased by as much as 75 per cent.

140

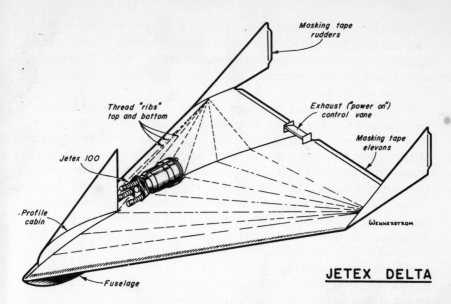

Masking tape rudders

Thread "ribs" top and bottom

Exhaust ("power on") control vane

Masking tape elevons

Jetex 100

Profile cabin

WENNERSTROM

Fuselage

JETEX DELTA

Fig. 12–4. Delta Model.

Because the power plant produces no torque, it is possible to have extremely low aspect ratios on the model plane. In figure 12–4 you will note that the plan for the delta 50 is approximately as wide as it is long! This radical type of machine was developed by Dr. A. M. Lippisch, one of the world's greatest aerodynamicists, designer of the Messerschmitt Me-163 rocket fighter of the last war. With a span of about 12 inches and a similar length, the Delta 50 weighs 1.1 ounces, and will climb to 250 feet for a one-minute glide, when well-made and well-adjusted. Construction is extremely simple. The wing consists of 4 pieces of $\frac{1}{16}$ sheet balsa butt-jointed and edged, along the sides of the triangle, with $\frac{1}{16} \times \frac{3}{8}$ balsa cut from $\frac{1}{16}$ inch sheet. The body or fuselage is $\frac{1}{8}$ inch sheet. The forward fin has been found to prevent spiral dives. Note the position of the C.G., location of the jet unit, and its angle of mounting with respect to the fuselage. Deltas with the jet mounted on top rather than the bottom were found superior. Incidentally, here is a useful tip for power-testing a new Jetex job. Cut the fuel charges in half for early flights.

With pulse jet and Jetex engines available, one might expect model plane inventors to rest on their laurels. But during 1951, Thomas Purcell, an aircraft engineer living in Philadelphia (and an experimental modeler), came up with a truly revolutionary idea. This was the ducted fan. A ducted fan is a stumpy prop placed in a passageway

141

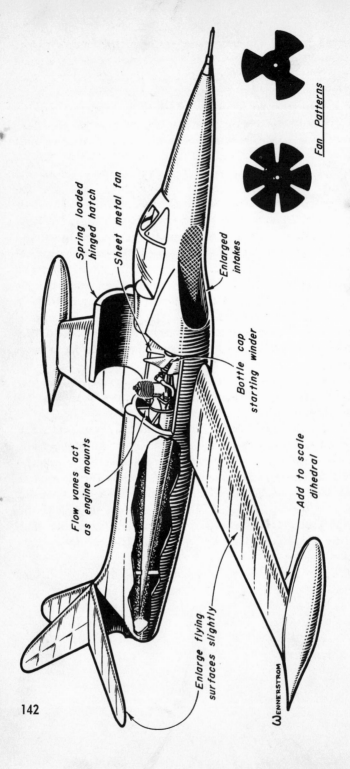

Fan Patterns

Spring loaded hinged hatch

Sheet metal fan

Enlarged intakes

Bottle cap starting winder

Flow vanes act as engine mounts

Add to scale dihedral

Enlarge flying surfaces slightly

WENNERSTROM

142

DUCTED FAN SYSTEM FOR LOCKHEED F-90

Fig. 12–5.

or duct. Purcell located his engine and prop in the middle of the tunnel to be found in scale jet jobs. Purcell's experiments were made with engines of .02 to .049 displacement and planes of roughly 20 inch wingspan. The ducted fan was found not practical for U-control.

Several requirements must be observed for efficient operation of the ducted fan. The shape of the air tunnel is important. The air intake or front orifice of the tube is larger than the tail orifice or exhaust exit. Also, the point at which the engine is located is in a relation-ship to both the intake and exhaust openings. The shape of the fan is important. It is essential that the tips of the fan just clear the tunnel wall. In the case of the .19 engine, this clearance should be $\frac{1}{16}$ inch or less. An access door should be provided to enable replace-ment of fans, adjustment of the needle valve, fueling, and motor re-placement. The motor may be attached to a hardwood cone whose front, flat face is the same size as the crankcase diameter, and this cone can be held in place in the plane by 4 or 5 sheet-wood fins. It is possible to make variations on this scheme; for instance, to have divided air intakes, one on either side of the fuselage, as found in such planes as the Cutlass and the Lockheed P-80 and F-94 series. More or less pitch can be imparted to the metal fan blades by twisting with the hand.

How is the engine started if there is no external propeller to flip? A flywheel is installed on the shaft. Cord is wound around it and a smart pull usually starts the engine without difficulty.

With the increasing enthusiasm for jet miniature aircraft, many modelers find it hard to obtain suitable plans. These tips will get you started. The best possibility is to obtain some suitable model airplane kit and modify it as necessary. A number of manufacturers, such as the Cleveland Model and Supply Co., have small scale kits intended for the Jetex 50. These can be modified to use a ducted fan with the K & B .02, .035, Cub .039 and possibly the various .049 engines. The more enterprising reader can scale up these small kit plans for engines of any capacity.

Write the model magazines for information about their plans for ducted fan models.

13

FREE-FLIGHT MODELS

FREE-FLIGHT machines fall into three general classifications. (See figure 13–1.) First, there is the contest type free-flight, engineered for maximum climb and an efficient glide. Second, there is the sport variation, more realistic looking than its thermal-hooking brother, somewhat heavier, and equipped with a smaller engine for more gentle flying. Third, there is the flying scale and semiscale job, most always rather small in size and powered with one of the little, but potent, Half-A mills.

What makes a good contest free-flight machine? Let's begin with the rules. Through the years, they have changed many times, always seeking to limit performance. In the beginning, one could make any kind of a design, equip it with any engine, and fly it with all the fuel he could cram in a tank. Then fuel became limited: ¼ ounce per pound of plane weight. Since big jobs weighed as much as 7 pounds, duration still was out of this world. Then came the 30-second engine run rule. Ingenious modelers responded with more efficient, faster climbing planes, getting them high for a long glide. The engine manufacturers created power plants that flew the ships to enormous heights in that 30 seconds. So the rule was changed to 20 seconds. Wing loadings (such as 8 ounces per square foot of area) were tried for a time but so many people entered contests that judges were kept busy weighing and measuring airplanes and little flying could be done. A weight rule based on engine displacement has been in force since well before the war. At first calling for 60 ounces weight per cubic inch of engine displacement, then for 80, then for 100, this rule has

144

FREE FLIGHT GAS MODEL TYPES

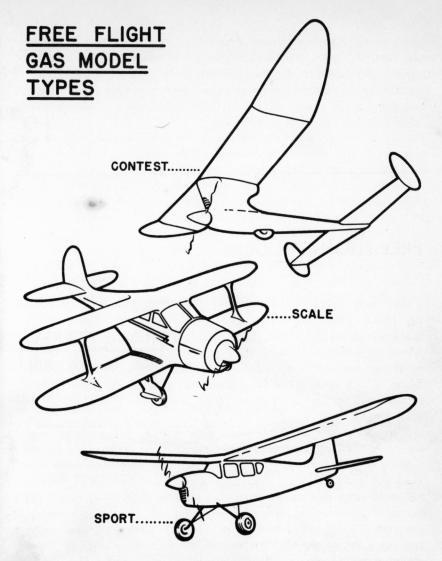

CONTEST........

......SCALE

SPORT........

Fig. 13–1.

been no more successful in curbing duration than any other rule of
bygone days. We even have to utilize dethermalizers—pop-up stabilizers or drag parachutes that drastically shorten the flight when they
are operated by a pre-set timing device—to get our planes down before they become lost.

It is evident that the two main factors in peak performance are a
fast, high climb, and an efficient glide.

The design of such an airplane centers about the engine. To put it more accurately, the problem really is one of controlling the amount of power developed by the engine. Ever since 1938, when Carl Goldberg's pylon appeared (the pylon is a finlike mounting for a wing) this configuration has been favored for stability and reliability under power in a machine of reasonable size.

Modelers usually associate increased stability with the high wing location. In other words, the lower the C.G. in relation to the wing—this is termed pendulum stability—the more stable the design is expected to be (within reasonable limits, of course). However, the pylon configuration has some unique characteristics which have a more direct bearing on its fine performance. Three principal factors stand out. First is torque.

In the low wing, and even a moderate cabin type layout, torque is a real problem. But on the pylon model, the deadly torque force is not nearly so effective and actually may be canceled by another force. This factor is the slip stream, the twisting mass of air that blows back

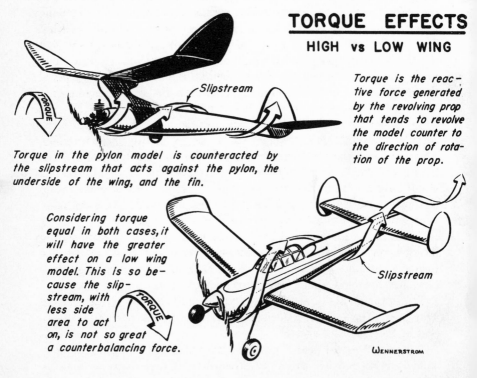

TORQUE EFFECTS
HIGH vs LOW WING

Torque is the reactive force generated by the revolving prop that tends to revolve the model counter to the direction of rotation of the prop.

Torque in the pylon model is counteracted by the slipstream that acts against the pylon, the underside of the wing, and the fin.

Considering torque equal in both cases, it will have the greater effect on a low wing model. This is so because the slipstream, with less side area to act on, is not so great a counterbalancing force.

Slipstream

Slipstream

WENNERSTROM

Fig. 13–2.

from the whirling propeller. This slip stream revolves in the same direction as the propeller so that it strikes against the upper left profile of the fuselage and vertical tail (looking forward from the tail). Of course the slip stream tends to roll the model over to the right and into a right-hand turn. By controlling the height and area of the pylon and the vertical tail, the builder is able to overcome the torque and have a ship that turns slightly to the right. With high-powered pylons, the slip-stream effect generally exerts a much greater force than torque so that the danger to be avoided is a right-hand turn or spiral into the ground. It can also be shown, although this is more complex and rather theoretical, that the gyroscopic effect of a whirling propeller will produce a right-hand diving turn tendency when the nose of the model is displaced in an upward direction. From the practical standpoint, it will be found that, if the slip stream is properly put to work, the airplane is controllable.

The third important factor results from the fact that the wing on the pylon model is high above the fuselage. Consider that the thrust line must obviously be considerably below the wing location and that the effect of the propeller thrust pulling forward, while the wing resists forward motion due to its drag, is to rotate the nose skyward. The reader who is given to drawing diagrams will quickly see that the thrust is being exerted through a moment or leverage arm equal to the distance between the thrust line and the center of resistance of the plane. To combat this nose-up tendency, the free-flight designer resorts to a type of stabilizer, which, having an airfoil section like the wing, generates lift. The faster the plane goes, the more lift the stabilizer develops to counteract the tendency of the plane to climb. At some point the lift of the wing and the nose-up tendency of the thrust will be balanced by the lift developed by the stabilizer. It would take an experimenter years to establish the precise relationship of these and other factors in the pylon, but inasmuch as the optimum values now are established, we can review them briefly.

The C.G. usually lies well back on the wing chord in airplanes using lifting type stabilizers, being positioned anywhere from an extreme forward position of 50 per cent chord, back to the trailing edge position, and averages about 75-85 per cent of chord.

The optimum stabilizer area appears to be about 45 per cent of the wing area. The stabilizer thickness ratio would work out to 8 or 9 per cent of the stabilizer chord.

A good, all-round aspect ratio for the wing that combines aerodynamic efficiency with structural strength is 6:1, perhaps as high as 7:1. Airfoil thickness varies between 9 per cent and 13 per cent, aver-

147

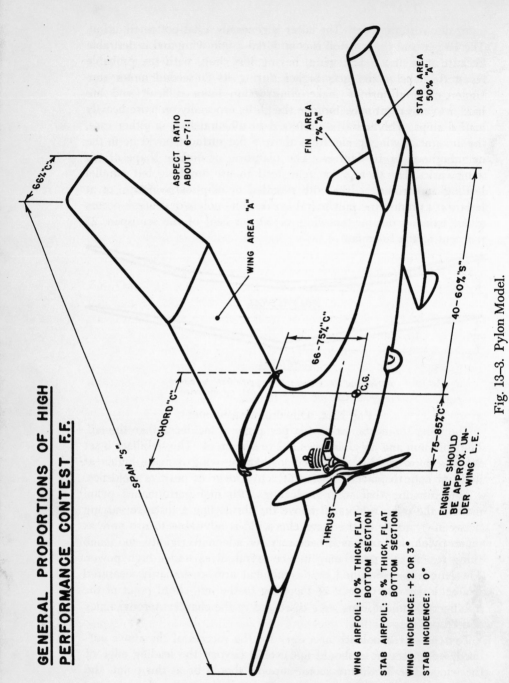

GENERAL PROPORTIONS OF HIGH
PERFORMANCE CONTEST F.F.

66½"C"

SPAN "S"

CHORD "C"

ASPECT RATIO
ABOUT 6-7:1

WING AREA "A"

FIN AREA
7% "A"

STAB AREA
50% "A"

66 – 75½"C"

C.G.

40 – 60% "S"

75 – 85%"C"

ENGINE SHOULD
BE APPROX. UN-
DER WING L.E.

THRUST

WING AIRFOIL: 10% THICK, FLAT
BOTTOM SECTION

STAB AIRFOIL: 9% THICK, FLAT
BOTTOM SECTION

WING INCIDENCE: +2 OR 3°

STAB INCIDENCE: 0°

Fig. 13-3. Pylon Model.

148

aging about 10 per cent. The latter is generally a flat-bottomed airfoil. The 10 per cent thick airfoil is considered a thin wing and is desirable because it is also a fast wing, having less drag, with the probable result that the model gets higher during its 20-second motor run. Undercambered airfoils make construction more difficult and are harder to cover but may improve the glide, especially on more heavily loaded ships. Polyhedral is preferred to dihedral but, in either case, the amount of wingtip elevation above a flat surface should be in the neighborhood of 10 degrees. The planform or outline shape of the wing varies, but there is no real need to use anything but parallel leading and trailing edges with rounded or elliptical wingtips, or at least out as far as the polyhedral break. The polyhedral break occurs about halfway out on the wing, or 50 per cent of the semispan, 25 per cent of the full span.

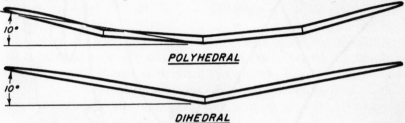

POLYHEDRAL

DIHEDRAL

Polyhedral is preferable to dihedral. In either case use approximately 10° tip elevation

Fig. 13–4. Dihedral Measurement.

The wing should be set at a larger angle of incidence than the tail. The optimum angular difference is 2 to 3 degrees. The stabilizer is set flat at zero degrees of incidence so that the wing is made higher at its front end, to place the wing at 2 to 3 degrees positive incidence.

Remembering that we are dealing with high-performance pylon models, the wing is situated above the thrust line a distance varying between ⅔ to ¾ of the wing chord. It is advisable to use only as much pylon side area as is necessary for adequate rigidity; too much side area at this point may induce spiral dives under high power. The length is determined by the moment arm, customarily measured from the mid-chord point of the wing to the mid-chord point of the stabilizer. Moment arms were discussed in the chapter Aerodynamics and Proportions.

To achieve the balance necessary for the success of the above outlined set-up, the nose should not extend beyond the leading edge of the wing. The firewall or motor support should be at this point: the motor may project beyond. Still shorter noses, as well as longer ones, are used, but longer noses usually affect the power turn characteristics adversely.

An overlarge fin area will cause the plane to head into the wind. This prevents the tight gliding circles essential for riding thermal currents and is therefore undesirable. Too small a fin area may cause the plane to rock to and fro as it climbs steeply and, when the plane is rolling from side to side, it may suddenly make a half roll until the nose is pointed down, when a fatal dive may result. The proper average fin area is about 6 or 7 per cent of the wing area.

Every high-performance free-flight job should be equipped with a dethermalizer. Wiser fliers know that no such machine should even be given its first short test hop unless the dethermalizer is set and ready for action. Contest rules do not allow for duration beyond six minutes. Therefore, even with no wind, when the plane might come down almost at the spot where it took off, the flier takes no chances and sets his dethermalizer for the time limit.

Although numerous devices have been tried, only two types have proved both effective and practical. By far the most popular is the pop-up tail. This is nothing but a stabilizer that is hinged in some manner at its leading edge, and spring-loaded by means of a rubber band so that it will tip up at the rear. When the stabilizer assumes a large negative angle, it abruptly raises the nose until the model stalls. The ship descends in a nose-high attitude at a steep angle and at a fairly high rate of speed. It will not be broken upon reaching the ground. The trick is to get the angle of tilt so adjusted that the airplane will remain in a constant nose-high attitude and not just rock back and forth between alternate dips and stalls; this angle is approximately 45 degrees. Another essential condition is to have the stabilizer so keyed that it will not slide or twist when tilted, which would cause the rudder to be turned and so spin the airplane. A piece of thread may be run from the rear edge of the stabilizer (about halfway toward the tips) down to the rear tip of the fuselage. This tether prevents the tail tilting beyond the desired angle and also keeps the rear of the tail from sliding to one side or the other. The leading edge usually is hinged or keyed in some manner—say by a plywood tongue fitting into a slot cut in the stabilizer mounting platform—so that the tail remains accurately centered.

Two methods are used to operate this type of dethermalizer. One is a standard pneumatic timer available in any hobby shop, and the other is a fuse. If the timer is employed, it is located well forward in the fuselage and has either a long, thin music wire pull rod, or a cord, extending back to the tail release. The timer is cocked with a

150

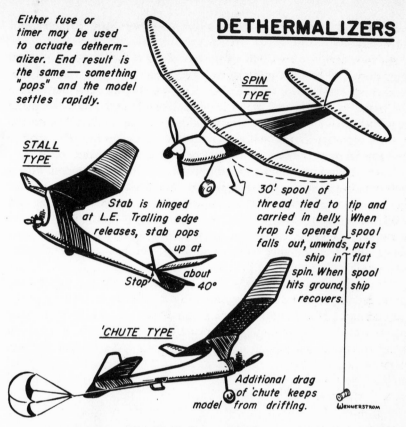

DETHERMALIZERS

Either fuse or timer may be used to actuate dethermalizer. End result is the same — something "pops" and the model settles rapidly.

SPIN TYPE

STALL TYPE

Stab is hinged at L.E. Trailing edge releases, stab pops up at about 40°

Stop

30' spool of thread tied to tip and carried in belly. When trap is opened spool falls out, unwinds, puts ship in flat spin. When spool hits ground, ship recovers.

'CHUTE TYPE

Additional drag of 'chute keeps model from drifting.

WENNERSTROM

Fig. 13-5. Pop-up Tail.

piece of pull cord which extends through a hole in the bottom of the fuselage. The fuse is simply a piece of string that has been soaked in saltpeter. The release for the tail consists of two short projections of music wire; one sticks out to the rear from the center of the stabilizer and the other, just below the first wire, is attached to the fuselage itself. A small rubber band is looped lightly around both wires; it should be just strong enough to hold down the back of the tail. The fuse is inserted through the rubber band. When the burning fuse contacts the band, it will break and then the tension of another rubber band tilts up the stabilizer.

The second dethermalizer idea is the drag chute, a small parachute which is folded and stored in a small compartment in the bottom of the fuselage, well forward beneath the wing. The compartment door is held shut by a rubber band through which a fuse is inserted. A small piece of asbestos attached to the underbody near the fuse will prevent igniting the model. When the door springs open, the chute falls out and is inflated, then drags out behind the airplane so slowing its glide that it descends quickly to earth.

In some sections of the country, a fuse could be a fire hazard so the use of a pneumatic or mechanical timer is recommended when practical.

How big a free-flight model should be depends on the power plant and this, in turn, where the contest or high-performance type is concerned, depends on the event or class in which the design is flown. Rules define these classes of engines in free flight: up to, but not including .05, Class AA or Half-A; from .05 up to, but not including .20, Class A; .20 up to, but not including .30, Class B; and .30 up to, but not including .65, Class C. The rules further specify that an airplane weigh at least 100 ounces for each cubic inch displacement. Therefore, to find the required weight of the plane you have in mind, multiply its displacement by 100. For example, a job would weigh $.19 \times 100$, or 19 ounces. The average model weighs about 4 to 6 ounces per square foot of wing area, running up to the lower figure in small ships and the larger figure in big planes. A 450 square inch machine for a .19 engine is known to be about the minimum that safely handles some of the newer engines and this works out to approximately 6 ounces per square foot of area. The little Half-A's, on the other hand, are considered best when they have about 200-250 square inches of wing area. Since the displacement of .049 times 100 equals a required weight of 4.9 ounces, you can see that the wing loading is much under the 6 ounces per square foot of the Class A ship. In fact, it is nearer to 3½ ounces per square foot. This variance is due to the fact that smaller wings have less efficiency than big ones, and therefore must be more lightly loaded to have comparable performance. A Class B plane would have upwards of 650 square inches, and a Class C ship, upwards of 850 square inches. The proportions of the plane will work out from the dimensions given the wing and these are a matter only of the area and the aspect ratio.

The flying scale and sport gas job tend to be Half-A designs. Larger sizes also result in prohibitively wide fuselages, excessive nose diameters, and great fragility in minor crack-ups. Wing areas should be slightly larger than normal. For the hotter Half-A engines (.049's), it is suggested that wing areas be made as large as 225-250 square inches. Engines of .035 cubic inch displacement power planes with about 175 to 200 square inches of area.

14

RADIO CONTROL

In 1949, the Federal Communications Commission approved for operation on 465 megacycles, without requiring the usual ham license or radio operator's license, the MacNabb Citizenship radio. In the late winter of 1951-1952, the Commission further approved for remote control the frequency of 27.255 megacycles. The transmitters for remote control of objects such as planes, boats, and cars are limited by FCC regulations to a maximum input of five watts to the final stage. Model planes are reliably controlled to the limit of vision on less than two watts output of the transmitter.

Actually, the transmitters are not license free, inasmuch as the purchaser or builder (465 mc home-built transmitters cannot be approved) of such equipment must fill out and file with the FCC Form 505, which obtains for him a station license. However, he does not have to take a code test or written examination. There has been much confusion over this point. The Citizen bands are examination free, but not license free.

For general information on this fascinating subject, it is suggested that the reader consult *Radio Amateur's Handbook; Hints and Kinks for the Radio Amateur, Vol. 4;* also the *Course in Radio Fundamentals,* published by the American Radio Relay League, West Hartford, Connecticut. Model airplane magazines publish news of radio control developments and print many plans of radio control planes and boats.

At the time of writing there are three controls of practical use on model airplanes. These are rudder, elevator, and engine. The number of controls desired by the individual modeler and the precision with which they may be applied are primarily pocketbook matters. By using construction kits for receiver, transmitter, and other devices, the builder may scrape by with an investment of about 50 dollars for the privilege of being able to make the model turn left or right in flight by use of a rudder-only system. Or he may spend up to 300 dollars and have selective controls for rudder, elevator, engine, and various or all positions of these control surfaces in combination.

Radio control, of course, can become a very complex matter. The hobbyist is urged to start with the simplest airplane kit and radio. By so doing he can learn his way into the practical matters of tuning a receiver and transmitter, adjusting a relay, and so on.

In its simplest form the system used to operate a miniature airplane by remote control consists of a transmitter that emits the signal, a receiver in the plane that picks up the signal, a relay (usually part of the radio) that is operated by the change in voltage flowing through the receiver tube when the signal is picked up, and an actuator, which may be either a servo (an electric motor device) or an escapement (an electro-mechanical device, somewhat similar to the escapement in a clock). The opening and closing of the sensitive relay makes and breaks a second electrical circuit to the actuator, which, when energized, moves the control surface, usually the rudder. The muscle for the escapement is provided by a twisted loop of rubber strand.

Most control systems are based upon a single-channel radio. By single channel is meant that only one control intelligence can be transmitted at a time. Usually, when the transmitter is turned on, and keyed, the signal it sends out is what the radio experts term a "carrier wave." This is a good name because it implies that the wave could be made to carry an additional signal. This is exactly the case when multi-channel equipment is used. Multi-channel transmitters "modulate" the "carrier wave," which means that they superimpose upon the wave various "tones." This may sound complicated but it is really quite simple when you consider your household radio. The voices and musical sounds you hear correspond to the "tones." The "tone" transmitter for a model airplane may send out from one to eight tones. The receiver, capable of sorting out these tones and responding to the particular one that is being transmitted at the instant, closes and opens circuits, by means of relays, to various actuating devices, giving up or down elevator, right or left rudder, high, medium, low, or shutoff to the engine.

Suppose we examine in greater detail the various popular combinations of radios and controls. First, by reason of its overwhelming popularity is the single-channel radio. The cheapest single-channel carrier wave receivers are of two types: a two-tube type, in which the first

154

tube is of the gas-filled or "soft" variety (sometimes both tubes are this kind), and the single, hard-tube type. A typical gas tube is the Raytheon RK-61, a typical hard tube, the 3V4, 1V5, etc. These are made by a number of different manufacturers.

From the beginning, the gas tube lent itself to small, light, compact, sensitive receivers. The difficulty was that the gas tube is relatively short lived when idled at normal current in a single-tube receiver. When, a few years ago, the single gas-tube receiver was the vogue, the tube idled at 1.3 to 1.5 milliamperes of current and had a life of a few hours at best. On signal, this receiver idling current was reduced sharply to .1 to .3 milliamperes, and this current change, as mentioned above, caused the sensitive relay to close the circuit to the escapement (servos are a more recent development). To get around the problems of tube life and more reliable relay operation, the two-tuber was developed. In this receiver, the first or detecting "stage," idled at but .5 milliamperes. The second tube idled at a current close to zero. Upon signal, the current in the first tube would drop to perhaps .05 milliamperes, and the current in the second tube, being triggered by the first tube, would shoot up to 2.5 or even 5 milliamperes. The hobbyist obtained longer life from his sensitive gas tube, and at the same time a more reliable relay action due to the large current change. This made the relay relatively immune to vibration from the engine; a consideration that makes the little two-tubers tremendously popular even today. A relay is one of the weak points in any control system.

Various limitations of the gas tube receivers led to wide use of the single hard-tube receiver. By hard tube is meant one from which the air has been evacuated—in other words, the familiar vacuum tube. On such a receiver, the idling current might stand at anywhere from 1.5 milliamperes up to about 4 milliamperes. On signal, this receiver has a drop in current, possibly from 1.5 to .4 milliamperes. Although the hard tube has an almost infinite life as far as the average modeler is concerned, the receiver usually requires additional adjustment controls and more careful adjustment (the manufacturer's directions always give such information). Therefore, these two receivers, the two-tuber using a gas tube as a detector, and the single hard tuber, are most popular with the modeler who has limited funds to spend. "Tone" receivers having three tubes for detection, amplification, and operation of the relay are most reliable and supply a current change of as much as 6 milliamperes to the relay.

Keep in mind that these are single-channel or one-control intelligence receivers. Now let's examine what can be done with such a simple unit. First, the signal is sent by means of a microswitch (the keying lead) on the transmitter. The end of the lead, with the control switch, is held in one hand. Signals are sent by pressing the button; the signal stays on—governing its length—as long as the switch or button is kept closed. What happens at this point depends on the type of actuator that moves the control surface on the plane.

For this kind of operation (hand pressing of a button to send signals) there are two types of escapements and servos. These are the self-neutralizing and compound types. The difference is simple. On the self-neutralizing escapement, or servo, the unit will move, say, a rudder to the full on position to turn the plane. As long as the signal is maintained, the rudder stays over and the plane continues to turn—as a matter of fact, it usually will begin to spiral steeply. When the signal is cut off, the actuator returns to a neutral position automatically, and the rudder similarly returns to its neutral position. Although the simplest of all actuators, the self-neutralizing types do not allow selective rudder, that is, choice of left or right, but compel a sequence, such as right, neutral, left, neutral, right, and so on. To make a turn, the pilot would hold down his signal button, then relax the button for the ship to resume straight flight. Then, if he wanted a turn in the opposite direction, he would simply press the button again. But, if he wanted to repeat a turn in the same direction, as a right turn after a right turn, he would have to press the button once for the first turn, then relax, then press twice more, once for the opposite turn, and once to come back to the original turn. This is done quickly so that the plane has no chance to respond to the opposite turn signal. Thus, two signals sent to the self-neutralizing actuator always gives the same direction of turn, whereas one will give to the opposite of the last turn made. It is necessary to remember which direction of turn was last made so that it will be known how many signals are required for the next desired turn. In a tight spot, close to the ground, this can be important, and a mistake may cause a crack-up.

The compound types of actuators, be they servos or escapements, allow the pilot to select his turn at any time. One signal usually gives a right turn, whereas two will give a left turn. Most of the compound actuators have a third position (takes three signals) in which an electrical contact is bumped shut; this contact closes a circuit to a secondary actuator, either escapement or servo, which can be used for motor or elevator control. When the secondary actuator in a single-channel system operates an elevator, the actuator usually is of the self-neutralizing type (it is difficult to key the required number of signals for a secondary escapement of the compound type); therefore, the self-neutralizing actuator on the elevators gives a sequence of up, neutral,

156

down, neutral, up, etc. Thus, if the pilot wishes up he will send three rapid signals through the primary compound actuator, which then triggers the elevator actuator to give up, if the last position was down. Three more rapid signals would move the elevators through neutral to down. While this system does facilitate dives, loops, and possibly inverted flying, it obviously leaves much to be desired.

One improvement is the Babcock Mark II escapement, which can be used in a number of ways to give additional controls. The third position contact can be used to work either elevator or engine by means of a secondary actuator. Or, a mechanical movement on the third position will "kick up" elevator whenever used, useful for loops and flared out landings; this leaves free the electrical contact to operate the engine control. Or, an additional electrical contact can be attached to this escapement (also to the Bonner Compounds) to allow engine control (another actuator needed) by means of a very fast, short signal; right rudder on one longer signal, left rudder on two longer signals, and up or down elevator, via a third actuator.

Some ingenious modelers, tiring of the necessity to transmit three, then three more signals to obtain desired elevator action, which is limited to a sequence of up, neutral, down, etc., created the "cascade system." By attaching microswitches to the escapements, it became possible to obtain up or down elevator at will by pulsing three or four signals, three being up and four down. This meant that any time four signals were transmitted, the elevators would go into the down position. This seems to be the ultimate in escapements: one quick signal for engine control, one steady for right, two for left, three for up, and four for down. These new escapements include a printed wiring circuit that replaces the microswitches in home-built actuators of this type and require no construction on the part of the hobbyist.

Unfortunately, this system puts a strain on the pilot and, in general, any control system requiring complicated count-offs or dialing systems makes it tricky to maneuver the airplane in an emergency. New cascaded escapements by Bonner, called the Varicomp, materially improved this "full house" of escapements. In servos, much has been accomplished by DeBolt's DMECO servos.

Still on the subject of single-channel equipment, there is another basic system for moving controls. This is the pulse system. An electronic or mechanical pulsing unit is attached to the transmitter keying lead in place of the microswitch control button. This unit sends out signals far more rapidly than is possible by hand.

For the airplane, an entirely different type of actuator is required. This is the magnetic actuator. Its operation depends on the fact that a relay has two contacts. Normally, only one contact is used, but in the pulse system both relay contacts are connected to the actuator. With signal on, one relay contact is activated, closing a circuit that causes the magnetic actuator to swing in one direction. When signal is cut off, the other relay contact is activated and the actuator swings in the opposite direction. By sending a continuous stream of signals, whose length is equal to the intervals between signals, the relay armature bounces back and forth, the actuator following its rapid motions, and the rudder, too, swings quickly from left to right, and back again. This motion is so rapid that the airplane does not respond, but flies straight, despite the wiggling rudder. If the pulser control is moved to one side or the other, either lengthening the signal length in relation to the interval between signals, or vice versa, the relay armature favors one contact over the other, the actuator and the rudder following suit, so that a turn results. Infinite variations by means of the control produce a shallow or steep turn, with the turn being in proportion to the movements of the control stick.

Hobbyists fortunate enough to understand electronics can achieve much with single-channel radios. It is possible, for example, to alter the pulse rate as well as the pulse length of a signal. When the pulse rate is altered on the control box in the pilot's hand, a second control is operated by the receiver. Simultaneous and proportionate action of both elevators and rudder, slaving to the actions of the control stick on the ground, is a remarkable achievement for a simple, single-channel receiver.

A big step up the ladder from this simple receiver is the two-channel receiver that allows the pilot to select either rudder or elevator at will, without having to go through one control to find the other. As a rule, the two-channel receiver would work two primary actuators of the compound type, so that either or both actuators could be hooked up to one or more secondary actuators. One channel using a compound actuator might give right, left, and engine control; the second channel could work up and down, plus—you name it: brakes, parachute, or bomb dropping, etc. The two-channel receiver is tuned to respond to two different tones sent out by the transmitter. Push one button and one set of controls operates, push the other button and a second set operates. Sometimes it is possible to push two buttons at once and to come up with a third tone for some additional purpose.

At a cost of about 200 dollars, complete with actuators, we get into three- and five-channel receivers. The most popular three-channel receiver features an electronic filtering system that sorts out the three tones that the transmitter may send out, and directs this intelligence to close a relay, one of three, that operates three distinct controls. Such a receiver is usually hooked up with one channel to operate a compound actuator for left and right rudder and, by means of a secondary actuator, to control motor speed; the remaining two channels are connected respectively to up and down elevator, by means of a trimming-type servo. The ground control box would have a stick control; pushed forward, the stick gives down; pulled back up; pushed right, right rudder; pushed left, left rudder. The trim servo means that the elevators do not come back to a neutral position but remain where last placed; thus, if a dive is started, the plane will remain in the dive until the servo is repositioned. This gives an infinate number of trimming positions for realistic flying but is awkward for full aerobatics because the pilot is continuously hunting neutral elevator. When stunting at high speed, this can be hard on the nerves—if not the airplane. Note that, since the rudder is being worked by an actuator, it is not fully selective but is restricted to a one signal for right, two for left, three for engine.

Moving up into the five- (or more) channel receivers, we encounter the reed bank. A reed bank consists of one to five or more individually tuned reeds (lengths are different), each of which will vibrate in response to the frequency of a tone sent out by the transmitter. When a reed is agitated, it closes a contact that operates one relay connected to a given control. With five channels, the usual system is to allot one channel for right, one for left, one for up, one for down, and one for engine. Engine is operated by a button on the transmitter that can be pushed quickly in emergency. A stick gives left, right, down, and up. If moved left, for example, the rudder goes directly left, not having to pass through right on the way. If the stick is returned to neutral, the rudder neutralizes; ditto for elevators when the stick is moved forward or backward, then to neutral. By repeated fast applications of stick, a crude sort of proportionate control is obtained. This is the most versatile of commercially available equipment.

The more expensive transmitters and receivers, when properly used and cared for, are more reliable than the simple, and especially home-made, single-channel 27.255-megacycle deals. Although the latter do render perfectly acceptable service, they perform a number of functions on one or two tubes that ideally would be performed by a number of tubes. The single-channel, single-tube receiver is capable of only so much current change when a signal is received; hence the contact pressure and reliability of the relay is relatively low. The receiver that has tubes for the separate functions of detection and amplification provides a large current change through the relays. Babcock uses

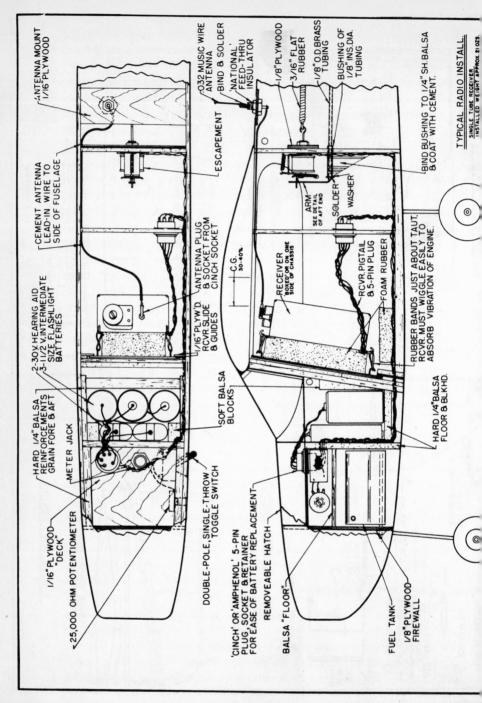

'ANTENNA MOUNT 1/16" PLYWOOD

CEMENT ANTENNA LEAD-IN WIRE TO SIDE OF FUSELAGE

.032 MUSIC WIRE ANTENNA

BIND & SOLDER

'NATIONAL' FEED-THRU INSULATOR

1/8"PLYWOOD

3/16" FLAT RUBBER

1/8" O.D. BRASS TUBING

BUSHING OF 1/8" INS. DIA. TUBING

ESCAPEMENT

ANTENNA PLUG & SOCKET FROM CINCH SOCKET

BIND BUSHING TO 1/4" SH. BALSA & COAT WITH CEMENT.

ARM SEE DETAIL OF AFT END

SOLDER

WASHER

RECEIVER SIDE OF ONE SIDE OF CHASSIS

C.G. 30-40%

2-30V. HEARING AID 3-1 1/2 V. INTERMEDIATE SIZE FLASHLIGHT BATTERIES

RCVR. PIGTAIL & 5-PIN PLUG

FOAM RUBBER

RUBBER BANDS JUST ABOUT TAUT. RCVR. MUST WIGGLE EASILY TO ABSORB VIBRATION OF ENGINE.

1/16"PLYW'D. RCVR. SLIDE & GUIDES

HARD 1/4"BALSA REINFORCEMENTS GRAIN FORE & AFT

METER JACK

HARD 1/4"BALSA FLOOR & BLKHD.

SOFT BALSA BLOCKS

1/16" PLYWOOD "DECK"

DOUBLE-POLE, SINGLE-THROW TOGGLE SWITCH

25,000 OHM POTENTIOMETER

'CINCH' OR 'AMPHENOL' 5-PIN PLUG, SOCKET & RETAINER FOR EASE OF BATTERY REPLACEMENT

REMOVEABLE HATCH

BALSA "FLOOR"

FUEL TANK

1/8"PLYWOOD FIREWALL

TYPICAL RADIO INSTALL.

SINGLE TUBE RECEIVER INSTALLED WEIGHT APPROX. 2½ OZS.

Fig. 14-1.
Typical Radio

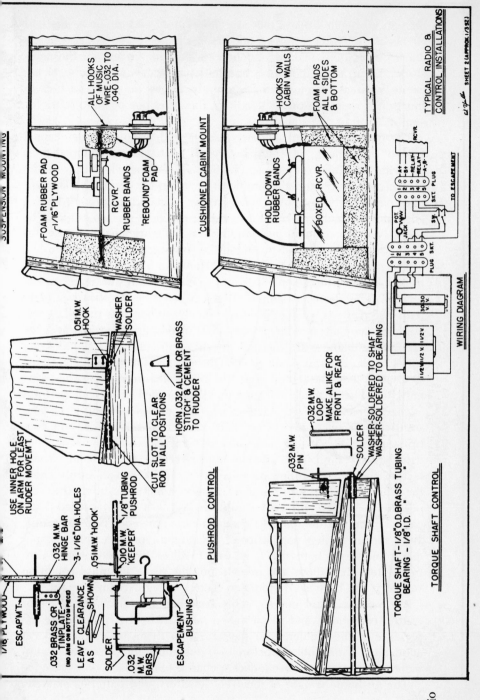

SUSPENSION MOUNTING

FOAM RUBBER PAD
1/16" PLYWOOD

ALL HOOKS OF MUSIC WIRE .032 TO .040 DIA.

RCVR.
RUBBER BANDS

'REBOUND' FOAM PAD

'CUSHIONED CABIN' MOUNT

HOOKS ON CABIN WALLS

HOLD-DOWN RUBBER BANDS

BOXED RCVR.

FOAM PADS ALL 4 SIDES & BOTTOM

TYPICAL RADIO & CONTROL INSTALLATIONS

SHEET 2 (APPROX. 1/3 S.)

USE INNER HOLE ON ARM FOR LEAST RUDDER MOVEMT.

.051 M.W. HOOK

WASHER SOLDER

HORN .032 ALUM. OR BRASS 'STITCH' & CEMENT TO RUDDER

CUT SLOT TO CLEAR ROD IN ALL POSITIONS

1/8" PLYWOOD

ESCAP'M'T.

.032 M.W. HINGE BAR

.032 BRASS OR TINPLATE (NO ARM ON BOTTOM PIECE)

3-1/16"DIA. HOLES

.051 M.W. 'HOOK'

1/8"TUBING PUSHROD

.010 M.W. 'KEEPER'

LEAVE CLEARANCE AS SHOWN

SOLDER

.032 M.W. BARS

ESCAPEMENT BUSHING

PUSHROD CONTROL

.032 M.W. PIN

.032 M.W. LOOP MAKE ALIKE FOR FRONT & REAR

SOLDER

WASHER-SOLDERED TO SHAFT
WASHER-SOLDERED TO BEARING

RCVR.

+ A+
RELAY
RELAY
– B –

TO ESCAPEMENT

POT.
JACK

SW.
V.W.

SKT. PLUG

PLUG SKT.

30/50
V.V.

1 1/2 V.

1 1/2 V.
1 1/2 V.

WIRING DIAGRAM

TORQUE SHAFT-1/8"O.D.BRASS TUBING
BEARING - 1/8" I.D. "

TORQUE SHAFT CONTROL

Fig. 14-2.
Typical Radio
and Control
Installations.

hermetically sealed relays that are tamperproof and minimize the bad effects of dirt, exhaust fumes, and electrical arcing across the contacts due to continuous making and breaking of the current on the actuators. Again, the single-tube transmitter often runs the tube to capacity, whereas the multi-tube transmitter allows the oscillator tube to function at more reasonable loadings, then uses one or more tubes for amplification of the signal.

The great majority of modelers use the rudder-only, single-channel type of equipment. It would be well if all beginners confined their first efforts to this equipment. Practically everyone who tackles radio control underestimates the problems of flying the airplane. This applies particularly to persons who, having profound electronics knowledge, automatically assume that existing practices are too crude. The result is a year of hard work and either no flights whatsoever or just the one flight that it takes to smash the complex rig to smithereens.

The reader will ask immediately, "How can a model plane be controlled by the rudder only? How can the machine be made to descend?" The answer is simple. When allowed to travel in a straight path, the plane is trimmed to climb slowly. When it is turned, it will hold the same altitude momentarily but, if the turn is maintained, the nose of the plane will drop and the ship will enter an altitude-losing spiral or, if the turn is sharp enough, a tight, spectacular corkscrew descent. When the motor stops, the pilot need only guide the plane until the wheels touch the ground. Experienced pilots can perform advanced maneuvers like wing-overs, stalls, spins, loops, and even consecutive rolls on rudder alone. The danger to the rudder-only-controlled plane is excessive power and/or poor trim conditions that cause it to kite sky high or to become unmanageable in the wind. These factors, combined with inexperience, result in "ballooned" turns, where the plane zooms up into the wind when completing a turn. Until experience is gained, the tyro should always fly with a throttled-down engine (rich mixture) and with short motor runs (don't fill the tank). With the increasing popularity of compound-type actuators, escapements and servos both, it is quite easy to affix a two-speed engine control system that allows the pilot to put the plane in cruise condition so that it can be steered around without gaining excessive height.

Multi-channels, of course, allow trimming the plane, extra motor control conditions, and so on, but a multi-channel requires more experience of the builder, who should master flying technique and get acquainted with problems before charging ahead into expensive equipment that may never have a decent chance to do its job.

The air-borne weight of receiver, actuators, and batteries may run

162

from approximately 10 ounces to 40 ounces or more, depending on the complexity and number of controls. Most starting modelers are confused by the question, "Where and how do I install this stuff?"

Let's begin with the single-channel lightweight receivers. At the front of the cabin, beneath the leading edge of the wing, is a thick sheet balsa bulkhead (usually ¼ inch thick). At the back of the cabin is another bulkhead which may be cut out for lightness. The escapement is generally mounted in front of this second bulkhead; the receiver, on a sliding plywood tray (¹⁄₁₆ to ³⁄₃₂ inch thick), which slides down into the cabin, in a vertical position, by means of a plywood track. The receiver is usually placed so that one side of its chassis can be bonded to a piece of foam rubber (not sponge), which in turn is bonded to the ply tray. Pliobond is a good bonding agent. On the floor of the cabin, or along one wall, is arranged a plywood strip or shelf with two sockets in place. The receiver cable plugs into one socket, the battery cable into the other. On the side of the ship, facing the launcher when he holds the plane, should be the switch, the jack (for inserting the phone plug on which is the meter for checking current), and the potentiometer. The batteries may be inserted in special battery boxes firmly affixed to the structure in some convenient and accessible spot, or they may be taped together in packs to which the cable leads are soldered. Sometimes the top of the nose is removable to permit access to batteries, sometimes the cabin floor. In the latter case, there is a false floor recessed inside, accessible from the bottom, to which the battery boxes are screwed tight. Or the batteries, in pack form, may slide down behind the front cabin bulkhead, in which case the receiver tray slides down against a second, false bulkhead, just behind the battery compartment. The actuator is connected to the rudder by means of a wire or wood pushrod or torsion rod which has a rocker action. If the escapements are used, the driving rudder reaches to a hook in the back of the ship, the hook being accessible for attachment of a winder.

Heavy, multi-channel receivers require different handling. Sometimes, where the fuselage is big enough, they, too, can be mounted on a foam rubber pad bonded to a sliding tray. But very often their weight makes it necessary to mount them by screws, etc., in a horizontal position deep in the cabin. They rest on thin plywood pieces bonded to foam rubber, which is bonded in turn to horizontal wood bearers. Servos, being heavier than escapements, generally are mounted detachably on special plywood platforms resting on thin but firm shock-absorbing material, such as ⅜ inch rubber weather stripping. As many as three escapements sometimes are grouped on the front face of a sturdy bulkhead—all being removable by screws for servicing.

Naturally, there are a thousand and one combinations for installing equipment. Directions show some methods. Individual ingenuity plays a large part. It is an excellent idea to make a study of methods used by other hobbyists. Radio fans usually operate as a group, and you can probably learn from your hobby shop where they fly.

Another reason why simple equipment is recommended in the beginning is that large, heavy planes may be required for heavier outfits. Even the expert finds it difficult to build a light but sturdy plane, and the beginner may end up with an overloaded monster of eight pounds or more with at least a .35 engine. The plane proves flimsy, even so; is hard to launch and requires utmost skill from the flier if it is not to be broken. A plane with an .09 for power should not weigh more than 16 ounces per square foot of wing area, and one with a .35, not more than 20 ounces per square foot of wing area. The all-round best figure is 16 ounces per square foot. For a full stunt machine capable of inverted flight and outside loops, the weight should be as low as 12 ounces per square foot of wing. Check your plane against these figures. Power loading, which is the gross weight of the machine, divided by the displacement of the engine in cubic inches, should be about 300 ounces for multi-control, not more than 400 ounces in any case, and this latter figure presumes a good engine.

The more experienced radio man who has yet to try remote control will be interested in the relays used for this purpose. For single-channel work, where current change is not great, a very sensitive relay, such as the Sigma 26F, should be employed. The Sigma 4F and 5F also are good. Kurman makes a useful relay and there are others. It is desirable to have screw adjustable contacts, and they should be easy to adjust and clean regularly. (Never clean contacts with an abrasive; sticking and smash-ups result.)

For multi-channel work (also on two-tube receivers) where there is a good current change, the lightweight relays such as Gem, Neomatic, etc., are quite satisfactory. Now, how about transmitters?

Disregarding the variations in functions, transmitters are of two types: the hand-held and the stationary. Hand-held transmitters almost invariably are operated by means of batteries contained in the case itself, whereas the stationary type may have self-contained batteries, or a self-contained power pack. The hand-held type offers superior mobility and flexibility on the field, but the smaller batteries must be replaced more often, a fairly expensive item; the stationary type may be trouble free for a year or more, even on its own batteries,

RADIO CONTROL PROPORTIONS

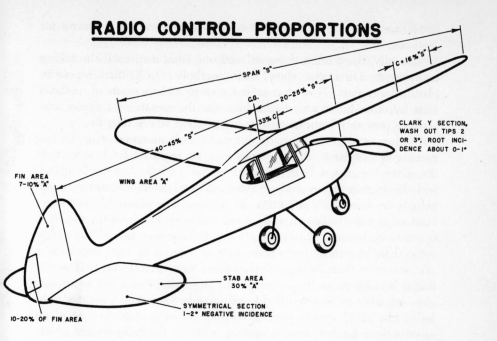

SPAN "S"

C = 16 % "S"

C.G.

20-25% "S"

33% C

CLARK Y SECTION,
WASH OUT TIPS 2
OR 3°. ROOT INCI-
DENCE ABOUT 0-1°

40-45% "S"

FIN AREA
7-10% "A"

WING AREA "A"

STAB AREA
30% "A"

SYMMETRICAL SECTION
1-2° NEGATIVE INCIDENCE

10-20% OF FIN AREA

Fig. 14–3.

because of their large size, but it is tied to one location, frequently the hood of a car. Many of these transmitters actually are connected to the storage battery in the car. The number of controls does not necessarily govern the type or size of transmitter case.

For instance, the three-channel Babcock transmitter fits in a box approximately 8 x 3 x 5 inches, all batteries included. The single-channel Citizenship transmitter on 465 mc measures about 9 x 3 x 4, batteries included. Some hand-held transmitters are considerably smaller than these. A typical stationary type, the Control Master, measures 12 x 6 x 7, but has plenty of space for batteries three or four times the size of batteries contained in hand-held types, or its accommodates a vibrator, or power pack, or power supply. A power supply is similar to the unit in the automobile radio that converts the voltage of the storage battery, 6 or 12 volts usually, into the necessary B-voltage, usually $67\frac{1}{2}$ in the car, but 135 or even 180 on the model airplane transmitter. Some transmitters are fitted with a small wet-cell storage battery, a power pack, and a charging unit, and are completely self-contained and capable of many dozens of flights without recharging, which is done by plugging the unit into a common light outlet.

The trend in size and weight of radio-control models is downward. Not only are single-channel receivers becoming more compact and lighter but the increasing use of transistors has decreased the weight and size of some multi-channel radios, notably the CG Electronics five-channel receiver, below that of some single-channel outfits. In 1956, Babcock introduced a two-channel outfit, the receiver fully transistorized, on 465 mc. Its only battery requirement is a 30-volt hearing aid. CG's transistorized equipment did use a sub-miniature tube for detection but required only a pencell and one small hearing-aid battery. Transistors spell low battery drain.

So the size of the model varies according to the weight of the equipment to be carried. The CG five-channel might even be installed in a so-called Half-A model, which is one powered by an .049 cubic inch displacement motor, the smallest available commercially. The weight of actuators for moving the controls would bring up the gross weight, however. For competition flying, fliers have found the 5 to 6-foot airplane, with about 5 square feet of wing area, to be supreme at complex maneuvers, such as outside loops and inverted flying. The average single-channel radio can be carried well in a plane of 4 to 6 foot span, with a good .09 or a weak .29 as the power limits, according to span.

The radio model design should have a comparatively long nose and a fairly short fuselage aft of the wing. An aspect ratio of 6:1 or 7:1 is good—the distance between the center point of the wing chord and the center point of the stabilizer chord should be about $\frac{2}{5}$ the wing span. The nose length—in front of the leading edge of the wing—should be at least 75 per cent of the chord.

The stabilizer area should not be more than 30 per cent of the wing area, as large tail areas make for poor stall recoveries, giving longer dives out of a stall. A good minimum is 25 per cent. The C.G. should be located not more than 40 per cent of the chord from the leading edge, and preferably should be forward of that, say at 33 per cent. The further aft the C.G. is located, the more abruptly the plane responds to nose-up forces, just as does the U-control model that has its C.G. located too far to the rear. A forward C.G. makes for smooth maneuvering and good wind penetration. The usual method of aligning the flying surfaces is to place the wing flat on the top of the cabin, which should not be slanted for incidence, and the stabilizer is then positioned at a slight negative angle, such as $1\frac{1}{2}$ or 2 degrees. The nose-heavy trim works against ballooning and zooming under power, or hanging on the prop with a mushing flight characteristic; in the

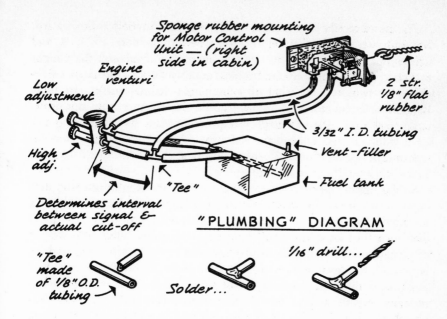

Sponge rubber mounting for Motor Control Unit — (right side in cabin)

Engine venturi

Low adjustment

High adj.

Determines interval between signal & actual cut-off

"Tee"

2 str. 1/8" flat rubber

3/32" I.D. tubing

Vent-Filler

Fuel tank

"PLUMBING" DIAGRAM

"Tee" made of 1/8" O.D. tubing

Solder...

1/16" drill...

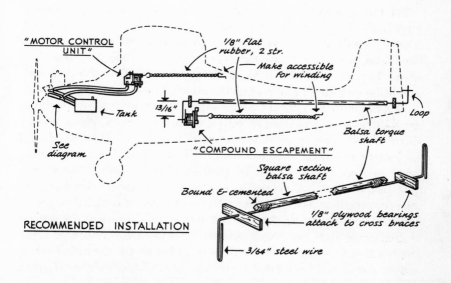

"MOTOR CONTROL UNIT"

1/8" flat rubber, 2 str.

Make accessible for winding

Tank

13/16"

See diagram

"COMPOUND ESCAPEMENT"

Loop

Balsa torque shaft

Square section balsa shaft

RECOMMENDED INSTALLATION

Bound & cemented

1/8" plywood bearings attach to cross braces

3/64" steel wire

Fig. 14–4. Two-Speed Hook-up.

glide, the required force to hold up the nose is derived from the negatively angled stabilizer. (Figure 14–3 shows proportions.)

With the above setup, an undue amount of downthrust (tilting down) of the motor may be necessary. So another alternative is to place the wing at a large positive angle, say 8 degrees angle of incidence, and then to place the stabilizer also at a positive, but not quite as great an angle—say six degrees. By doing this, the motor appears to be pulling straight ahead but actually, relative to the angle of wing and tail, is pulling downhill. This downthrust is necessary as a rule to prevent nosing up or stalling under power, even when the ship has a normal gliding angle. If the plane glides correctly, never alter the angle of the tail to prevent nosing up under power; rather, tilt the engine down as necessary.

Still another arrangement is seen with full stunt matchines. These may have a fully symmetrical cross section to their wings (the rib is not flat on the bottom, but has a convex shape to the bottom surface that matches its top contour). Or the top camber or curve of the wing may be two-thirds the depth of the rib above the chord line of the rib (the line drawn through leading and trailing edges), and one-third its depth below. When using such sections, the difference in angular setting between wing and tail should be between $\frac{1}{2}$ and $1\frac{1}{2}$ degrees.

The amount of dihedral governs turn characteristics as much as any other factor. Large dihedral requires that the rudder be held on to maintain a turn and, in holding on rudder, a spiral dive eventually results. Recovery, once the rudder is returned to neutral, is jerky as the plane practically bounces back to level flight. Shallow dihedral will permit applying rudder and immediately neutralizing, after which the plane will maintain a turn on its own, perhaps as much as 360 degrees before breaking out to straight flight (if the C.G. is properly located). The maximum dihedral necessary may be considered 7 degrees.

It will be obvious that the rudder will have more effect while the engine is running than when the plane is gliding. This is due partly to the slip stream but mainly to the increased forward speed of the machine which causes the rudder to be more sensitive. If the plane has slow glide but high speed under power, this difference in degree of rudder response becomes a definite handicap. If adjusted for mild power turns, it may prove inadequate during the slow glide so that the plane cannot be controlled. If more rudder action is used for good glide control, it then may be so sensitive that long application with the engine running can roll the machine, placing it in an inverted dive. Therefore, compromise is indicated between a somewhat touchy reaction under power and an adequate control during the glide. Remember that windy weather requires a sizable increase in rudder action for the same responses. The ideal solution to this problem of rudder action is to so adjust the plane that its power-on and power-off speeds lie closer together. With the loadings described above, a rudder area of approximately 15 per cent of the total vertical tail area, itself perhaps 10 per cent of the wing area, should have a movement of approximately $\frac{3}{16}$ inch to either side. In practice, this may work out to $\frac{1}{8}$ or $\frac{1}{4}$ inch movement but only trial and error will determine the precise amount. As the flier gains confidence, more rudder action can be safely used.

Inasmuch as some wind will almost always be encountered, it is important to know the technique of flying a radio-control job in a breeze. To begin with, it is characteristic of all free-flying models that they cannot be properly flown both in calm and windy weather without readjusting their flying trim. The ship that glides perfectly in a calm will stall in a wind; the ship that is trimmed for wind will glide steeply in a calm. Since a plane is first adjusted in calm or near calm conditions, it follows that trim for wind must be in the direction of increased nose heaviness, accomplished by adding weight to the nose, moving the wing back, decreasing the angle of incidence in the stabilizer.

Failures occur frequently because the builder does not check his batteries often enough or exhausts them by excessive periods of bench or ground testing. It is essential to test the batteries under load.

Escapements frequently fail because of battery exhaustion. Be sure to check the escapement batteries under load, as well as those in the receiver. Many times, flights are made with the pilot forgetting to wind the escapement rubber.

Too much power will make any ship unmanageable. Do not add power for wind. Overpowering builds up vibration at diving speeds. Vibration can cause skipping of the escapement or relay with the possibility of a crack-up.

15

FLYING AND ADJUSTING

THE control-liner has several unusual factors that tend to spoil its flight. One is the weight of the steel wires, tending to pull down the inside wing. Another is the air drag of the wires, tending to turn the nose in toward the center of the circle. Another is torque, which, on an airplane that flies counterclockwise, tends to roll down the left or inside wingtip. Added together, these forces create a pronounced tendency to roll the ship in toward the flier. On a windy day, the force of the wind against the plane as it flies upwind of the pilot on one side of the circle considerably magnifies this rolling tendency. Should the airplane move sideways toward the flier so that the control lines become slack, control is lost and the plane dives full speed into the ground. Fortunately, these are simple difficulties to overcome. One expedient which quickly becomes second nature to the practiced flier is to step back whenever the lines become slack. Tension is restored and control preserved.

While taking up the slack is a necessary part of any U-control flier's technique, it is also essential to reduce any tendency of the plane to come in on the lines. These are the few simple adjustments. Torque is compensated for by tilting the thrust line 2 or 3 degrees toward the outside of the circle. Further insurance is provided by setting the rudder toward the outside of the circle. On a large plane, the rear edge of the rudder should be displaced as much as ½ inch; on a small Half-A-powered ship, ¼ inch should be sufficient. To

170

overcome the weight of the lines, lead weight is placed in the outside wingtip. The proper weight may be determined by a simple test. Having put a weight in place, hold the nose and the rear tip of the fuselage between fingers with unweighted side of the wing pointing at the ground. The counterweight should roll the plane back to an upright position and continue rolling until the weighted tip is pointing at the ground.

The fore-and-aft sensitivity of the ship, which determines the response to elevator movements and the smoothness with which the plane flies when you try to hold level flight, is determined by many things. C.G. position is most important, just as it is in free flight.

Not only does the location of the C.G. govern the sensitivity, if not the very flyability of the ship; the placement of the bellcrank pivot point, and the amount of area, and movement of the elevators, all contribute to the flying characteristics of the plane. In fact, the bellcrank pivot point and the C.G. usually are considered as a combination. For example, if the ship is supported at both wingtips by the finger tips so that it teeters back and forth until the exact balancing point is located, the bellcrank pivot should then be so placed that the C.G. falls somewhere between the pivot and the front line hole in the bellcrank. The nearer the C.G. is to the pivot, the more sensitive the ship will be, other things being equal, and the further forward the C.G. is, as on the front line hole position or even further forward, the steadier flying but less responsive the ship becomes. Therefore, a very fast machine to be used for speed should balance on or about the front line, whereas the stunt ship which requires quick changes in position rather than extreme steadiness in flight, should balance between the front hole and the pivot. Trainers balance forward, sport models at an in-between position.

The speed plane does not have an offset rudder, usually does not have offset thrust and never has a weight in the wingtip. This is true for several reasons, the important one being that the plane is not stunted and is not allowed to get high off the ground. Its timed run usually is made not higher than the flier's head. At its very great speeds, the heavy racing job develops centrifugal force which keeps the wires taut despite wind that would tend to slide the ordinary job in on the lines toward the flier. Some racing planes even have thrust toward the inside of the circle to decrease pull on the lines for more efficient flying. Team racers fly level and do not require as much compensation as stunt jobs. Some stunt models utilize tricky features in design to eliminate the wingtip weight.

The beginner should make a special effort to remember that the wind, however slight, should be allowed for in planning a flight. This is why. If the plane is permitted to take off into the wind, it is apt to climb high right after take-off and will be positioned at high altitude on the upwind side of the circle before speed is built up to guarantee sufficient force to keep the lines taut. Most accidents happen at this point, as lines go slack and the plane dives into the ground. Take-offs should always be made downwind. For similar reasons, all possible stunts, such as loops and vertical 8's, should be made on the downwind side of the circle, where the wind tends to blow the ship away from the flier and to keep the lines taut. Stunting on the upwind side is always dangerous. It is easy to know where to begin a stunt because the wind can be felt on the back, and some quickly identifiable object, like a house or tree, may be picked up out of the corner of the eye.

Since free-flying models are not restricted in any direction their adjustment is more demanding. The flier must know what the ship was doing on its last flight to make proper corrections for the next hop.

What makes the glider fly? When it is thrown into the air, the momentum from the launch provides the flying speed necessary for the wings to develop lift. Why, then, doesn't the glider tumble to earth as soon as this momentum is used up? The answer is that the glider noses down and the force of gravity then becomes a substitute for a propeller, providing thrust to maintain forward speed and lift. The glider then coasts down hill. Assuming that the glider is properly proportioned and hence inherently stable, the modeler has only to balance it fore and aft, so that it does not dive or stall, and then turn the rudder slightly for any desired turn. This fore-and-aft balance is the factor upon which all further adjustments are based. It is this simple: if the glider stalls, add weight to the nose; if it dives, remove weight from the nose.

Directions and plans for hand-launched gliders always show clay, lead pellets, or other weight attached to or inserted in the nose. Gliders require weight in the nose in order to have the C.G. properly located in relation to the chord of the wing. Select an open area—covered with tall grass if possible—and throw the glider lightly ahead. Do not point the nose skyward. Point it at a spot on the ground about 25 feet away. If the nose rises abruptly so that the model seems to falter, drop its nose, and dive to regain speed, it is stalling and requires more nose weight. On the other hand, if it dives to earth, re-

172

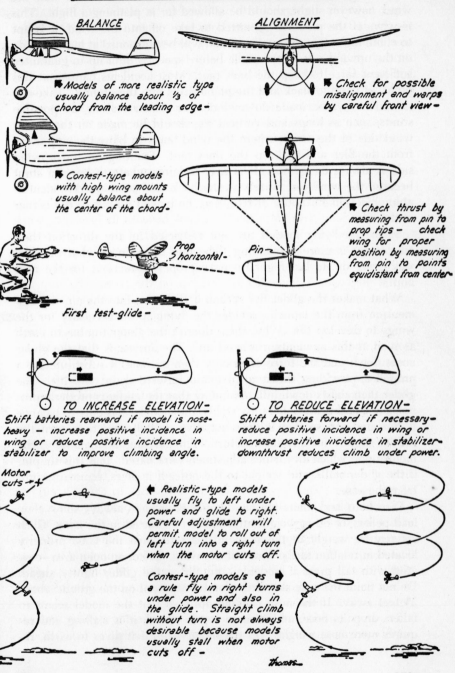

BALANCE   ALIGNMENT

▶ Models of more realistic type usually balance about ⅓ of chord from the leading edge—

▶ Check for possible misalignment and warps by careful front view—

▶ Contest-type models with high wing mounts usually balance about the center of the chord—

Prop horizontal—

First test-glide—

Pin

▶ Check thrust by measuring from pin to prop tips— check wing for proper position by measuring from pin to points equidistant from center—

TO INCREASE ELEVATION—

Shift batteries rearward if model is nose-heavy — increase positive incidence in wing or reduce positive incidence in stabilizer to improve climbing angle.

TO REDUCE ELEVATION—

Shift batteries forward if necessary—reduce positive incidence in wing or increase positive incidence in stabilizer—downthrust reduces climb under power.

Motor cuts—+

◀ Realistic-type models usually fly to left under power and glide to right. Careful adjustment will permit model to roll out of left turn into a right turn when the motor cuts off.

Contest-type models as ▶ a rule fly in right turns under power and also in the glide. Straight climb without turn is not always desirable because models usually stall when motor cuts off—

Fig. 15–1. Free-Flight Adjustments.   173

move some of the weight. Properly balanced, the machine will slide along smoothly and travel 6 to 10 times as far as the elevation above the ground from which it was launched. Once trimmed, the glider may be thrown harder, with the nose pointed up a little and the ship slanted off slightly into a right hand turn (or left hand, if you are left handed). If the ship is still tail heavy, it will loop smartly. The trick is to bend the rudder slightly to the left, then throw the glider in a natural right hand turn. After the momentum of launching is dissipated, the glider will gradually come out of the right turn and, putting down its nose to maintain speed, will enter a left turn in response to the rudder.

The soaring or towline glider may require an extra touch. In order to catch thermals or rising currents of air, a miniature plane must circle tightly. But since the towline glider must be towed aloft by means of a long string attached to a hook beneath its fuselage (when overhead, a small piece of rag tied to the end of the string causes it to slide off the hook, releasing the model), deflection of the rudder will cause the towliner to turn during the launch and possibly dive. If the flier doesn't immediately ease up on the string, the ship will continue around and down into the ground. To make possible a straight launch, the hooks beneath the fuselage are mounted more to one side than the other. These hooks are placed opposite to the direction of the turn. Thus, if the ship is to turn right, the hooks are mounted beneath the fuselage close to the left side. The off-center pull of the towline then equals the turning force of the rudder and the climb is straight ahead until the model releases the line and the rudder takes over unopposed.

Sometimes a circling glide is desired, but inasmuch as an offset rudder would make it impossible to high-start the model in a straight line, a special rudder control becomes necessary. This usually consists of a small spring or rubber-loaded adjustment tab on one side of the rudder. This tension holds the tab offset to cause a circling glide. To obtain a straight launch, the towline is caught over a movable hook which in turn is attached by a fine wire or string to the side of the rudder opposite the string or rubber adjustment device. The result is that the pull on the towline, during launching, is transmitted to the rudder, holding it straight despite its trimming device. When the towline drops off the hook beneath the body, the trimming device is free to move the rudder.

Once you understand the simple tricks of balancing a glider, you can readily master the rubber-powered prop-driven ships.

174

The first thing to be sure of is a calm day. Early morning or late evening is usually the best testing time. Avoid wind because it will buffet the ship and make it difficult to judge the effects of the adjustments you make. If the plane is a small, simple one, the kind of terrain doesn't matter but, if the ship is at all fragile and of built-up construction, select a grassy area for maximum protection. The ship is hand glided (with the motor unwound) from a standing position; aim the nose at a spot on the ground about 25-35 feet away and give the plane a light forward toss, not much more than a gentle shove. A severe throw will cause the craft to zoom up steeply, where it will stall and then dive into the ground. Too easy a launch will not provide enough flying speed and the ship may seem to fall to the ground. Vary the strength of the launch on several attempts in an effort to get the plane to glide smoothly toward the imaginary spot. This will quickly indicate if the ship is nose-heavy or tail-heavy.

Let's correct a stalling tendency. Pieces of solder may be added to the nose, moving the C.G. forward. This is satisfactory for sport flying, but contest fliers prefer not to add weight because it may subtract seconds from the flight duration. If the wing is strapped on with rubber bands, we may slide the wing back a trifle, moving the C.G. forward in relation to the wing. Or we can decrease the amount of lift exerted by the wing by placing a thin sliver of hardwood under its trailing edge; or increase the lift of the tail—tending to force the nose down—by adding such a shim under its leading edge. Use any of these corrections or all in combination, making repeated test glides until the plane appears to glide properly. If the ship had been nose-heavy, the exact opposite measures would be taken. (That is, less nose weight, more wing incidence, less—or even negative—tail incidence.) Now, at last, the motor may be used.

One of the secrets of good adjusting is to iron out glide faults and then pass on to final adjustments which have to do with the effects of the working propeller. On the first short power test, put perhaps 50 turns in the rubber and hand launch the ship just as if you were making a hand glide. Don't throw the craft and don't point its nose upward. If a stall or dive results, don't forget that the ship already is in gliding trim and that previous adjustments must be left alone. Any bad power effects must be controlled by altering the position of the thrust line. If we wish to stop the stall, a sliver of hardwood is inserted behind the top of the nose block, which angles the thrust line down at the front. This is called downthrust. If the ship dives (this is extremely unlikely) the opposite correction is made. On the low-wing types, the opposite can be true and upthrust might become necessary. Rotation of the propeller will bring into play two forces not encountered in the glider, torque and slip stream. Torque is compensated for by adding right-thrust. If slipstream takes effect, it will decrease the effects of torque. The important thing to remember is to make all corrections a little at a time, making short flight after short flight until the ship performs smoothly. Only then begin to add power, either more turns on the rubber job, or a hotter engine run on a gas job. Additional adjustments to the thrust line will be evident from time to time as power is increased.

The rubber model performs most satisfactorily when it is caused to circle to the right, both under power and in the glide. You will note that until now nothing has been said about turn. It is all but impossible to set the rudder for the proper-sized turn when making hand glides because the plane is not airborne long enough to see a complete turn performed. But as those 50 motor turns are applied for the first power tests, the plane will be high enough when the prop stops for you to see how the ship glides, and then to set the rudder slightly to the right to cause a barely perceptible turn. If you can, make this rudder setting before arriving at the full amount of right-thrust necessary to make the plane turn right under power because the rudder also will have its effect on the power portion of the flight. On most rubber-powered planes, it will be found that it is necessary to set the rudder to the right for the right turning glide and to offset the thrust line to the right as well, to keep the plane from spiraling into the ground to the left under the effects of torque. As power is increased from flight to flight, the glide will stretch out, giving the flier a better opportunity for judging its quality. He may detect a slight stall or dive which can be corrected by the methods used during the first hand glide tests.

POWER-TO-GLIDE TRANSITION IS QUICKER
IF MODEL IS ADJUSTED FOR TURNS

Fig. 15–2.

The expert sees his plane circling wide but stalling slightly, as its nose rises and dips. At this point, he will turn his rudder more severely to make the turn still tighter, and the stall disappears. If the turn was too tight to begin with and the ship was gliding too fast, he would apply less rudder, increasing the diameter of the turn and creating more lift to help support the craft.

Some bright modeler once noticed that an airplane could be made to turn tightly without banking steeply and that this appeared to boost the duration of the glide. He did this by tilting the stabilizer so that one tip was higher than the other. The model will always turn toward the higher stabilizer tip. Or it will turn toward whichever wingtip is lower in relation to the stabilizer. Sight along the ship from the rear when tilting the stabilizer. Modern contest planes utilize the tilting stabilizer almost exclusively because by some odd quirk it has little or no effect on the power flight, but radically affects the gliding portion of the flight. Therefore, thrust is controlled by tilting the thrust line while the glide circle is determined by tilting the stabilizer. On high-powered machines, every slight bit of rudder offset has an acute effect on power characteristics so that, in the case of such ships, it is wise to leave the rudder tab alone, or even to eliminate it entirely.

In the case of the rubber job, which turns right both under power and in the glide, it may help to warp up the right or inside wingtip. An increase of $\frac{1}{16}$ inch in the incidence at the wingtip of a 6 inch chord wing should be sufficient. The warp itself may be engineered by holding the wingtip over a steaming kettle until the paper softens slightly, then holding the wing with the tip at the desired angle until the covering becomes taut again.

Another condition that the practiced flier allows for is the wind. No model will fly the same in a wind as it does in a calm. Wind will cause the calm-weather plane to stall. It is necessary, therefore, for the modeler to learn as quickly as possible how much nose weight, or shimming of wing or tail, is necessary to balance his craft for windy weather gliding. The power adjustments remain the same.

Adjusting and flying the free-flight gas model involves much the same procedure as for the rubber-powered job, although the builder has more of a choice as to how he wishes the plane to fly. It was noted that a rubber model should be adjusted to circle to the right, both under power and in the glide. This adjustment is referred to as right-right. In gas modeling, the plane may be made to circle either way, either under power or in the glide. For example, the most popular system is to circle right under power and left in the glide. This would

MAXIMUM SAFE TURNS - $\frac{1}{8}" \times \frac{1}{30}"$ BROWN RUBBER

Strands	TURNS/IN	20"	22"	24"	26"	28"	30"	32"	34"	36"	38"	40"
2 STR	115	2300	2530	2760	2990	3220	3450	3680	3910	4140	4370	4600
4"	80	1600	1760	1920	2080	2240	2400	2560	2720	2880	3040	3200
6"	64	1280	1408	1536	1664	1792	1920	2048	2176	2304	2432	2560
8"	55	1100	1210	1320	1430	1540	1650	1760	1870	1980	2090	2200
10"	50	1000	1100	1200	1300	1400	1500	1600	1700	1800	1900	2000
12"	44	880	968	1056	1144	1232	1320	1408	1496	1584	1672	1760
14"	40	800	880	960	1040	1120	1200	1280	1360	1440	1520	1600
16"	36	720	792	864	936	1008	1080	1152	1224	1296	1368	1440
18"	34	680	748	816	884	952	1020	1088	1156	1224	1292	1360
20"	32	640	704	768	832	896	960	1024	1088	1152	1216	1280
22"	30	600	660	720	780	840	900	960	1020	1080	1140	1200
24"	27	540	594	648	702	756	810	864	918	972	1026	1080

MAXIMUM SAFE TURNS - $\frac{1}{4}" \times \frac{1}{30}"$ BROWN RUBBER

Strands	TURNS/IN	20"	22"	24"	26"	28"	30"	32"	34"	36"	38"	40"
2 STR	80	1600	1760	1920	2080	2240	2400	2560	2720	2880	3040	3200
4"	56	1120	1232	1344	1456	1568	1680	1792	1904	2016	2128	2240
6"	44	880	968	1056	1144	1232	1320	1408	1496	1584	1672	1760
8"	37	740	814	888	962	1036	1110	1184	1258	1332	1406	1480
10"	33	660	726	792	858	924	990	1056	1122	1188	1254	1320
12"	29	580	638	696	754	812	870	928	986	1044	1102	1160
14"	27	540	594	648	702	756	810	864	918	972	1026	1080
16"	25	500	550	600	650	700	750	800	850	900	950	1000
18"	23	460	506	552	598	644	690	738	782	828	874	920
20"	21	420	462	504	546	588	630	672	714	756	798	840

TO DETERMINE MAXIMUM TURNS OF ANY MOTOR, CARRY HORIZONTAL LINE TO RIGHT FROM NUMBER OF STRANDS UNTIL IT INTERSECTS A VERTICAL LINE REPRESENTING THE MOTOR LENGTH. I.E.: 12 STRANDS OF $\frac{1}{4}"$ FLAT, 30" LONG, HAVE 870 TURNS MAXIMUM UNDER IDEAL CONDITIONS. ON VERY HOT OR COLD DAYS, TURNS WILL BE CUT DOWN APPRECIABLY.

THE MAXIMUM SAFE TURNS GIVEN ARE FOR MOTORS THAT ARE STRETCHED WHILE WINDING. FOR HAND-WOUND MOTORS, DEDUCT 20 TO 30%.

MAXIMUM SAFE TURNS - $\frac{3}{16}" \times \frac{1}{30}"$ BROWN RUBBER

Strands	TURNS/IN	20"	22"	24"	26"	28"	30"	32"	34"	36"	38"	40"
2 STR	94	1880	2068	2256	2444	2632	2820	3008	3196	3384	3572	3760
4"	60	1200	1320	1440	1560	1680	1800	1920	2040	2160	2280	2400
6"	54	1080	1188	1296	1404	1512	1620	1728	1836	1944	2052	2160
8"	46	920	1012	1104	1196	1288	1380	1472	1564	1656	1748	1840
10"	42	840	924	1008	1092	1176	1260	1344	1428	1512	1596	1680

Strands	TURNS/IN	20"	22"	24"	26"	28"	30"	32"	34"	36"	38"	40"
2 STR	38	760	836	912	988	1064	1140	1216	1292	1368	1444	1560
4"	35	700	770	840	910	980	1050	1120	1190	1260	1330	1400
6"	32	640	704	768	832	896	960	1024	1088	1152	1216	1280
8"	28	560	616	672	728	784	840	896	952	1008	1064	1120
10"	25	500	550	600	650	700	750	800	850	900	950	1000

Fig. 15-3.

be called right-left. Some builders even prefer to circle left under power and right in the glide, or left-right.

First power tests for a free-flight can be ticklish. It is desirable to limit the amount of power. Most builders set the needle valve for a very rich, slow-running mixture. Plug the intake leaving only a small air hole.

A better system is to put the propeller on backwards during early tests. The reversed prop seems to develop from $\frac{1}{2}$ to $\frac{2}{3}$ the normal thrust and, what is important, to have approximately the same amount of torque. If your new pylon persists in nosing up, it means that more lift must be had from the tail. If the area is proper, the stabilizer should be replaced with one that is slightly thicker. If this has been done and it is felt that the stabilizer airfoil section is at the practical limit of thickness, the best solution is to remove some of the incidence from the wing and to move the C.G. further back on the chord.

A common difficulty on the cabin type of original design is a pronounced tendency to nose down—as if to start an outside loop—when extra flying speed develops. It is common of cabin jobs that there is less nosing up tendency under power so that stabilizer areas may be somewhat smaller, down to as small as $\frac{1}{3}$ the wing area, and not as thick in cross section as on the pylon model. When the cabin plane is trimmed to balance at $\frac{1}{3}$ the chord, it won't require a lifting tail section and a symmetrical one is substituted. Balanced further back so that the tail carries part of the load, a slight lifting section may be required, such as a ratio of tail thickness to tail chord of 6 to 8 per cent. The diving tendency may be cured by adding wing incidence, using less tail incidence, or moving the C.G. back, provided the plane still is able to glide properly. Otherwise it is necessary to make a smaller and/or thinner stabilizer.

Low-wing airplanes frequently prove bad fliers in model plane size. The low wing has its thrust line positioned high in relationship to the center of drag of the machine, therefore creating a nosing-down tendency at high speed. This is exactly opposite to the normal tendency for the pylon. However, the long-wing model may glide excellently which makes the solution seemingly a mystery. The secret is to maintain an angular difference between the incidence setting of wing and stabilizer.

179

16

SCALE MODELS

THE BEAUTY of the solid type of replica (see figure 16–1) lies in its adaptability for copying any airplane in existence. One does not have to be concerned with thoughts of whether or not the machine would make a good flier. The solid also is a pleasant project for those long winter evenings and bad days when one can't go out-of-doors.

It is customary to build solid scale aircraft to some convenient scale. Popular scales are ⅛ inch to the foot, ¼ inch, and ¾₁₆ inch. Thus a plane that is 40 feet in span in real life would come out at 5 inches as a scale job in ⅛ inch scale, or 10 inches in ¼ inch scale. The scale used depends on the types of planes the builder wishes to make. Storage space, cost of materials, and the amount of labor are factors in choosing a scale. So is the size of the big airplane. In ¼ inch scale, a B-36 superbomber would have a wing span of almost 6 feet! Even in ⅛ inch scale this would be a walloping big 3-foot ornament. It would seem that ¹⁄₁₆ inch scale is the largest scale practical for larger types of aircraft. The trouble is that one likes to make all one's models to a standard scale so that a fighter is in proper relationship to a bomber companion. So, weigh all these pros and cons before picking your scale.

Most home-built replicas are made of solid pieces of wood. Balsa is most used but many builders interested in durability and ease of finishing favor a harder wood like pine. The building procedure is

180

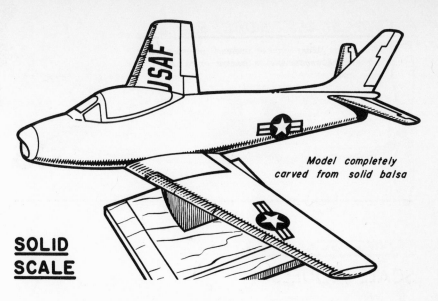

Model completely
carved from solid balsa

SOLID
SCALE

Fig. 16–1.

to draw the side view of the fuselage—its profile—on a clear grained block of the proper length, width, and depth, allowing a slight margin for safety. The profile is then cut out, preferably with a power jigsaw, or with a coping saw. The cut is made sufficiently far outside the pencil marks to permit final sanding without reducing the accurate dimensions of the part. After cutting the side profile, the top profile is marked and the process repeated. The blanked out fuselage is then shaped to the cross sections indicated on the plans. The wing and tail surfaces are made in the same manner. As a rule, external details, like an extended landing gear, are sacrificed, the model being placed on some kind of an attractive stand.

The flying scale model is a more exciting challenge. Some planes have excellent reputations for fliers in model form. Others are mysteries. Dare you try one? Some, obviously, will lend themselves to free-flight gas construction, such as the Monocoupe with its squared fuselage, generous wing, and short nose for balancing the weight of an engine. Others, like the long nosed Fairchild 24, will make good rubber-powered ships because the weight of the rubber will be sufficiently far forward to prevent tail heaviness. (See figure 16–2.) Prop driven planes of many types, like Mustang fighters (figure 16–3), will work wonderfully well when flown on wires with a control handle. Even the spectacular modern jet fighters can be made to fly by means of Jetex, Dynajet, and ducted fan power plants. All these engines are

FLYING SCALE RUBBER

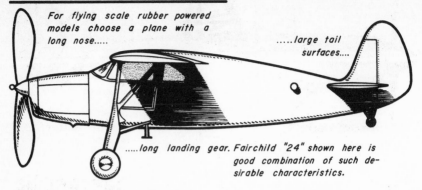

For flying scale rubber powered models choose a plane with a long nose.....

.....large tail surfaces....

.....long landing gear. Fairchild "24" shown here is good combination of such desirable characteristics.

FLYING SCALE GAS

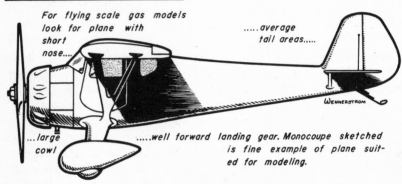

For flying scale gas models look for plane with short nose....

.....average tail areas.....

WENNERSTROM

...large cowl

.....well forward landing gear. Monocoupe sketched is fine example of plane suited for modeling.

Fig. 16–2. Free-Flight Scale.

described in the chapter "Jet Models." Jetex has made practical flying replicas of almost any superhot fighter now in existence.

What famous Navy and Air Force planes are adaptable to models? Let's start with the Navy's carrier-based jobs. First, there is the Grumman Panther and its swept-back wing successor, the Cougar. Then there is the McDonnell Banshee and its successor, the Demon. Or the Vought Cutlass, that weird tailless plane with side-by-side jets. All of these will fly when powered with one or two Jetex units as the design may call for. The spans and weights depend on the size and power of the Jetex unit employed. In all probability you'll want to work with the Jetex 50 or 100 (figure 16–4), with replicas of, perhaps, 2-foot span. Bigger, more powerful, and really fast-flying machines can be made with the Dynajet, but this is for the advanced modeler. A very

182

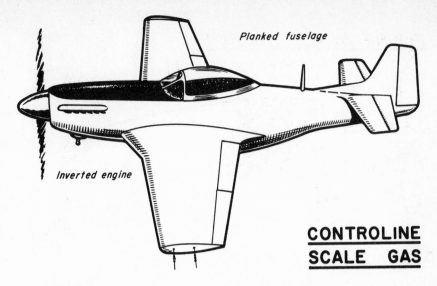

Planked fuselage

Inverted engine

CONTROLINE
SCALE GAS

Fig. 16–3.

pleasant variation of the scale jet flier is a semi-scale approach where a sheet balsa fuselage is substituted for a built-up fuselage. In other words, the plane has a profile like the real job but its top view reveals no width to the body. Such a model is extremely simple to construct, especially when the wings and tail are made from sheet balsa.

The Navy has first-line propeller-driven fighters and dive bombers, as well as jets, on carriers. The old Vought Corsair, that rugged fighter-bomber of World War II, has done a bang-up job in Korea as a close-in support plane for the Marines. Although it has a prop, the Corsair would be a tricky flier in any form but U-control. The Douglas Skyraider, a postwar type that has seen duty in Korea, is another prop job useful in U-control. They are highly useful in the Navy Carrier Event in which the modeler tries to fly a scale plane for a certain number of high speed laps, low speed laps, and then land the job on a simulated carrier deck. Both jobs may be built successfully as U-controllers with any power from an .09 to a .60, but engines of the .29 category are recommended for best results. With such an engine, the span will be in the neighborhood of 36 to 40 inches.

The picture is the same with the Air Force ships like the Lockheed Starfire, a rocket-firing jet interceptor which homes on its prey by radar; the Thunderjet, a rugged carrier of rockets and bombs in Korea; the Sabre, a graceful, fast-flying killer of the Migs; the Northrop Scorpion, a twin jet night fighter, massive and powerful; McDonnell's dart-

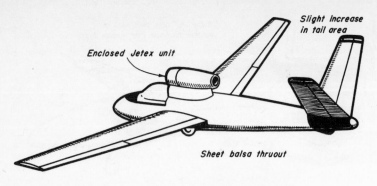

Enclosed Jetex unit

Slight Increase
in tail area

Sheet balsa thruout

SCALE JETEX SAILPLANE

Fig. 16–4. Free-Flight Jetex Sailplane.

like Voodoo, an all-weather interceptor, a slugger among fighter planes. These and others of their kind can be flown in miniature with Jetex, or, if you are more expert, the Dynajet (figure 16–5) or ducted fan. The prop-driven Mustang will fly well on wires as a U-control with engines of .19 to .35 displacement. Well-known trainers, like the North American AT-6 or Texan, make grand U-control models. The Army Ground Forces go in for grasshopper types, like the Cessna Bird Dog, used for spotting fire and directing jet plane attacks on ground targets. The Cessna is a most beautiful-looking free-flight model with the finest performance.

The world is full of exciting jet jobs and special purpose propeller-driven planes. The DeHavilland twin jet 110 night fighter and the Gloster GA-5 delta interceptor represent the latest sensational British fighters. The French Mystere, the Swedish Saab, the Mig 15, all are first-line fighters with performance roughly the same as our Sabre. Their plans all have been published as scale outlines in the model magazines.

Most of us will want to build flying duplicates of the civil type fight planes. Here, too, the matter of low or high wings has a great deal to do with the choice of the plane as either a U-control type or a free-flight machine. In general, free-flying scale planes are apt to be tricky when of a low-wing layout. For either gas or rubber power select some well-known high wing. If for gas, try to pick a short nose, due to the weight of the motor; pick a long nose for rubber power. This distinction is especially true of relatively small planes. If the model becomes large in relation to its gas motor, then a longer nose will be safe.

184

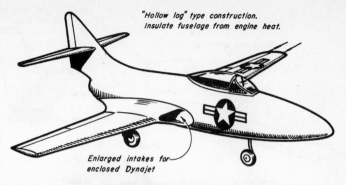

"Hollow log" type construction.
Insulate fuselage from engine heat.

Enlarged intakes for
enclosed Dynajet

CONTROLINE SCALE JET

Fig. 16–5.

The scale fan avidly examines any airplane picture he sees. Pictures serve to show the planes that are in existence, what they look like, to what country and what service they belong, and what their duties are. The best sources of pictures are the various aviation magazines, such as *Flying, Model Airplane News, American Modeler, Aviation Week,* and *Aero Digest. Aviation Week* and *Aero Digest* are trade magazines and therefore do not appear on the newsstands. However, larger libraries may have files of these publications or they sometimes may be found in shops that deal in secondhand magazines. The annual directory number of *Aero Digest* frequently contains three-view drawings on a small scale of all American military ships on which information has been released.

Kit manufacturers are a good source of scale drawings. The rub is that you'll have to buy a kit to get the drawing! All the popular light planes, as well as a fair variety of other civil types, and a huge variety of military planes have been manufactured in kit form. Most of these kits are solid scale jobs, or cheap flying models with rudimentary structures. However, the outlines of the drawings are useful and may be scaled up to a size appropriate for the service you expect the ship to give. Some manufacturers have larger kits, both free-flight and U-control—usually the latter—of better known military and civil types. A number of these may be had in larger spans, ranging from about 2 to 3 feet or even 40 inches.

Flying scale designs are often published in the model magazines. Very often, these magazines have full-size plans available at a nominal fee.

17

PAYLOAD MODELS

Shortly after the war, Dallas Sherman, now Regional Director of Orient, Pan American World Airways, persuaded his firm to sponsor a model airplane event which quickly won world-wide acceptance. This was the PAA Load event. As the name suggests, it could be entered by airplanes that carried a certain specified load. As far back as 1940, Sherman had played experimentally with the idea. What he suggested in 1947—the first PAA Load event at the Nationals was run at Olathe, Kansas, in 1948—immediately captured the fancy of all miniature plane designers. The payload was to be in the form of weighted dummy occupants.

Before Class Half-A payload was included in 1950, the rules provided for two classifications of free-flight ships, the conventional Class A (top displacement, .20 cubic inches) and B (top displacement .30 cubic inches). While the complete rules cannot be reproduced here, the important feature was the specified shape, dimensions, and weight of each occupant, and the conditions pertaining to the placement of the dummy inside the plane. To begin with, each dummy was required to weigh 8 ounces and a Class A plane had to carry one dummy, while a Class B had to carry two. The dummy was crudely human in shape, consisting of a rectangular block 3 × 3 × 1 inch, surmounted by a head at least 1 × 1 × 1. The occupant was to be carried in an upright position, be removable for inspection and checking,

PAALOAD PROPORTIONS

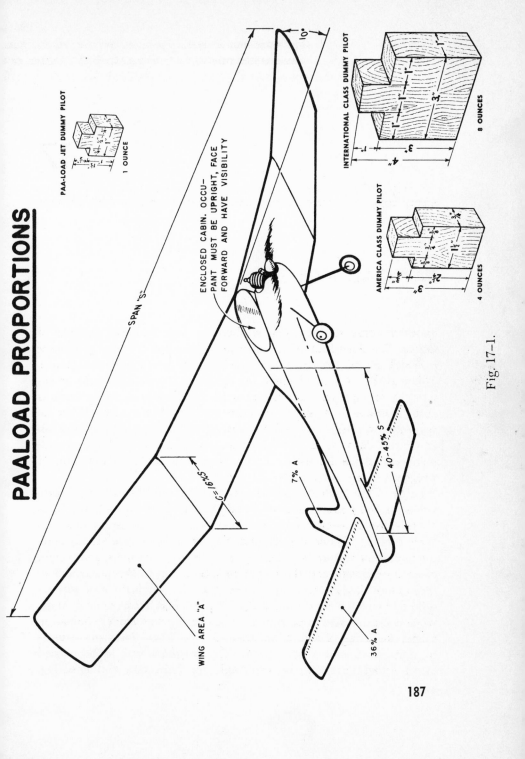

PAA-LOAD JET DUMMY PILOT

1 OUNCE

INTERNATIONAL CLASS DUMMY PILOT

8 OUNCES

AMERICA CLASS DUMMY PILOT

4 OUNCES

10°

SPAN "S"

ENCLOSED CABIN. OCCU-
PANT MUST BE UPRIGHT, FACE
FORWARD AND HAVE VISIBILITY

C = 16% S

WING AREA "A"

7% A

40 - 45% S

36% A

Fig. 17–1.

187

and have a certain minimum visibility through a windshield. The payload model was so speedily accepted by hobbyists that Pan American then extended rules to cover the popular Half-A engines, or those with a maximum displacement of .049 cubic inches. In this case, the dummy was smaller, measuring 2¼ × 1½ × ¾ inches, surmounted by a head that measured at least ¾ inch in all three dimensions. Initially, the weight was 3 ounces but the little Half-A's proved much better weight-lifters than expected, so the weight of the dummy was increased to 4 ounces in 1952. (See figure 17–1 for a PAA-Load model.)

In 1951, Dallas was inspired to write Pan American rules for a Cargo Clipper (figure 17–2) competition. This competition has proved an interesting challenge to designers. It is for Half-A competition with the greatest load lifted for a minimum duration after take-off of 40 seconds winning the prize. Since mere weight was specified, not a dummy, planes took weird configurations. In 1952, the rules were changed to call for a dummy plus load, the dummy counting as part of the load. Some idea of what was achieved by designers can be gleaned from the fact that a Half-A model usually weighs in at 5 ounces or so, and that the Cargo record stands at more than 40 ounces, a far better performance percentagewise than has been realized by full-scale aircraft.

Rewritten in 1955 the PAA Load rules now include the America Class, where engine displacement is less than .05; and the International Class, for engines of .15 maximum displacement. A Jetex event was added, the first time that jet models have toted a pay load. Though all experts agreed that such models would never take off, winning jobs have pushed five minutes in the air and have been lost while soaring in thermals!

The America Class model is required to weigh at least 5 ounces, less fuel and pay load, and the International Class design must weigh a minimum of 15¼ ounces. Because of the many engines of somewhat more than .049 displacement, the America Class model may be powered by an engine of not more than 1 cubic centimeter displacement provided an additional ounce of payload is lifted. The latest rules dictate that a dummy, plus a simulated cargo, be transported—this because performance was climbing too high! This cargo weighs 1 ounce in the America Class (2 ounces if a 1-cubic centimeter engine), and 8 ounces in the International Class. Thus, the required 4-ounce dummy plus the cargo gives a payload of 5 ounces in the America Class, an 8-ounce dummy with 8-ounce payload, a total of 16 ounces in the International Class. The small dummy has a body 1½ inches wide,

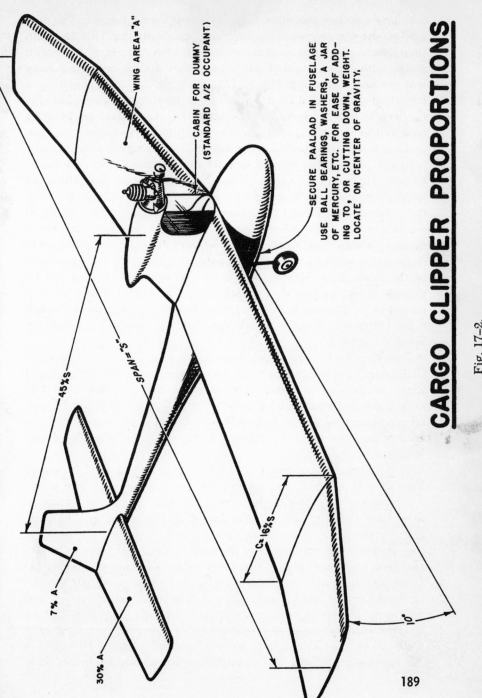

WING AREA="A"

CABIN FOR DUMMY
(STANDARD A/2 OCCUPANT)

SECURE PAALOAD IN FUSELAGE
USE BALL BEARINGS, WASHERS, A JAR
OF MERCURY, ETC. FOR EASE OF ADD-
ING TO, OR CUTTING DOWN, WEIGHT.
LOCATE ON CENTER OF GRAVITY.

45%S

SPAN="S"

7% A

30% A

C= 16%S

10°

CARGO CLIPPER PROPORTIONS

Fig. 17–2.

2¼ high, and ¾ inch thick, surmounted by a head that is a ¾-inch cube. The International Class dummy is 3 inches square, 1 inch thick, with a 1-inch cube for a head.

The jet powered, or Jetex, payloader presents an interesting challenge. First, the model must not span more than 36 inches, and it must not weigh less than 5 ounces, gross weight. When this was written power was specified as the Jetmaster 150 but it was expected that other appropriate power plants will be allowed in the future. The dummy pilot in this case weighs 1 ounce, is 1 inch square, ½ inch thick, and has a ½-inch cube for a head.

The rules for jet payload specified two flights, one R.O.G. (Rise-Off-Ground) and the other hand launched. Scoring was the total time of two flights. This is mentioned because performance increased so quickly that what could have been a Nationals winner was lost out of sight on the first flight, which was R.O.G. Since the rules specified two flights, this entrant was disqualified. But as you read this, new rules will govern this point.

In 1954 Pan America instituted the PAA Load Endurance Event for control-line models. Here an engine of .15 cubic inch maximum displacement was specified. These weight lifters had to carry an 8-ounce International Class dummy, plus a cargo of 1½ pounds, making up a load of 2 pounds. Gross weight was restricted to 7 pounds maximum. A maximum of 1 pint of fuel was permitted. Control lines were 52½ feet.

For full information on the fascinating payload, or PAA Load (for Pan American Airways), address Educational Service, Pan American World Airways, 28-19 Bridge Plaza North, Long Island City 1, N.Y.

Load-carrying models necessarily show differences from the unloaded contest free-flight job which simply points its nose well up and bores into the sky. When a ship climbs vertically, its wings are contributing no lift: the entire weight is being supported by the propeller. Therefore, if engine thrust as developed through a propeller is equal to the plane's weight, the craft will hang motionless. If thrust exceeds weight, the forward speed in a vertical climb would depend on the amount of thrust that remained after lifting the weight of the airplane. Some extremely light but powerful models climb at breath-taking speed. It is obvious, however, that the added weight of a payload plane makes it undesirable to have an excessively steep climb. —

Another interesting difference between the dummy-lifter and the unloaded free-flight is the fuselage profile. It was found many years ago that the pylon layout gave the best results for a high-climbing

190

free-flight. A lifting stabilizer was used and the plane was balanced rather well back on the wing chord. The result was a peculiar tendency to assume and maintain a certain angle of climb as if the plane was following an invisible string. Mistakes in adjustments, or warps in construction, could throw the ship into a disastrous spiral like any other type but, in general, the pylon type was by far the most consistent flier. The very high wing location caused the machine to assume a steep nose-up angle and, after that, the lifting stabilizer held the ship in that position. Now, as we have seen, the load-carrying plane must avoid steep climbing angles. The dummy-carrying payload jobs, therefore, seldom if ever use the familiar pylon. Their wings usually rest upon the cabin. The cabin, containing the one or two dummies according to class, is barely deep enough to hold the dummies.

This highlights another interesting factor in obtaining peak performance from the payload plane. We know that the ship is somewhat bigger than the free-flight of the same power. It certainly must have more cross section in order to hold the dummies. And it must have a reasonably sturdy gear to take off—usually a two wheel gear. These things spell air resistance. While no one seems to point out that a ratio exists between the drag of the model and the available power, or thrust, of the engine, it is a fact that a real effort must be made in the payload plane not to overload the power plant. Overloading it with weight is something modelers easily understand; overloading it with sheer aerodynamic drag is something not always clearly perceived. The more cross section a plane has the more drag it creates. Therefore, the wise builder makes the fuselage of his payload job as small as possible.

A sliding hatch is provided for insertion of the dummy. Sometimes it is on top of the fuselage; very often it is beneath. Naturally the dummy must be firmly in place. Its concentrated weight would cause damage in a crack-up if it shifted. One method of holding the dummy is to pass a dowel through the fuselage and dummy at the same time. Where the holes are drilled in the fuselage sides, a metal or fiber or ply washer should be cemented to the fuselage to prevent the dowel from ripping the wood.

To give the "pilot" the visibility required by the rules, builders use a bubble canopy on top of the wing. The canopy may be bought from a hobby shop or taken from some U-control scale model or kit. Or you can build one from pieces of celluloid cemented together at the seams.

To produce the proper angle of climb without overloading the engine to the point of a stall, the engine is usually placed in a nacelle above the wing. Or it will be located as high on an ordinary fuselage as possible, with the thrust line running very close to the bottom of the shoulder-mounted wing.

A significant factor is the small proportion of stabilizer area to wing area. Whereas the normal proportion for a free-flight contest job is 40 to 50 per cent, this Cargo Clipper winner had a stabilizer with but 30 per cent of the wing area. In the case of weight-lifters it is better to trim the plane so that the wing carries as much as possible of the load, using the stabilizer for stability purposes, and not to use the large type of stabilizer which carries a fair share of the load. The former combination is most efficient for producing minimum drag on the propeller, while the plane itself is carrying a maximum load.

GLOSSARY

Aerodynamics—The science or study of the forces acting on an airplane in motion.

Actuator—An electrical or mechanical (or combination) device used to move the control surfaces of a radio-controlled model.

Airfoil—The cross-section shape of a wing taken at right angles to the wing span; also known as the wing section or the rib section.

Antenna—An aerial for the transmission of radio signals to a radio-controlled model airplane.

Aspect ratio—The relationship of the wing span to the wing chord, expressed numerically as the number of times the span can be divided by the chord.

Attack, angle of—The angle at which the wing chord strikes the air stream.

Autogiro—An airplane that flies by virtue of freewheeling rotating wings, set "windmill" fashion above the fuselage.

Baffle—A kind of wall or partition, as inside a fuel tank to prevent sloshing or surging of the fuel, or on top of a piston to prevent the fresh gases from being blown out the exhaust opening.

Balloon tank—Common toy balloon occasionally used to hold fuel in stunt type U-control models or a rubberized, flexible tank especially manufactured for such use.

Bank—A turn made in flight with one wing tip lower than the other.

Bearing—A tubular fitting in a wood wheel to prevent elongation of the axle hole, or a washer or flat metal plate used between the propeller and the nose to reduce friction, or the part of an engine that holds the crankshaft.

Bellcrank—A pivoted metal, wood, or plastic arm which converts the motion of the control lines to up and down movement of elevators.

Boom—A wood tube or strip that extends rearward from the wings or from a short fuselage to support the tail surfaces.

Booster—A dry-cell battery of the door bell variety temporarily plugged into the ignition system of a model plane to supply a strong spark, or to a glow plug for heating, for starting.

Bore—The diameter of the inside opening of the engine cylinder.

Bulkhead—A wood former cut from sheet balsa or plywood. Used in fuselages that have varishaped cross sections to support the stringers.

Bushing—A hat-shaped tubular fitting used in wood wheels to prevent elongation of the axle hole.

Cam—An eccentric revolving part mounted on the crankshaft to raise the engine timer contact spring once in each revolution.

Camber—The curvature of the wing or horizontal tail from the leading edge to the trailing edge.

Cap strip—A thin, flat strip of wood attached to the upper and lower surfaces of a wing rib to support the covering.

Carburetor—A device for mixing and feeding a vaporized mixture of fuel and air into the engine.

Center of gravity—The spot where the mass or weight of the airplane can be said to center.

Center of pressure—The point on the upper surface of the wing, relative to the chord, where the lift can be said to center.

Chassis—Landing gear.

Choke—To block the air intake of an engine to admit fuel for starting purposes rather than a mixture of gasoline and air.

Coil, spark—A device for raising the voltage sufficiently to fire a spark.

Condenser—A cartridge-like device used in ignition systems as a reservoir for electrical current.

Contra piston—A second piston, fitted into the top of the cylinder of a diesel engine in such manner that it can be adjusted to decrease or increase the space between it and the movable piston for the purpose of raising or lowering the compression of the engine.

Control handle—A stick or shaped device to which the control wires are attached; held in the hand, its movements are transmitted through the control wires to the plane's elevators.

Control-line flying—A method for tethering a model to fly in circles around its builder or a pole.

Cowling—A specially shaped nosing to enclose a motor.

Crankcase—The lower section of an engine in which is housed the crankshaft.

Crankshaft—The revolving shaft in a motor to which the piston is connected by means of a connecting rod.

Crutch—Backbone for a gas-model fuselage, consisting of two longerons with cross pieces.

Cubic-inch displacement—The volume of the cylinder as calculated between the top of the piston in the up position and the top of the piston in its down position.

Cylinder—The upper part of the engine which houses the movable piston.

Dethermalizer—A timer-operated wing flap, spoiler, or rudder control tab, that functions after a desired period of time to force the model into a steep descent to prevent loss in a thermal current.

Diameter, propeller—The size of the propeller measured from tip to tip.

Dihedral—The uptilt of the wing panels toward the tips for purposes of stability.

Double-surfaced wing—A wing having thickness of cross section so that both a top and bottom wing surface are covered.

Dowel—A round, hardwood strip.

Down thrust—The tilting down of the propeller, hence the thrust line, to pull slightly downward to offset stalling tendencies.

Drag—The resistance of the plane to movement through the air.

Drop—The amount of current change, from a higher to a lower current, in a radio receiver upon receipt of a signal.

Drop out—The point at which a relay will relax, or release, due to the change in current flowing through its wire winding.

Ducted fan—A small-diameter metal rotor, used as a substitute for a propeller on jet-type models in which both fan and engine are mounted internally.

Dummy—The weighted wooden "occupant" required by rules to be carried by all PAA Load models.

Dummy motor—A nonworking copy of a real radial type airplane motor used to enhance the scale appearance of a model.

Electrode—The wire points of a spark plug that form the gap across which the spark jumps to ignite the fuel vapor.

Elevator—The hinged control section of the horizontal tail.

Entering edge—The front edge of the wing, the first to strike the air stream. Also called the leading edge.

Escapement—An electro-mechanical ratchet that applies the power of a rubber-band or electric motor to the controls of a radio-controlled model airplane.

Exhibition model—A nonflying model that is built for appearance only.

False rib—A very short wing rib used between full-length ribs at the leading edge.

Filler—A pastelike substance used to seal the pores in the wood or covering before painting.

Fillet—A special streamlined contour between wing root and fuselage sides, at the junction of vertical and horizontal tails to reduce wind resistance, or at any exposed assembly joints.

Fin—The forward fixed portion of the vertical tail.

Firewall—A plywood bulkhead placed immediately behind the engine.

Flaps—Hinged surfaces attached to the trailing edge of a stunt model wing to increase its maneuverability.

Flight timer—A mechanical device that cuts the ignition of the motor after a desired period of time, thus preventing the model from flying away.

Float—Pontoon. A boatlike part that supports the model on the water.

Flood (or flooded)—The condition of an engine brought about by the entry of excess fuel into the cylinder before successful starting.

Flywheel—A small-diameter, thick, heavy wheel attached to the engine driveshaft to dampen vibration.

Flying boat—An airplane with a fuselage shaped like a hull for operations off the water.

Flying scale model—A flyable miniature of a real airplane, usually rubber powered.

Form—A jig consisting of pins hammered into the bench to hold pieces in position while they are being assembled.

Former—Bulkhead.

Four cycle—An engine that requires two revolutions of the crankshaft to achieve one power impulse.

Freewheeler—A propeller fitted with a special attachment that enables it to continue revolving after the rubber motor has fully unwound.

Fuselage—The body of the airplane.

Fuel proofer—A liquid brushed over the painted surface to make it impervious to the bad effects of glow fuels.

Geodetic—A latticework or basket-weave construction.

196

Glider polish—A special preparation rubbed into the wood surfaces of a balsa glider to give them a super finish for efficient gliding.

G-line—A form of control-line flying in which the model is flown on the end of a fish line or fine wire from the tip of a short pole held in the hand.

Glow plug—A device like a spark-plug which contains a heated element to explode the fuel charge within the cylinder.

Guide plate—A piece of plywood, sheet metal, or formed wire with two holes through which pass the lead-outs that connect to the control wires; attached to the wing in cases where the lead-outs are not placed inside the wing.

Hand-launch—To start a model in flight by releasing it or throwing it from the hand.

Hand winder—A heavy hand drill equipped with a special wire hook for the speedy winding of rubber strand motors.

Helicopter—An aircraft that can rise or descend vertically by virtue of large overhead power-driven propeller or propellers.

Hydro—A model that can take off and land on the water.

Idling current—The normal reading shown on a meter when the receiver is not being given a transmitted signal.

Ignition—The electrical system providing the spark that explodes the gasoline vapor in an internal-combustion engine.

Incidence, angle of—The angular setting of the wing chord relative to the thrust line.

Induced drag—The resistance of the wing to forward movement due to the disturbance of the surrounding air.

Jig—A fixture or form for holding together parts for assembly.

Keel—A wide precut piece of sheet balsa used as a backbone in the construction of bulkheaded fuselages.

Kit—A construction set.

Landing gear—The wheel and strut, or skid chassis, that supports a model while at rest on the ground and during taking-off and landing.

Lapped—The process by which the piston is fitted close to the cylinder walls when piston rings are not employed.

Leading edge—The front or entering edge of a wing or a tail.

Lead-out—The heavy wires which attach to the bellcrank and which extend to join to the control wires.

Lean—A condition of improper engine adjustment consisting of too little fuel in the fuel-air mixture.

Lift-drag ratio—The relation of total lift to total drag, expressed as a mathematical proportion, 6 to 1, 15 to 1, etc.

Longerons—The principal fore and aft strips in a fuselage.

Lubricant—A greasy, paste like mixture rubbed into the rubber strands to increase their turn capacity.

Master stringer—A wide, flat strip cut from sheet balsa. Used like a keel piece, but on the sides of a bulkheaded fuselage, as well as on the bottom.

Microfilm—A very thin transparent covering for indoor models made by pouring a special liquid on water.

Moment arm—The distance from the center of gravity at which a force is applied. The distance between the C.G. and the tail, or between the C.G. and the propeller, etc.

Motor bearer—A wood-strip motor mount.

Motor stick—A heavy strip used to support a rubber motor. The body of a stick-type model.

Mush—A nose-high, slow speed flight attitude resulting from a slight excess of tail heavy trim.

Needle valve—The adjustable valve which extends through the venturi for the purpose of adjusting fuel mixture.

Neoprene—Fuel tubing made of a special material impervious to the degenerating action of glow fuels.

Nose plug—A shaped wood block used to support the propeller-thrust bearing.

Ornithopter—A freak-type airplane that flies by flapping its wings like a bird.

Parasol—An airplane in which the wings are mounted on struts above the fuselage.

Pay load—The weight carried by an airplane over and above its own structural weight plus the weight of the fuel (and crew in a big plane).

Piston—The moving part which moves up and down within the cylinder to transmit the power of the exploded fuel to the crankshaft.

Pitch—The distance forward traveled by a propeller in one revolution.

Pitch-diameter ratio—The relation between the propeller pitch and the propeller diameter, expressed as a mathematical proportion, 1½ to 1, 2 to 1, etc.

Planform—The outline of wing or stabilizer when viewed from above.

Planking—Wood covering accomplished by gluing thin flat balsa strips side by side.

Plywood—Sheet wood with high resistance to splitting or warping, made by gluing together thin layers of wood with the grain of each at right angles to the adjacent layer.

Pod—A short, streamlined fuselage fitted with a boom to support the tail surfaces.

Pod-and-boom—A type of model that derives its name from the appearance of its short body and tail-support boom.

Polyhedral—A modification of dihedral, by which the different panels of a wing are tilted upward at varying angles to achieve lateral stability.

Pontoon—A float or boatlike device which supports an airplane while on the water.

Poppet valve—Either an intake or exhaust valve actuated by a cam that causes the valve to open and shut at precise intervals.

Port—An opening used in an engine to admit or exhaust gases.

Prime—Unvaporized fuel squirted into the exhaust port of an engine to facilitate starting when cold.

Pull test—A controlled strain placed on the wires and control mechanism of a control line model to insure its meeting safety requirements before being flown in competition.

Propeller—An airscrew that bores its way through the air pulling or pushing the airplane, depending on the motor installation.

Propeller hangar—A metal fitting used to mount the propeller shaft on a motor stick.

Pterodactyl—A tailless airplane; a flying wing.

Pusher—An airplane in which the motor is mounted ahead of the propeller so that the propeller pushes instead of pulls.

Pylon—An enclosed or solid fin-type wing mount.

Reel—A storage device for control lines when not in use.

Regulator—A metering device which admits controlled amounts of fuel to an engine on demand when a pressure tank is used.

Relay—A device used in radio-controlled models to convert the radio signal into motion of an escapement that connects a rubber-band or electric motor to the controls.

Resistance—Air drag, or the opposition of the air to being displaced by the forward movement of the plane.

Restrictor—A plug of metal or wood inserted into a venturi of an engine to decrease the opening when lean running cannot be eliminated.

Rib section—The cross-section shape of the wing taken between the leading and the trailing edges.

Rich—A term that describes the running condition of an engine when the fuel mixture contains too little air.

Riser—A thermal or upward moving column of air.

Rudder—The vertical tail surface on a model airplane. Actually only the hinged or movable section of the vertical tail on a real airplane.

Sailplane—A highly efficient form of glider, capable of gaining altitude higher than its launching point.

Servo—A motor driven device for moving control surfaces of a radio model.

Sheet balsa—Thin, flat slices of balsa wood.

Shut-off—A timed device for terminating the flow of fuel to an engine for purposes of limited flight duration.

Side thrust—The offsetting of a propeller to pull slightly to one side for the purpose of flying adjustments.

Single surface wing—A wing with a very thin cross section or rib, covered on the top side only.

Slip-on—A device to connect booster wires to a glow plug.

Solid model—A miniature airplane that has been shaped from solid pieces of wood.

Spars—The span-wise, load-carrying, structural members in a wing or tail.

Spiral stability—The characteristic of a model that permits high-speed banked turns without diving into the ground.

Sponson—Stubby, winglike projections on either side of a pontoon or hull that prevent the model from tipping over on the water. A "sea wing."

Squirt gun—A fuel can of the pump type.

Stability—The tendency of an airplane to remain in level flight or to return to level flight after any disturbance by an upsetting force.

Stabilizer—The fixed horizontal tail surface.

Stall—The complete loss of lift resulting from too steep an angle of attack.

Stalling point—The particular position at which any given wing will lose its lift. Expressed in degrees, 10 degrees, etc.

Step—An abrupt break or crosswise edge in the bottom surface of a pontoon or hull to assist in breaking the water suction during a take-off.

Stick—A type of model having a motor stick for a body.

S-hook—A special wire fitting for making a rubber motor quickly detachable from a permanent rear rubber hook. Used when a winder is required.

Stooge—A device attached to the ground which restrains a U-control plane from take-off until a release is actuated.

Streamline—To shape the contours of an exposed part of an entire airplane to reduce air resistance or drag; round at the front, pointed at the rear.

Stroke—The distance up and down that a piston travels within the cylinder.

Sweepback—The angling back of a wing from the center toward the tips as seen on the planform, to increase directional stability.

Tab—A small, adjustable section on either a horizontal or a vertical tail or on a wing for delicate flight adjustments.

Tail—The smaller flying surfaces at the rear of a conventional-type airplane.

Tail skid—A wire, bamboo, or wood piece at the rear of a fuselage or stick to support the model while on the ground, and to protect the rear of the fuselage from damage during take-offs and landings.

Team racer—A special type of U-control model flown simultaneously with similar models over a specified number of laps.

Template—A stiff pattern for scribing the outlines of parts to be cut from sheet wood or sheet metal.

Tensioner—A device for keeping taut unwound rubber motors which normally have slack, for a greater turn capacity.

Thermal—A rising column of relatively warm air.

Thinner—A liquid used to cut or thin dope and cement.

Thrust—The propulsive force developed by a whirling propeller.

Thrust bearing—A washer, tube, or metal plate attached to the nose block or nose plug to take the propeller shaft; a propeller hangar.

Thrust line—An imaginary line drawn through the propeller shaft and extending rearward through the model. Used in designing and drawing plans.

Tip loss—The reduction of lift near a wing tip due to the seepage of air from the high pressure area beneath the wing to the low pressure area above the wing.

Torque—The reactive force generated by a revolving propeller that tends to revolve the model counter to the direction of rotation of the propeller.

Tow line—The launching cord or string used for towing aloft a sailplane or tow-line glider.

Tractor—A puller propeller. A model equipped with a puller-type propeller.

Trailing edge—The rear edge of a wing or tail surface.

Transmitter—A radio device which generates the signal that is sent out to, and picked up by, the receiver.

Tricycle—A three-wheeled landing gear, consisting of a nose wheel and two rear wheels.

True pitch—A type of propeller so designed that all points along the blades travel an equal distance forward during a revolution.

Tungsten wire—The strongest available wire used in very thin diameters to brace the fuselages and motor sticks on featherweight indoor models.

Twin pusher—A type of model equipped with two motor sticks assembled in the form of a V, fitted with two pusher-type propellers.

Two-cycle—A type of engine that requires one revolution of the crankshaft for every power impulse.

U-control—A method of control-line-flying for gas models.

Undercamber—The convex curve incorporated into the bottom surface of certain airfoils.

Veneer—A form of plywood having extremely thin plies. A thin, laminated sheet wood used for covering, cowls, etc.

Venturi—The air intake passageway of an engine.

Vortices—The peculiar twisting air disturbance resulting from the forward movement of a wing through the air.

Washin—Twist incorporated into a wing tip to raise the leading edge.

Washout—Twist incorporated into a wing tip to raise the trailing edge.

Wedge tank—A control stunt model fuel tank with a cross section shaped like a wedge to insure steady running of the engine during maneuvers.

Wing—The principal flying or supporting surface of an airplane.

Wing section—Airfoil; rib section. The chord-wise cross section of a wing.

Zoom—An abrupt steep climb.

INDEX

aerodynamics, principles of, 17-18
airfoil shapes, 17-22
    Clark Y, 19-22
    Eiffel 400, 21
    of free-flight wings, 21
    Goldberg, 21
    NACA 4612, 21
    NACA 6409, 21
    of pylon wings, 147, 149
    RAF 32, 21
angle of attack:
    of tail, 28-29
    of wing, 18, 28-29
angle of incidence, 30
angular difference of wing and tail, 29-30
aspect ratios, 22-25
    of control-line models, 6
    of jet models, 140
    of pylon models, 147
    of rubber-powered models, 111
    of rudders, 30
    of stabilizers, 30
axes of rotation, 14-15

balsa wood sizes, 42
    for fuselages, 46-47
    for tails, 60
    for wings, 53-58
bellcrank, *see* control systems
Booton floats, *see* floats
bulkheads, 12
    construction of, 47-51

Cargo Clipper, *see* payload models
center of gravity, 14-15, 27-28, 34-35, 171, 172, 175, 179
    in free-flight models, 166
    in pylon models, 146, 147
    in radio models, 166

center of pressure movement, 25-26, 34
Civy Boy, 21
Clark Y, *see* airfoil shapes
Class Half-A, *see* payload models
Class B, *see* payload models
combat planes, 120-121
control-line models:
    aspect ratios of, 25
    carrier planes, 123
    characteristics of, 16-17
    endurance flight, 124
    Firebaby, 2-4
    fuselages of, 60-61
    hazards of flying, 134
    landing gears of, 65-67
    specifications of, 134
    speed models, 123-124
    stunt models, 119-120
        proportions of, 131
    team racer, 122
    types of, 118-123
    typical model, parts of, 119
control systems, 120, 124
    bellcrank and linkage, 118, 124-125, 129, 130, 131
    hinges and horns, 125-126, 130, 131, 133
    ignition, 132
    lines, 118, 125-130
    Mono-Line, 126-128
    two-speed engines, 123
covering:
    application of, 81-89
    of fuselage, 82-85
    grain of paper, 87
    lettering of, 88
    materials for, 82
    of tail, 89

covering (*cont.*):
tools for, 81
of wing, 85-86
crutch construction, *see* fuselages

Delta, *see* jet models
dethermalizers:
drag chute, 151-152
pop-up tail, 150-151
Diesel engines, 95-96
starting technique, 101-103
dihedral, 15, 30-34, 149
construction of, 51-54
joints, 59
in pylon models, 149
in radio-control models, 168
directional axis, *see* vertical axis
drag, 18-19, 21, 24
parasite, 24
of payload model, 191
of propeller, 76-77
from skin friction, 76-77
drag chute, *see* dethermalizers
ducted fan, *see* jet engines
Duster, Joe Bilgri's, 116
Dynajet, *see* jet engines

Eiffel 400, *see* airfoil shapes
engines (*see also* Diesel engines,
glow plug engines, venturi
and needle valve, wiring) 4,
7
breaking in of, 97-98
four-cycle, 90
ignition, 91-92
mounts for, 103
spark plug, 90-91, 93
testing of, 97
two-cycle, 90-91

Firebaby, 2-4
floats:
Booton, 69-70
construction of, 72-73
design requirements of, 67-72
flying boats, 67
proportions of, 72
forces acting on plane, 38
freak models, 5, 7

free-flight models (*see also* gas models, pylon models, rubber-
powered models, scale models):
aspect ratios of, 25
determining size of contest type,
37
dethermalizer for, 150-152
types of, 144
fuel tanks:
balloon, 107-108
construction of, 109
for control-line models, 108
speed model, 134
for free-flight models, 105
placement of, 104-105
wedge, or stunt, 106
fuselages:
construction of, 40-51
control line, 60-61
covering of, 82-85
crutch construction of, 51-52
moment arm of, 34
planking of, 49-50
profile of, 36
of rubber-powered models, 61
of speed planes, 61

gas engines, *see* engines
gas models:
flight adjustments of, 177, 179
landing gear of, 62-64
Sailplane, 21
glider, hand-launched, 6
jet-propelled, 138
glider, towline, 6
glow plug engines, 93-94
correcting troubles of, 100-101
starting technique of, 98-99
Goldberg section, *see* airfoil shapes

handles, *see* control systems
hinges and horns, *see* control systems

jet engines:
ducted fan, 141-143
Dynajet, 4, 135
Jetex, 4, 136, 138
operating principle of, 135
types of, 135-138

jet models, 4
  construction of, 138, 140
  glider, 138
  Jetex Delta, 140-141
  payload model, 190
  scale model, 140

landing gears:
  construction of, 64-67
  types of, 62-64
lateral axis, 15
lift:
  of stabilizer, 27-28
  of wing, 22-23, 25
lift-drag ratio, 19, 25
lines, *see* control systems
linkage, *see* control systems

model types, 2-7
moment arm:
  of fuselage, 34
  of nose, 37
  of tail, 37

NACA 4612, *see* airfoil shapes
NACA 6409, *see* airfoil shapes
nose:
  construction of, 46-47
  moment arm of, 37
  typical, 48

PAA Load contest, 186, 190
PAA Load model, 181
payload models:
  American Class, 188
  Cargo Clipper, 188-189
  Class B, 186
  Class Half-A, 186, 188
  design characteristics of, 188, 190-192
  flight characteristics of, 190
  International Class, 188
pendulum stability, *see* stability requirements
planforms:
  of stabilizers, 31
  of wings, 22-24
plans:
  enlargement of, 8-11

plans (*cont.*):
  full-sized, 11-13
plastic models, 2, 119
polyhedral, *see* dihedral
pontoon planes, 67
pop-up tail, *see* dethermalizers
propellers:
  carving of, 75-76
  folding, 77-78
  freewheeling, 76-77
  gas model, 79
  indoor model, 80
  one-bladed, 77
  pitch of, 79-80
  pitch-diameter ratios of, 74
  for rubber-powered planes, 113
pylon models, 146-149
  stability of, 26-28, 35

radio-control planes, 7
  flight in wind of, 169
  rudder action on, 156-159, 162, 168-169
radio control systems, 153-154
  effect on plane design of, 164, 166-168
  multi-channel control, 154, 158-159, 162, 164
    installation of, 163-164
  reed bank, 159
  single-channel control, 154-158, 159, 162, 164
    installation of, 163
  transmitter, 164-165
  two-channel control, 158
  two-speed engine control, 162
radio frequencies for model planes, 7, 153
RAF 32, *see* airfoil shapes
reels, *see* control systems
ribs, 12
Rise-Off-Ground, *see* rubber-powered models
rubber motors:
  characteristics of, 113
  installation of, 114-115
  tensioning device for, 113-115
  winding of, 117

rubber-powered models, 6
  aspect ratios of, 111
  characteristics of, 37, 110-113
  fuselage construction of, 61
  Joe Bilgri's Duster, 116
  Rise-Off-Ground, 110
  scale model, 175
  turn adjustments of, 176-177
rudders, 15-17
  action on radio models of, 156-
    159, 162, 168-169
  aspect ratios of, 30
  construction of, 60
  shapes of, 32

scale models:
  control-line, 121-123, 181-183
    jet powered, 184-185
  free-flight, 7, 181-182
  landing gear of, 65
  rubber-powered, 7, 181
  solid type, 2, 6-7, 180-181
sea wing, see sponson
skin friction, see drag
slip-stream effect, 35
  on pylon models, 147
spanwise axis, 15, 17
spark plug, see engines
speed models:
  airfoils for, 21-22
  fuselages for, 61
spiral stability, see stability require-
    ments
sponson, 67
stability requirements, 14-17, 34-35
  pendulum stability, 34
  spiral stability, 35

stabilizers, 15, 17
  acting as dethermalizer, 150-151
  aspect ratios of, 30
  construction of, 60
  planforms of, 31
  of pylon models, 147
  of radio plane, 166, 168
  types of, 26-30
stalling point, 28-29

tails:
  construction of, 60
  covering of, 89
  moment arm of, 37
templates, 11, 13
tools, 41
torque effect, 32-33
  on pylon models, 146-147
two-speed lines, see control systems

U-control models, see control-line
  models

venturi and needle valve, 96, 98-102
vertical axis, 14-15

wings:
  aspect ratios of, 111
  construction of, 51-59
  covering of, 85-86
  planforms of, 22-24
  of pylon models, 147-149
  of radio plane, 158
  structure details of, 57
wiring, one- and three-volt, 93-94,
  96